Tale of a
Sky-Blue
Dress

Also by Thylias Moss

Poetry:
HOSIERY SEAMS ON A BOWLEGGED WOMAN
PYRAMID OF BONE
AT REDBONES
RAINBOW REMNANTS IN ROCK BOTTOM GHETTO SKY
SMALL CONGREGATIONS
LAST CHANCE FOR THE TARZAN HOLLER

For Children:
I WANT TO BE

Tale of a Sky-Blue Dress

THYLIAS MOSS

AN AVON BOOK

Avon Books, Inc.
1350 Avenue of the Americas
New York, New York 10019

Copyright © 1998 by Thylias Moss
Interior design by Kellan Peck
Published by arrangement with the author
Visit our website at http://www.AvonBooks.com/Bard
ISBN: 0-380-97550-5

Library of Congress Cataloging in Publication Data:
Moss, Thylias.
Tale of a sky-blue dress / by Thylias Moss.
p.   cm.
I. Title.
PS3563.08856T35   1998   98-17552
813'.54—dc21   CIP

First Bard Printing: August 1998

Always for Wesley
This one for Deidre too
and also for the others all of them

In that space of silence, Platero brays.
And his gentleness becomes associated
with the bell, with the rocket, with the Latin,
and with the music of Modesto, which return
then to the clear mystery of the day;
and his bray, from haughty, turns sweet;
from humble, becomes divine.

—JUAN RAMÓN JIMÉNEZ

Platero and I

This is a prayer to save the soft gray dresses of evening.

—LINDA HOGAN

"Prayer for Men and Children"

Acknowledgments

The author wishes to thank the John Simon Guggenheim
Memorial Foundation, the John D. and Catherine T.
MacArthur Foundation, and the Mrs. Giles R. Whiting
Foundation for support that provided the time needed to
complete this book.

Parts of "Washing the Storm Out of Cumulonimbus"
appeared in slightly different form in *Going Where I'm
Coming From: Memoris of American Youth*, Anne Mazur, editor,
Persea Books, 1995.

CONTENTS

Washing the Storm Out of Cumulonimbus

In Wade Park, a girl no bigger than a good-sized goose runs after birds, her parents watching, her skirt tail rising, it the color of the color coming into their cheeks. They sit on a bench that faces Mount Sinai Hospital in Cleveland, Ohio, where I was born during a blizzard that my mother says buried cars. Even the cab taking her to the hospital in the early morning's darkness supposedly tunneled through snow. Every winter she tells me that no winter has been like that winter, the tone of her voice sometimes impressed with my involvement in the severity for its proving the power of something half hers, and the tone sometimes critical of my apparently having caused it, the perfect timing of birth and storm not coincidental. The snow line rose as she looked out the cab window whenever contractions permitted, and soon the snow prevailed.

As she says this, I envision suds in the Laundromat's front-loading Speed Queen triumphing over filth. And I can see then that her washing diapers in the commode was like washing the storm out of cumulonimbus, then flinging plump white geese back into the sky. Every moment if I listen carefully, I can hear her telling me something, although usually we are two hundred miles apart. Mostly she tells me that I've been blessed. As if I had caught those pigeons, sprinkled salt on their tails and grabbed them. My father could turn his hands into wings; they flew away with him in 1980. *Blessed.*

A night of love in Tennessee in May made that birth and bird chase possible.

By the day of our discharge from Mount Sinai, the city of Cleveland was all plowed; snow piled high on both sides of the street, higher at corners, seemed, I've been told, the supports of bridges that had collapsed. She said I did not cry until wind shrill through an ill-shutting north-facing window of the attic where we lived stirred a feather that drifted down from the sill as if it had been lost just then in flight. First chance I get, a girl no bigger than a good-sized goose chases pigeons. First chance I get, I commit to a reunion of bird and feather.

In the park that day, two of us, Mama and Baby Girl, are there with pecan skin glowing and Rh-negative blood warm underneath it, but the woman, her hair in such excellent curls they are uncrushable, does not know that we share this blood feature. Her positive husband does not pass the Rhesus factor to me, but she doesn't know this. She decides not to have another child for fear her own Rh-negative blood would put it at risk, my blood having sensitized hers to the presence of a harmful protein. She's not that kind of woman, one who could deliberately hurt her child no matter what vile personage her issue might become. Imagine her own blood attacking, shooting antibodies across the cord, the baby's blood devastated, the child stillborn or born suffering when upon exposure to air and light, brown pigmentation should begin to surge; born needing a transfusion, risking damage of the brain, destruction of all the possibilities you want to hold no matter who you are, where you are, what you are. There was no Rhogam in 1954 to destroy these antibodies; just one injection after the miscarriage, abortion or birth of an Rh-positive baby and the antibodies disappear. Still, I am without sisters.

At the park again later in the year, ice and snow dazzle me so much I don't seem as interested in pigeons. My parents, watching as before, are so glad it doesn't take much to delight this girl still no bigger than a good-sized goose. In fact, her father is going to tell her that night, the story of a girl that geese will surround, their feathers locked as

tightly as a snow house. Around her they honk, their circle tightening, their feathers brushing against her, some of the feathers working their way into her skin until, when the circle widens, in the center is the Goose Princess who prefers wings to crown, and whose movements become more balanced and graceful. At times, her feet skim the ground.

Then I am invited to finish the story. I tell him what she can do with the wings. The imagination soars colossal. *Is that all?* he asks. *Of course not,* I say, then try to push something else out of my brain. It shouldn't be this difficult if, as he's told me, indeed there are no limits.

Although he doesn't say so, I know this has been elevation of wing, not denigration of crown. I know from this that dark little girls can assert themselves and boost the power of darkness without despising the pale wonders like him. I know that it is fine to think myself fine, that his fineness and mine can coexist, that one fineness does not detract from the other although these finenesses may seem opposed. The goose princess's little preference, despite its amplification since it is also my preference, does not affect crown. Crown is whatever it was before his little demonstration of choice. Its status remains. My father's paleness is a tower that as the sun sets, at the blessing hour of slanted light, takes on a radiant pecan hue.

In my notebooks, I begin drawing feathers. After the jelly's gone, Welch's jars are stuffed with feathers that come into the windows and that layer the yard. Looking at them closely, quill feathers mostly, the down feathers looking too likely to melt, and I want things lasting; looking closely, I see ribs radiating from shaft and calamus that seem like closed plastic-toothed zippers. I learn that feathers are a hundred million years old, that the first fossilized feather was found in a Bavarian quarry, set in limestone, as if an ancient flying reptile was first to try to make an angel by sweeping the ground.

I have liked this story. I have liked walking home from the park with him, a bag of groceries in one of his arms, my hand in his other hand. I think that I'm the Goose Princess and that those wings are making life so easy. We are just walking along a gilt corridor; the trees become iridescent. This will end when we move from Lills Drive to Trunt Avenue and my father, who always did the marketing, never my mother, would from then on hire a jitney to take us home, although on Trunt we lived closer to the supermarket than we did on Lills. I remember once when I was ten returning to the market Jiffy corn muffin mix that was laced with webs; very pretty but unappetizing. Like our dusty wires. We never cleaned the basement's pipeworks. I walked alone that day.

We slide and fall on the ice, the smooth, cold pearl path that goes all the way home. A box of vanilla wafers spins, oranges roll, turnip and mustard greens stick out of snow as if they grew there. We laugh and rise, still holding hands, pick up the groceries and go home understanding better than ever what we have chosen.

Such a happy girl. Glad to be no bigger than a good-sized goose. Not that much bigger now. Was big only when she looked as if she had swallowed a good-sized goose, but that was a baby who right now is no bigger than a good-sized goose.

*

I begin with these parents. I begin with the structure of a beatitude.

*

In Tennessee in the late nineteen-forties and early fifties my mother worked in a dry cleaners and briefly in the hat factory where some of her siblings and cousins eventually worked for a while. Those not as mindful of their souls could work in a distillery or cement plant. Growing up, she worked in the fields, a farm girl in the Appalachian foothills; she lugged milk that couldn't be any fresher. By the time she was ending adolescence, the farmlife was gone, but not the unpaved roads and paths. Five sisters wore her shoes.

There are no photographs of her childhood, her adolescence; no picture of the happy couple the night that she and my father became engaged; not one wedding picture. For those moments, I conduct deep searches into her face when she falls asleep, more and more easily now, while we talk or attempt to watch a film together. I take away lines, yellowing of the eyes, pounds; I blacken her hair, lengthen it, braid it and tie on it ribbons made from reeds that grew by the creek along the road she walked to the colored school until she stopped going, having learned, she was told, all a colored girl would ever need to know.

Barely five feet tall, she was good at basketball despite mild curvature of her legs. Did my father see her a first time as she leaped into her reputation? She was a forward, genuine trophy material. However, her real love was art; I have drawings of hers from ninth-grade biology, illustrations of frogs and paramecia that look like diagrams from impressive reference books so detailed are they. I have her Dream Home notebook in which she drew plans for each room and attached magazine clippings of home furnishings and her possible trousseau. Variation after variation of the "Draw Me" head from an art school advertisement, each one better, more exact. Where would the money have come from?

I've been to a house she grew up in, sturdier than shack with its stone walls (in my memory a fortress), but size of shack for a family with twelve children. I remember three small rooms. No basement. No convenience. Being territorial was impossible, not even privacy for a bath had there been indoor plumbing. I remember a pump just outside the kitchen. Laundry done in the yard in the same galvanized tubs they bathed in, water heated on the wood, and much later, gas stove. Soap so strong, lye and potash, it couldn't help but purify. Fertilizer sacks bleached practically into linen hung outside between sycamore and sapgum, flagging down the locomotives churning through the yard at the top of the hill; the outhouse would tremble. Pleated skirts, sailor suits, shorts and envy made from that linen.

Roaches had the run of the kitchen, congregating in the dark like a black wall-to-wall rug, scattering, in sudden light, like marbles. To use the outhouse, my mother had to make a run through roaches fat as thumbs and the black licorice their father would bring them from Alabama, had to carry sticks and stones for snakes. But at night, maybe after she woke from her pallet on the floor to go to the outhouse, pencils and paper that she hid under her pallet were probably pulled out, and curtains were pulled back exposing the moon lamp, the table hers until dawn and crowing, her need for art turning roaches into dark chalks and charcoal. A need her mother had too, drawing her daughter drawing.

My father probably would not have met my mother had her family not resettled in Marrakech County, Tennessee, from Valhermosa Springs, Alabama, which sounds like a marvelous place to be from. I expect that spring to be blessed, as if it were water diverted from Lourdes. "Valhermosa" perhaps is a corruption of Spanish words for beautiful valley, *valle hermoso,* with special water flowing through its center, water that helped the Watkins family, into which my mother was born during the Great Depression, survive all that the south, in the days of unlimited sharecroppers and unlimited difficulty in asserting nothing more than what was deep in the nest of one's heart, had to offer.

You didn't want to use your senses, for interpretation of their use could get you killed, yet to repress the senses was to deny your own humanity, and you didn't want personal complicity in a denial at that moment rampant in the southern culture. So you, head of the Watkins household, risked your eyes anyway and beheld a pristine flowing right by the fields where sometimes you danced with your daughters, two-stepping and the Charleston, where the steer lay down and needed a fire lit under its tail to get it going again. You saw twelve children in the cotton and after a sip from the spring, you could see only the softness, the heaven, though short-lived, of the scene. Then the full sacks were taken to the gin where they yielded a five-hundred-pound bale to bank on, forty-nine cents a pound; sticks of bologna soon could be bought, sliced and frying in lard or butter. Not much of your crops were yours to keep.

The spring water touched your throat, Curtis Montgomery Watkins, grandfather I never knew, like paint, the artist surprised and proud, the artwork too splendid for the artist to claim. Oh but some things your farm couldn't do in the prevailing hardship of sharecropping in the nineteen-thirties and forties, so you had to leave your children to work it while you worked at the arsenal back in Coryville for the war effort, coming home to them on the weekend, taking all your daughters and sons, one in linen diapers, to the restaurant on pay day, finding explanations in the Book of Daniel, finding excuses in your harmonica and three-man band, finding pleasure and forgiveness in huge sacks of oranges and peppermints practically as big as plums that you took home for Christmas as long as you lived.

No corruption for the beautiful valley until the stream one day ran dry. The father took the last drink and died at the hands of another man who said Curtis was looking at the wrong woman, was cheating on his wife with the wrong woman, the killer's woman so delicate and pale, even the killer, who had a right to, shouldn't touch her. The killer was not persuaded by the water that lacked the substance of flesh he needed to annihilate. My mother's father was dead. Stabbed. A casualty of the war. I think of him whenever I think of Emmet Till. The valley in the pale shadow of death.

There's not much talk about this, the details of finding the murdered body, lifting it by the shoulders, the head resting limp in the new widow's arms. Much evidence at the crime scene, but none of it used to convict anyone. Scot-free in the freest country of them all. But his children did not grow up bitter; although a few displaced rages onto spouses, most marriages endured. Theirs is preposterous faith that rage really won't soothe them and is a form of suicide the way it consumes. Their anger rises; my mother storms with the best, but she misses the sun too much while she conceals it and then is angry with the anger, so lets it go. Much of their prosperity is in the form of their attitude; my mother's still a maid.

Their mother did not remarry; there was no need to—the love within her (and the betrayal) was as strong as it ever was. It all came with her to Tennessee. And with Big Ma, what the grandchildren called her, came the dozen that she made with Curtis, bathed in the legendary water, a dozen as effectively established as the more famous twelve tribes of Israel. It is quite a legacy for my mother who is named for battlefields and victories: Florida Missouri Watkins.

How different it was at my father's house in many, many ways. His was a family of mixed bloods, the mother brown as burnt honey, the father brown only if he worked in the sun; not a black man. They lived in The Bottom, bottom of the hills. Every summer, until I was thirteen, I would visit both of my grandmothers, maternal great-grandmother, my aunts, and cousins in Drummond, Tennessee. My cousin Daney—Pretty Daney—and I would walk to the gas station, Texaco I believe—the town had only one—to use the bathroom. Eventually we were given our own key. Daney didn't like the outhouse anyway, whether or not I was with her, her brother liking me, his friend liking me when I was eleven and twelve, Tyson Somerville playing marbles with me, shooting some of them into my blouse. She also didn't want her refined cousin with long hair and long fingernails from up North to use a steel tub in the yard as she did, so we walked up the hill to Miss Helen's house that smelled like a spice forest. Her soap smelled good too, perhaps not expected of a Caucasian spinster. Back at Daney's house, her siblings who were too proud to bathe in Miss Helen's swan-footed tub would sit near us to sniff in secret our skin.

Up and down that same hill I walked between grandmothers, dividing myself as best I could, from Big Ma's cramped quarters to Grandma Leila's expansive white house and the porch that seemed to wrap around three sides of it, so impressed and excited I was the first time I saw it.

It is actually more modest, but still more porch than I've ever had. My father's was evidently a family of property, I thought, having lived in an attic, having lived in stacked apartments where the porches were not nearly as substantial. I remember important-looking (white shirts and dark ties) white men driving up in late-model cars and knocking on her door, perhaps to collect insurance premiums. I remember books in that house, expanse, pictures on the walls, braided rugs, bedrooms, one that could accommodate two full beds with case; a sitting room, a kitchen as large as half of the whole house my mother's family inhabited, widow as head of household, one child still in diapers.

I remember in my father's boyhood yard, geese white and fat as the pillows on the beds. A photograph of me, toddler in black patent leather shoes I still have, standing on the steps of that house, the porch grand behind me, and a photograph of the pale grandfather I never knew, my father a baby in his arms. I remember a photograph of my father early in his manhood, a brimmed hat cocked to the side—he looked like a sailor, like someone easy for my mother to fall in love with.

My father enjoyed indoor plumbing all his life, but an outhouse was still standing, a memorial to what his family was supposed to be. Grandma Leila Taylor Sterlin was a descendent of abolitionists of Philadelphia, or at least she wanted to be from that far east, near the ocean of her dreams; it was Civil Rights work that brought her parents, as she recalled, to Tennessee. When I was nearly three, Grandma Leila ordered the demolition of the outhouse. She was finally sick of that monument. My father, a high school graduate, tore it down with his bare hands as I sat on the ground shelling peanuts, sunflowers around me like bright cameras of dozens of reporters.

On the cusp of things, neither one nor another; mine are blended people. I enjoy multiple actualizations of self and mergers of what is believed disparate. That is my root. I love its complexity for what can grow from it. According to the research of my uncle (husband of one of my father's older sisters) who was a history professor at a university in Minnesota by way of Tennessee, Coon Rapids, and Anoka, my paternal great-grandmother actually came to Marrakech County, Tennessee, by way of West Virginia (my younger son's name is a town there, linking him to that inheritance) from a life among the Quakers (who were dedicated abolitionists). She was literate, constantly read the newspapers and wrote condemningly of racial intolerance and injustice, never forgiving whites for slavery although she was free all her life, unlike her husband who spent his childhood enslaved.

My paternal grandmother Leila was born just three decades after the Civil War, a child of the post–Reconstruction Era who eventually found writing social commentary irresistible. Until her death, she remembered horror stories from her parents about white redemption, but she did not condemn the entire white race or else could not have comfortably married into its fringes. Nor am I stranded in the past.

As for my paternal grandfather, Uncle Arthur C. said that Frizell Sterlin was most likely the son of a Cherokee woman and a free quadroon man related to whites in the county who were Frizells of French origin, in Marrakech County by way of North Carolina, some of them slaveholders and some not, my grandfather issuing, my uncle believed, from the slaveholding part of the family. Frizell's parents died early in his life, and he was raised, informally adopted, by a white family, the Sterlins, becoming literate and being sent to live for a while among blacks where he learned a trade and met Leila. Because Frizell was an orphan, it is particularly difficult to trace his genealogy.

In Drummond, it was widely accepted that this Frizell was not a black man; that creamy skin of his caused problems for his children who were known as mixed-bloods and were studied in the nineteen-thirties, I've been told, by the Mayo Clinic; all of the illnesses, especially those fatal, of my father and his eight siblings were attributed by both professionals and laymen alike to mixed-blood syndrome and accordingly were considered vigorous proof of the physiological disaster of miscegenation.

Frizell died young, Huntington's we know now, long before I was born, and of the nine siblings, only one survives, a woman who passed for a while as a full-blood white woman in the forties and worked for the government.

While in Marrakech County, my father, born Calvin Theodore Sterlin in 1923, worked for R. H. Brock's automobile dealership, DeSoto and Plymouth, maybe just polishing the cars, sometimes sitting behind new steering wheels and hitting the road in that mind of his that I still envy for the way it schemed and traveled, when he cooked right after high school for the railroad, beyond stops and layovers in and out of Oklahoma, as far west as Arizona. Somewhere between state lines and rules challenged by endless scenery, the idea for his slaw emerged, and the protocol of its preparation: cabbage shredded with an emptied can stripped of its label, his fingers aligned with the grooves. He cut with the can even after the invention of Ronco's Veg-o-Matic that he did not buy although it briefly tempted him. As much hot sauce as he could stand, his thumb obscuring the label's devil, passengers fanning themselves, some thinking it flashes of lust for the passengers next to them, my father knowing it was his slaw's success.

Although I can picture him easily in that position, my father could not have been a new car salesman in the early fifties in that insular southern town. That was not allowed; that was too much status. Even a mixed-blood man's privileges usually did not extend beyond mixing. I hope that he did not want to sell the cars, and was relieved not to exclaim the benefits of Plymouth although he would have known them as well as he knew the benefits of mixing, as well as he knew Mr. Brock's generosity, as well as I know that the fire of his slaw never leaves you. So if he waxed and shined them, I hope he loved getting his face close to those hoods, the rag supple in his hand. It is possible to love that, make a devotion of it as his brother-in-law did in the midsixties through the early seventies, beginning with the first of many new Thunderbirds. I too was enticed by the totemic white winged outline in the taillights.

Every Sunday belonged to the black auto; *Muncha Baby,* my father's brother-in-law whispered over and over, calling his baby daughter that too, a *Muncha Baby.* When I would witness this, I was not bothered by the gloss that as it brightened permitted deeper and deeper gazes and fattened my thighs, compressed my torso; the car controlled me and I just shut my eyes as my uncle rubbed himself into the finish. This was the uncle who also ate my egg yolks for me and talked me into eating the hard-boiled white parts that I wanted to refuse because halved with yolk removed, they looked like toilet bowls. I called him Uncle Spoon. Uncle Spoon and his first wife would separate, divorce in a few years but not before her trip through plate glass door to a balcony on which she placed pots of flowers she couldn't make hardy; her preoccupation was arguing with him, accusing, and there she was, flung as if they were trying to dance, she going into an otherwise magnificent twirl.

It had been such a problematic door. Its glass so clear at times, it wasn't there. A bird once had been knocked out cold. Wings do not necessarily make a difference; we need not covet only wings. Some birds were sucked into jet engines and ground to death by maybe some of the very blades my husband polished on second shift so long ago in the forge shop of the factory. But a bird soars on the way to this destruction; it soars.

They are fine now, the former spouses, in separate nonconverging lives.

I like the fire walkers, the snake handlers, swallowers of sword and flame. *I like those who come back from clinical death. And the one at whom the knives are thrown so that she walks away from wood, revealing her glowing stainless steel outline like a full-body halo, a total body crown.*

The truth is, my father was not in maintenance and was not a sharecropper although many Negroes, the etiquette then (though *negro,* in Spanish means *black,* so in some circumstances could remain the etiquette) were. Before 1953 could end, he would be in Ohio and his R. H. Brock experience securing him a job as a recapper for the Cardinal Tire Company. Many Negroes, even those who were educated, were encouraged to learn trades, destined for blue-collar employment, not positions of authority and power. He would rent an attic in the Wild-wood area of Cleveland and send for my mother in time for me to be born the next year up north. They wrote love letters back and forth; I have but a few of them. She keeps two hidden. In the south was his apprenticeship, his move into the lower middle-class independent of his family already there, and staying there even after his mother had to manage nine and then eight, the youngest died of a sports-related head injury, children alone.

When my parents migrated north as so many blacks did in the nineteen-fifties, my mother became a maid, and I sometimes went to work with her when Mrs. Feldman, and later a girl name Lytta, could not baby-sit. Mostly on Saturdays and during school vacations, sometimes just as a special treat, I was the maid's guest. We didn't have a car. My father claimed to have had a Mercury, sometimes a Studebaker or DeSoto, but only before I was born. After that, he didn't need to hold a steering wheel; it seems that until the day he died—when I didn't drive him fast enough to the hospital—there was no place else he wanted to go. I rode to work with my mother on the bus and dreamed dreams for the tight-lipped and the sour-looking.

I folded my hands and kept dreaming at the tables where she wouldn't let me eat though I wanted to badly; our table did not have the elegant scrolled legs or the oak and mahogany tops whose wood grains were like an artist's signature. I wanted to know if the peanut butter (never mixed with jelly; jelly would be on its own slice of un-crusted bread as a separate sandwich) or fried egg-white sandwich would taste differently on such tables; I knew I would bite the sandwiches differently, that I'd try for the most distinguished chewing possible, without moving my mouth or jaw.

We ate instead in a cool emergency stairwell of the high-rise, on Cleveland's gold coast, in which my mother worked. We spread Cannon towels, from boxes of Breeze detergent, over our laps. We ordered elaborate dishes from the menus we'd packed and would tell unusually tall waiters (we'd tilt our heads all the way back) to hurry as we had to return to the office in just half an hour; our work was much too important for us to be away from it any longer, and no else could do our jobs as well. These were menus we'd cut from ripped pillowcases and on them had stitched and embroidered entrees, appetizers, and desserts. The waiters served us everything on the house or the customer in the igloo hat or the customer with pelican pouch galoshes took care of our bill. My favorite dish was tiger stripe, a specialty of this establishment and a substitute for bacon.

In those cool stairwells, wrapped up in so much dim grayness, we found the place inside ourselves to which we could always return. Words we spoke there were like stones skipped on water falling with mild echoes to the bottom and becoming treasure.

I saw only the women my mother worked for, the wives, but for some reason I didn't think that odd. To this day, I can't picture them with husbands or even with fathers. It seems natural only when I picture them alone, or if not alone, then with my mother who sometimes would wash and style their hair, commenting on its fineness; how impossible it was to hold a single strand; when she thought she had one, it was at least a dozen, some of them twisted around her finger. She would say a ring was not practical; she'd have to remove it so as not to pull out their thinning hair that really was white, not the beige and ivory that were the colors of their often age-spotted skin.

She said she was glad she didn't have one, that a ring was not the most reliable sign of marriage. But the night I became engaged, she held the ring, turning it over and over in the light for an hour. She kept asking if it were real, she meant the world, its wonders, a small piece of which she was holding even though she'd have to give it up to me, the person for whom it was meant.

My mother wasn't able (still isn't) to come home from work without bags of cast-offs these women would give her: clothes, shoes, handbags, jewelry, kitchen gadgets, ceramic ware, porcelain figurines, lamps, mismatched pieces of fine china, and food, many forms of dark breads: zucchini, cranberry, applesauce, pumpernickel, and caraway. She'd be given furniture too, paintings, assorted business machines, small appliances, books, including the law books and stationery of a retired institutionalized lawyer once his wife heard that I was going to college, but these gifts, some showing their age and use too much, did not come daily. When she had enough of them locked away, she'd get someone with a van or light truck to help her take them home.

Dresses, some of them evening gowns I hope she won't actually wear, brought to her closet the perfumes of other women, sweetnesses and stories that won't wash out. She took every gift, helped them by deceiving them, letting them think they were helping her have what she'd never have if it weren't for them. But most of it she gave away to victims of natural and man-made disaster, and those held fast by poverty.

By now, my mother's house is furnished entirely with gifts. It is as if she lives in a museum, the Kitsch Hall of Fame. In the dining room is a fifty-gallon glass tank that once was home to tropical fish, mostly cichlids, but now is home to gaudy plastic flowers, plastic fruit, wooden, crystal, and soapstone eggs; cut-glass pieces of chandelier, that she thinks would make fabulous clip-on earrings; bills, a hand-carved bust of a beatnik, two Hummels, a Limoges dish, and Christmas cards.

My mother has visited some of these white-haired women more faithfully than their families, providing more than maid service. Sick, of retirement age, she won't retire; loyalty, friendship—and Christmas bonuses—get in the way.

Home for me first was in an attic, a walk up six flights of stairs in the rear of the house. There was no access from the front. Sometimes your father carried you up. Sometimes your mother and father each held one of your hands and you bent your knees so that your feet would not touch the steps; in that way you rode all the way to the attic door. My father would say *next stop: the penthouse.*

It was the attic of a two-family home owned by Mr. and Mrs. Feldman who lived on the first floor. Whenever I recall the scene, the Feldmans home enjoying everything they had, I make the scene botanical; the shavings from Mr. Feldman's carpentry seemed like petals. I place him outside although he worked in the basement that smelled of turpentine, varnish, metal, and acetylene, a fan always running. Reaching into pockets, stepping into shoes was the couple's deep entry into flowers. Petals would curl around their toes, fingers; seal them into the good closed night of a flower.

There was wiring in the attic, electricity to power our few machines and appliances, but not in my dormered room, a small space in which only I of my family could stand fully upright to see out the window. Thinking a long extension cord too hazardous, in my room, my parents placed lanterns and candles, the flames flickering, animated, excited. Long warm shadows moved along the spines of my books like fingers choosing the story best for that night. And when my father extinguished the flame, there was a faint white tail that dissipated slowly, too beautiful to be death.

I loved the blue walls and ceiling (my parents painted them blue and my Easter chick suffocated from the fumes); I lived in a box of sky. We were attic dwellers until I was five and the Feldmans sold the house to the Dorseys and we moved to the second floor, real tenants. The Feldmans moved to Wilmot Avenue, a street one block south of the street I would move to five years later. We stayed in touch with them, and helped them move, shortly after we arrived in the neighborhood, from Wilmot to Coventry as they stayed one step ahead of decline.

While we inhabited the attic, a family I don't recall occupied the second-floor apartment. Were they relatives of the Feldmans? Recluses or hermits? Bigots? I don't know. We kept our distance, perhaps with their encouragement, but once they vacated the apartment, it became our spaciousness, our hallways, our porch, front entrance, knocker and bell. Our moving down a level from the pinched and constricted top was easy; transition quiet and gentle—as if every article we owned were fragile. The Philco refrigerator and Muntz television floated down the stairs.

When I went back into the attic next, we were about to move again, almost five years had passed, and there was no blue anywhere, just darkness, fraying cords, a crack where pigeons entered and molted, wooden floor planks exposed through harsh-colored linoleum. It did not look habitable. Yet we had lived there, and it had seemed beautiful. As soon as I read it, *Diary of a Young Girl* by Anne Frank—my sister of the attic—became my favorite book. I think of Mrs. Feldman as Miep Gies.

Whenever I would visit the Feldmans, opening their kitchen door produced effects such as those when Judy Garland as Dorothy opened her farmhouse door to the land of Oz. I was overwhelmed by the brightness, as if all the walls were clear and glass and her original paintings were hung on air. There were baskets of vegetables in her kitchen and knit or embroidered throws and coverlets and doilies on everything. So many delicate objects, little porcelain dolls and figurines, miniature pieces of furniture, intricate carvings, crystal sparkling colored beads and pendants, books, pillows, mismatched place settings, but Mrs. Feldman would place spoon, locket, gravy boat in my hand so that I could feel the history of sumptuousness she would tell me; I wish I had not forgotten the details.

What a difference it made that I was allowed to touch, to handle her precious things, the entire inventory of treasure. What an honor that I was entrusted with the fate of delicate survival. While I held the breakable, it surrendered its future to me, and strangely that responsibility did not make me panic, but rather I stroked the object so gently it was more like the touch of a memory than like a real event. Then back into its tissue nest or back into its case or back onto its padded shelf. No object was tainted after being with me, not even by my breath. I am five and not yet given slim pencils in kindergarten; just those Laddie pencils and those thick crayons so fat they are awkward in my slim hands and therefore I sometimes think that I'm behind the other children. But in Mrs. Feldman's kitchen, I have printed my name with a golden pen. And she has told me that I will always be able to do this.

In my spare room is the metal electric stove that Mr. Feldman made for me when I was four. It was part of a complete wooden and metal kitchen that he built as I watched him saw, solder, hammer; as he screwed in hinges and tried the cabinet doors, opening and closing wooden wings. He was the only grandfather I ever knew, and he and my father were the same color.

In the stove, I used to bake tiny cakes, and his wife helped me make small challah loaves. I was allowed to plug it in. The stove has four eyes—the heating elements are all internal—but each eye consists of a circular grouping of small holes that allow heat to reach the bottoms of metal pans he also made. In one of those toy pots, I made a tiny serving of soup for my best and first friends outside my parents. The game of soup and bread. The flour on our hands, the grainy white mittens of cooks.

Above the eyes of the stove is a socket for a bulb of small wattage. And next to that is the oven itself, all metal, the door as well; the oven handle is wood that is painted silver to match the dominant metal. Inside the oven are holes grouped into a square that cover the entirety of the oven floor. The oven is lighted also. He made my stove from a kit from Metal Ware Corporation, but amplified the basic design with lights, a working oven where the kit had specified only a flat and basic stove top. Kenner's Easy-bake Oven does not compare! Mrs. Feldman made oven mitts and pot holders for me, but these have been lost. It is not possible to retain everything.

I always knew, although the situation did not ever present itself, that I could provide for myself, that I could make the small meal that I could eat. Food in the Philco refrigerator upstairs would last me for years; like a mouse, I'd break off nibbles and cook them. One pot roast for the rest of my life. Of course the stove has become a shrine, and yes; even a Holocaust shrine. I know what kept that man alive; he was a skilled metallurgist and carpenter. One of those cabinets that he crafted for my dishes and dolls, I still have in my mother's basement. I want soon to rescue it and explain to my sons that the ability to make something kept alive the man who made it for me. It's so important to know as much as you can about as many things as you can; the time may come when knowing something might save your life.

Mr. Feldman lived, and so did his wife, she probably because of her beautiful stitchery; she charmed the needles into doing anything for her. Did she allow a saved daughter to claim this stitchery as her own? Mrs. Feldman was gentle with her needles, even when she poked their eyes with thread. But maybe she survived because of more cunning.

Not a particularly robust child, I liked activities, sewing, that required long attention; sitting with Mrs. Feldman who would sit in a wicker chair and ease needles into cloth as if she were helping slender silver fish she had nursed back to health reacquaint themselves with water. In her calligraphy, she made for me the marriage license that proclaimed my relationship with Mickey Mouse legal. He already lived with me. I have lost the document. Mrs. Feldman and I both come from histories where fate, survival depended sometimes upon one's papers, one's official, authenticated papers. I realize that her hands were not soft at all, and that she always wore long sleeves, her husband too—I thought little of this as my father, lean man, also wore long sleeves all the time, but I'm sure now that there were numbers under the cloth, special treatment of the wrist.

Yet her hands knew the gestures of softness; she pampered with her touch the food she cooked.

~

Once, before the Feldmans moved, I had been able to walk by stoves without undue caution. There were knobs to regulate heat and make fire obey. Besides, gas was not strict in keeping to itself the odor purposely added so that it could not easily sneak upon me. A potential monster was under control. So I walked well by the stove in the Lills Drive kitchen, my braids loosening and bouncing when the gas surged blue, sucked the loose and flirting hair into itself.

What was it really? Ten seconds of burning? Probably not even that long. Mrs. Feldman put on oven mitts and suffocated the fire as I hollered, but I was ruined. To this day I will not strike a match; I will not light a candle to save a soul or wait out a storm-induced electrical loss. I will not do it, not even for the sake of romance. But neither will I deny fire; when it's near, I look at the burning fountains. The way fire grabbed at my braids, it was my first lover. It prepared me for all others.

Mrs. Feldman knew what to do. While my mother worked, Miep Feldman washed, brushed, braided my hair over and over again, my two braids hung over the back of the kitchen chair to dry. *There,* she said, her nose deep in a braid after what seemed to be hours of this, *no one will ever know you were burned.*

After the Feldmans' departure from Lills, house fires remained rare in my immediate neighborhood, but daily I could hear the soft whine of distant sirens. When there was a fire, all the neighborhood came out to witness the whipping flames and scorpions of smoke. Something irresistible tugged us all so that in nightgown, Oil of Olay dotted pink all over her face, my mother came out too.

Big, bad wolves, that people kept telling me about, could blow themselves silly and not even wrinkle the fire, at most just annoy it into shifting the wind so as to burn the wolves. Sometimes the wolves were made of fire and these could not be stopped if they wanted to come in, as one did that day to take Gladys by force. I watched as fire ravaged her brick apartment building, the flames spreading like a peacock's tail, so beautiful, so successful in attracting a mate: a willing peahen. Then thick black smoke gushed, erasing the beauty, dumping on it soot and burden. Gladys jumped to the ground, let spinal cord injury, that led to her death, have her rather than the wolf who thought her developing body was developing for him.

Gladys jumped; Gladys executed a great dive disappearing into smoke. These may have been two separate tragedies merging in my memory: Gladys fleeing a rapist, Gladys fleeing a raging fire; in my mind, she jumped but once. All arcs curve into Gladys. All winding roads.

You read about Icarus, Superman and that's the range of it right there; failure or success. Nothing else can happen. It is simple. In between comes Gladys, who learns from the mistakes of Icarus, flies away with a flock of birds, planes, no; with a flock of flying Africans. Nothing on the ground but a crumpled sheet, laundry that fell when Gladys whooshed by. Someone picks it up, folds it, puts it away. Martyr to chastity. Saint Gladys. On the way to her demise, she soared.

Moonlight and its deal with romance didn't motivate the neighborhood the way the fire did. Until Gladys was hurt, we observed with some pleasure the incineration of wood and brick by something that surely wasn't God yet was doing what God could do. As I stood there, I tried to feel what those involved with the flames and wolves were feeling, but as close as I may have come, I could not advance all the way to burning with what was burning inside the building. I would be singed, then I would back away my thoughts and feelings until they were no longer in danger of being consumed. I saved myself; made no attempt to save anyone else. I have felt responsible for Gladys although there was nothing I could have done. We stood there, I may even have been at the front of the pack, watching her like fanatics at the airport loving the takeoffs, holding our breath for the landings.

By the time we moved away, no one Jewish lived on Lills Drive. Little by little, the faces all became browner and the cooking smells in the evening were different, though they remained deep, rich smells. It was obvious the atmosphere had changed even if you drove or walked down the street and saw no one; there were different musics resounding through the brick and clapboard. There were street dances and block parties. I did the shimmy and the twist. I rode a bike with a wire basket on the handlebars down the hill that ended Alyssum Drive. I bought a jug of milk and fell off my bike, breaking the glass jug, cutting my leg. My mother picked out the glass, used peroxide; I was taken to the hospital by taxi, as she was too, soon after, when she broke a green coffee cup while washing it, glass wedged deep as bone in the web of skin between her thumb and first finger. And though she was cut, bleeding, she still braided my hair, tied ribbons on the ends and said how fine I looked, ribbons soaked in her blood, braids that got caught in the stove fire. But I did look fine, and my mother was determined to care for me no matter what disaster came along.

Doctors removed the glass from her hand and earlier, more easily, from my leg, but she had to know for herself that not the minutest particle remained to threaten me, so she squeezed the cut every day, prolonged the healing. But healing happened; there's no denying that. That is what is so remarkable: healing happened. Some sort of healing happened every day.

It was shortly after he finished high school that my father was christened Moe-lay by his brothers-in-law; my mother's five younger brothers, all born after all six of their sisters and one brother who was the eldest, never called him anything else. They sat around him in a circle; they were his flock. In Tennessee, Moe-lay managed and coached a Colored baseball team and had then his first circle, circle of *The Hawks*.

Always circles. Stirring the slaw. Pinto beans. Recapping tires. Hugging me. Phonograph records; a dozen 45s stacked on his thumb. Facial hair so trained and subdued, so scant, he could shave with the edge of a 78-rpm vinyl disk after my mother spread Barbasol on him as if she were icing a cake.

I didn't call him Moe-lay although I rather liked the name; I wanted to name him myself. No one else could call him *Daddy, Teddy.* I was with him as much as possible. He never thought that I was in his way. He spent evenings and much of Sundays fixing and improving the house. He liked to sing while he did this, and I loved to listen. Sometimes he told impromptu stories into which he incorporated what was happening around us. He'd begin with a question: *Do you know what happened when Samuel threw turpentine at the moon?* Even if I'd known, I would have lied just to hear him tell the story.

On one occasion, I watched Moe-lay take a crude nest from the gutter, one hand under it, one hand over its top. The universe became comprehensible the moment he touched it. For those few minutes, all meaning relocated inside two eggs that already held rock dove embryos, yet there was no crowding. Meaning fit perfectly, the nucleus it should be. He told me to study that nest and come up with the best place to put it so that hatching and dove life could proceed. Then he told me about other less obvious nests, and I watched him with his chin in my mother's straightened hair when I peeked in their room in the morning.

On Easter, there were many hard-boiled eggs though Moe-lay didn't eat them and I wrecked them disposing of the yolks. After Uncle Spoon, who had eaten the yolks for me, moved away, I had had to dispose of them myself. Hard-boiled was not always consistent although it was always twenty minutes of heavy boiling in the pot. Some yolks were like clay and I worked them in my fingers as if for Moe-lay or my mother I might sculpt small treasures: lucky yolk monkeys. Some yolks crumbled so easily that in my hand there was gold dust or pollen. Intact, the yolk was clown nose or yellow uninhabited planet, but that did not change the fact: I thought I'd wrecked what could have been chickens. So fine the way Moe-lay hid them, so shocking that my hunt failed so utterly, then it was even finer when he'd find them all on my person, pulling from behind my ears boiled eggs still white as the lilies on the table, and pulling them from my nest of hair, and from my mouth, full I had thought only of surprise.

With both hands on the nest, how did Moe-lay climb down?

Every Saturday night, his brothers-in-law formed a circle around him. He sat in a chair. They sat on the floor. His words would make life plain, the way his adolescent brothers-in-law needed it to be, the way his little girl thought it really was while he spoke. What was Moe-lay but the griot or shaman? He invoked magic, a sense of the world bigger than *"god."* My young uncles assembled to hear Moe-lay's dialectics of the soul. They all came north where poor lives resembled what they knew, from a distance, as rich lives in the south. They divided their weeks among their sisters until they found jobs in automobile factories and could afford bachelor apartments, breaking the circle. Moe-lay's disciples disseminating the word.

Sometimes the centerpiece, instead of conversation, seemed to be a bottle of Mr. Boston, and sometimes I, just nine, went with him to the state store where he had to sign to purchase these bottles from which he filled small, just-right-for-my-tea-set glasses like upturned bells, enough for all of us, even me, although it was strictly for our eyes. The liquor was the color of ringing.

No one was allowed to lift a glass or take a whiff, but after the session, I knew he drank them all and when he did, I imagined him taking on bourbon's translucence, this man who had so little color, but more color than two of my cousins who were albinos and were still in Marrakech county. Mr. Boston pulled from deeper dermal layers, deepened tonal values. He was a happy, harmless drinker, like Elwood Dowd in *Harvey*.

He sat with his legs crossed twice, at both knee and ankle, and explained the workings of the soul, the maintenance of the nest within. He insisted first that the soul be fed so that what hatched in it would have the strength to fly at the time of the body's demise; the soul must not get caught in death where, if caught, he thought it must remain. The soul being eternal only if free. My father said I didn't have to worry about Gladys. *It's better when the flight doesn't have the turbulence hers did, that's what you aim for, but her soul flew.*

He explained how some people, especially the weak, went to church to feed the soul; he wasn't going to attack that—how could he? It was something his wife loved and he loved her, waking her mornings by singing *Put on your Easter bonnet*. But he thought feeding the soul meant taking in the world, cataloguing it with all your senses, so he walked more than he rode, his body collecting all the data that his soul interpreted. Sensed presences meant nothing without the soul. Still, the senses would fall short, with ultraviolet wavelengths and gamma rays for instance, so for all the cataloguing, there'd be just a drop in the soul, and barely a beginning understanding of the infinite.

Though I'm not sure whether or not my father ever did it, he explained shouting and Pentecostal abandon as the soul trying to break free of the body, but the body understandably not ready to die does not let go and therefore has to participate in an ecstasy the body really can't handle or interpret, so the tongue starts speaking the soul's untranslatable language, the eyes roll back in the head trying to see the soul, and sometimes the body actually goes stiff or limp and stops breathing air because it's breathing something better, leaving the body no recourse but to either expire or recommit to oxygen just in time. The church nurses stand ready, a fence around the body, but they are really outfielders, and they won't let the soul out of the ballpark although a fly ball is on its way to glory and in its best interests should not be stopped. It is trying to fly free.

Moe-lay said not to worry. He said there is nothing but confusion about God. He said the confusion is understandable because God is beyond our experience as a body, but God is the ideal partner for our souls, which are just as eternal as God, because God does not want to be alone in eternity.

Moe-lay just didn't see the logic in the existence of hell. So the church had no use for Moe-lay, and he had no use for the church. He said good sense didn't allow that a God made entirely of love would create hell. Moe-lay got me thinking: *What could possibly motivate benevolence to create damnation? Why would mercy conceive of a place where mercy could not exist, forcing its own extermination?* I knew early that there must be other logic.

Evil, presumably the only product of hell, perhaps is like a virus, but given what certain strains of virus can do, given the way these viruses can completely possess (and usually ravage) their hosts, given that disease must be nearly as old as life, present soon after autotrophs (bacteria so entirely self-sufficient that they were likely earth's first life) became, in their simple division, sufficiently plentiful as to be available as food and habitat and a nudge toward complexity (as the numerous molecules collide and enact various chemical processes); given that virus is inactive and incapable of activity until it enters a living cell at which point it tries to establish dominance, then a virus actually becomes a possible model of God. Whether or not He is the creator, God does not function as *God* until there are believers and proselytizers. From what appears evil emerges the best established symbol of goodness.

God as a virus network traveling molecular and biological pathways; the choir sings: *I went to the church last night, and my heart was not right— something got a hold of me.* A virtuous virulence. God the virus, able to reproduce only in living cells. Being full of the spirit: being full of the virus of God. Wonderfully sick with God. The ecstasy and rapture when the virus that is God fully infests and dominates so that the body is no longer body, but is a mass of virus, a universe of virus, virus incarnate— a chain reaction for which plutonium is not required. No devastating strontium 90 fallout. Then are we one with him. God this way is not something vast whose profundity comes from enormity, but something unseeable whose profundity comes from its ability to invest billions of itself in dots and pinheads—what stars look like to the naked eye.

I like very much how Moe-lay conceded this: if hell is in fact established, don't worry; God, if he is any kind of father, will not send anyone there. He would not abuse his children; being love, he would venture no further than threat. At the last minute, if necessary, the fiery glow of the pit would become reflection of a profound sunset, and the father would forget why he was supposed to punish you since he didn't send you to hell when it would have done the most good: right at the moment of the transgression. Don't worry. And I didn't worry; my father never spanked me; I don't spank my sons; Frizell never spanked Moe-lay. *Hell,* my father said, *does not make sense.*

God cannot do this, Moe-lay insisted, but if he actually forsakes his identity and goes through with hell—because there's no denying the hell in the diaspora, middle passage and many similar displacements, craziness, detonations, the tidy eugenics and bell curves as attractive as the jump ropes of double-Dutch, the sonic appeal of the names of places whose actual poetry was disrupted, for instance: Alamogordo, Bikini, Chernobyl, Sarajevo, Bhopal, Birmingham, Buchenwald, Nagasaki, Three Mile Island, Rwanda, Oklahoma, another kind of bomb in Kikwit; if his hell is a success, then he would become our most challenging menace. Yet how we depend on nuclear energy; how we need the sun.

A soul needs more ambition than just keeping out of hell. A body needs more ambition than just keeping out of jail, said Moe-lay.

What is the soul? he'd ask at the end. My mother said from another part of the house that she hated for that liquor to start talking. She'd start her moaning song, minor key notes hummed adagio, full of the weariness of the ages, her original spiritual that she never finished composing. It was the same minor notes of overture: when she was upset with the bottle of Mr. Boston on the table, when her head or tooth hurt and Anacin packed in the molar's cavity had no effect, when she knew someone was about to die, anyone, strangers. The pathos of the song, beauty of the song; he loved to hear it, loved to provoke it.

What is the soul? he'd repeat, telling us to work on that question. We weren't supposed to forsake obligations just to concentrate on that question, but whenever we paused, just looked out a window or into a new car's finish, we were supposed to work on an answer. He would ask us whether or not a soul could tie a knot. My mother would fume. He told us that magicians wanted to pull a soul out of those top hats, and while the rabbits proved something was in there, they also revealed how dismally far magicians were from getting their hands on a soul.

After she was fully aggravated by my father's Soul Circle, my mother went outside, busied herself with flowers in the yard; she could make a bud bloom when she touched it, once even in winter, but she didn't know the names of flowers, only roses; she just knew roses. Actually, my mother loved getting out of the house, maybe because she couldn't think of herself without thinking also of travel, being named as she is after two states: sunshine and show me.

Most of the time, traveling for her just meant getting out of one house and going to another, either to work or to God's house where she also worked: cooking, cleaning, bookkeeping, praying. Only occasionally did she journey to a neighbor's house for a Tupperware party or Bingo. She did visit her sisters' places, but that was the same as staying home.

She was at church for the Tuesday Usher Boards Number One and

Two combined meeting, for the Wednesday prayer service, for the Thursday and Friday choir rehearsals, for BTU (Baptist Training Union) meeting, and all day on Sunday for Sunday school, morning worship, afternoon program, and evening service, coming home briefly between events. All those neighborhood churches, at least one struggling on every block, provided a place for the working class to rule; every member was part of the church's aristocracy; each one had a title, and most, including my mother, had several titles. I went with her from the beginning of my life, but did not devote the entirety of my Sunday; I split it between my parents: sacred mornings, profane afternoons.

While we were gone, my father worked on the house and completed the last hours of the ten hours necessary for the perfect cooking of pinto beans, onions cut up in them like small teeth. We came home to those beans, a cast iron skillet of corn bread, his secret recipe slaw, rice. I stayed and ate with him while the food held the initial hotness of its preparation. My mother would eat later, after church was over, the food reheated; she would eat my father's food even if at church she had already eaten, often her own cooking.

Rose of Sharon Baptist Church changed my life in unexpected ways. I was only five in my first clear memories of going there, so it was suspect just how much religion someone who couldn't tie her shoes (I was left-handed and had trouble with the right-handed lessons) could get. It was impossible, however, not to get something just by being in the presence of the choir robed in magenta satin and in the presence of all the hats, all the opulence of Sunday finery. For me, what made Sundays exceptional was the man elevated in the center front of the sanctuary, golden white lights turned upon him, the rest of the sanctuary dim and cool. He wore a white robe with gold brocade tippets, sleeves as full as wings; as he gestured through his sermons and speeches, he seemed to be flying.

Then there was the preacher's voice itself, soothing as distant thunder, then loud and pointed as if his tongue were a whip, then rhythmic and hypnotic like singing and dance, a hula of the voice. Those sounds filled my ears with an unrelenting numinous buzz. I thought honey would ease from them and fall thick in my lap. With just his voice he was able to bring women and men in the congregation to tears. They would shout and writhe, jump and run through the aisles, or simply stand and quiver, so overwhelmed were they by the power and intensity of the spirit that the voice of the preacher stirred within them.

And I was mesmerized, shocked by what a voice could command; the force of words that could touch, hammer, catapult, and bring down joy like rain. I wanted to do that too. Only with words. Nothing but words. The deacons lied in the prayers in which they pleaded for mercy for all those "under the sound of their *weak* voices." No; it was a baritone like my father's, shimmering when he sang like Crosby and Como, orated like President Kennedy, that really saved. It was the preacher's spirit-born bellowing so Herculean it kept heaven from crashing down on us. What was it made me feel so adored and special? The words my parents spoke that could heal what other words had injured. Words that could console when everything else was powerless. Words that made it possible to call upon magic you couldn't find unless you called it.

C# was a word that made me joyous; I saw poems when I looked at sheet music before I could read it at all in the church hymnals. I adored what an arpeggio looked like, the movement of it, the near spiraling effect of cuttlefish fins negotiating water. I understood it because it looked like what it really was: transcription of the praise song of my father's *good morning* to me.

I started to write stories when I was six on the heavy paper around which my mother's stockings came wrapped. She would discard the stiff paper, and when I first noticed those squares in the wastebasket, I immediately saw the mistake of the discarding; possibilities had been trashed. I retrieved the paper and on it formed words for the first time. More words the next day. Every day. Well into the night. Getting up when

I was supposed to be sleeping because the ideas had me so energized; they flooded me. Words wouldn't stop. Viral phraseology. Words came out of my fingertips as if I'd cut myself and bled stories.

Often I wrote as my mother sat sewing organdy for the curtains, our identical holiday aprons, dresses for my dolls; as she adapted her song to harmonize with music of the black Singer, for years a treadle model. I didn't have the steady sound of ocean, but I did have the steadiness of hum and stitch, a pacific background nonetheless, and I thought of myself as an embroiderer when with that rhythm I sat and put down words.

I wrote, not of what I really saw, but of the worlds I could not see but that were real once words revealed them. Worlds that could not be visited except through words. Write *river,* read *river,* and you can't stop one from flowing in your mind. A fully contrived world. For me, this was tenaciousness; this was fierceness. I made the world I wanted; I was perhaps a better maker of worlds than the maker(s) of this one. Time was under my written control. What couldn't I change? For me, this was empowering, the seemingly passive act of generating words, for language was the only context through which I understood anything; my life depended upon language. A mere idea could subvert the forbidden.

There was some alchemy going on: living graphite; living ink; rutabagas and beets giving blood to young vampires sucking on them in carriages so that they wouldn't have to tap the veins of friends, or so my story went. Special blood clouds, blood cakes. A generous animal. Story called "Many Heavens."

Anytime you spoke (or wrote) your mind, you were not lying, according to Moe-lay. I think the soul is made of the purest language.

When I was nearly eight, I wrote my first poem, after a two-year loyalty to prose, "Little Boys and Little Girls," on the back of the front cover of the church bulletin as I sat in the choir stand during the sermon. *Bible verses,* I lied when the choir director caught me writing. I thought it strange that he did not intercept especially that first note, opting to trust and believe me. A poem immediately had power. I was praised at the next junior choir rehearsal for taking notes. Others were told to follow my example. Deirdre and I passed notes about him. And notes about stinky boys.

It helped that the organist, who was also the junior choir director, at that time did frequently favor me above the other children. I was a runt so therefore likely the one with the puniest voice, in need of coaxing and protection, easy target for ridicule, an assumption borne out in rehearsal when Clarence Mipps, who was dominated by his own thinness and processed hair so receded it seemed about to slide off the back of his head, decided that I would lead one of the junior choir's A and B selections: "The Battle Hymn of the Republic." Mr. Mipps barely tapped the keys and instructed me to almost swallow the microphone to amplify my toned breath. He kept motioning with the hand not playing the melody for the choir to keep quiet while I sang the verses. The rehearsal microphone did all the work; I did not project, as if there were nothing substantial within me. I was not in the places where I knew I could succeed: at home with my mother, walking with my father or in Louis Pasteur elementary school. I didn't believe in myself anywhere else, where others controlled the language that defined me. Where girls jumped off porches. I didn't believe that anyone in any other place believed in me. I needed to be believed in, in order to exist.

And I was not self-sufficient; the kind of support that my parents, especially my father, provided, while ideal for my vulnerable self, did not lead to self-sufficiency. I was made for a dreamy world that existed in the mind, and I had the power to make any number of such worlds, but a world of thought differs much from a world of steel and concrete, that one being reinforced although it too began with an idea. My architecture was flimsy, required mental tenacity to maintain, but it was enough in my academic and household settings, enough when I walked with my father, collected feathers, ate with my mother in the stairwell. It was all too impractical a power, but no other power really interested me, really was not suspect in my thinking.

As rehearsed, Mr. Mipps restrained the organ, and the congregation was prepared to be polite. My mother beamed more intensely than usual when she was in the proven presence of God. But as Mr. Mipps played the tiniest sound, something happened. Unlike the vacant coldness of the sanctuary during rehearsal, the pews were full and the air was warm. I looked into faces focused upon me that were prepared to value what I presented. They filled me with power. Realizing that I had an audience, I seized my chance to be heard and took the microphone in my hand. It felt like a scepter. The part of me that was willing to fight to the death took charge of my larynx and endowed my voice with every unarticulated hope I had, hiding the specifics of my hopes in the lyrics of the "Battle Hymn," but committing to their future realization when I ruined the microphone and raised the roof of the church, erecting a steeple where there'd been none and ringing the bell that came with the new steeple. *Mine eyes indeed have seen the glory.* The stone rolled away. Attack of the voice that sounded as if it came from a Fifty-foot Woman.

On that Sunday, I introduced myself to a girl unashamed of fists, who could forget for an hour that the fist was a crude model of the heart. She was fortified by the robe, bodiless, snatched away from threats. Audience was a key to the kingdom. Audience completed the story. In fact, it wasn't a story, not really, until it was read or heard by someone. The preacher's words could not make women scream and swoon if the women were not there. I knew the effect my mother's song could have, knew that my father's singing was so perfect, its spiral matched the spiral of the cochlea because I heard them; I was their audience. I saw Moe-lay hypnotize us all so that on Saturday night we did not age until his voice stopped; the whiskey in the glasses rocked as he spoke, his voice pulling on the liquid like gravity.

~

My mother would take me to church with her to save me from her husband's corruption. It is interesting that her sisters became active in the church whereas the five brothers of the circle did not. I did not submit to God quite the way she wanted and didn't tell my mother that I wasn't worried. And I stopped calling myself a *wretch* in the singing of *Amazing Grace:* . . . . *that saved a* _____ *like me.* I filled in that blank, silently, any way that I wanted.

She, however, was worried and without problem became a wretch that she never was to me. Why would God require her to become something despicable? Why wouldn't his grace manifest itself in her more radiantly? But she did not realize that church was not the pure enterprise she wanted it to be. It was involved in as much loss as rescue, as I was finding out in Sunday school.

The teacher, Miss Kint, thought that dolls were idols. That Catholic saints were idols. To worship them meant the forfeiting of Glory. God didn't want us to focus on anything but him, she explained, and since we didn't have a correct image of him to focus on, we should keep our minds blank. We should try to be brain dead, visualizing nothing. Toys in general were sinful, made in the devil's workshop, not Santa's, each one a representation, false, not the real thing, so an idol. She said that what she was telling us came straight from the Bible's Ten Commandments.

Miss Kint hated most to see a baby with a pacifier, abhorred the phony suckling. She told us the parables that had been omitted from the Bible because the writers weren't listening to God except for when they wanted to hear him; they suffered from selective deafness. Didn't take good dictation as she did on her job; wrote down everything, even the gossip. She told us about the child she saw downtown, had ten pacifiers around her neck on shoestrings, sucked one for a minute, spat it out, sucked another, always sucking one of them; Miss Kint said the child should have spent her day up under a cow, but since Jesus was a lamb, she had idols around her neck. *She's going to that place I been telling you about; hot place, Children; going to burn all night, Children; skin going to burn off all night, cool off long enough to jump back on her bones in the morning, then burn off all the next night. She's on her way, Children. Get back! Get back from her ways.* She had a James Earl Jones voice half an octave higher.

Believing that there was no obedience without fear, Miss Kint threatened us that God was watching everything we did and would strike us dead if he caught us sinning. *Get back! Girl's about to sizzle. God's finger's pointing at her. Strike her like a match.* I worried that God may have brought down Gladys. That he could easily find reason to bring me down. Anyone down. For the longest time I had trouble going to the bathroom, not because I thought that urine or feces were sinful, but because I wanted privacy; I didn't want God to watch me pee and strike me dead for taking too much tissue or forgetting to flush.

Miss Kint was an incredibly bitter woman.

No matter; from my mother's born-again Baptist (Methodist while she lived in Tennessee) assessment, it was Moe-lay who taught heathenism; his vague and loose sense of God was not trustworthy. Moe-lay wanted to make sinners of all who were within the sound of his voice. Damnation was his destiny, though at his funeral, only his salvation was considered. His unchanging role as a cornerstone of the community. She wanted my father to be baptized, and he was, but according to his own spiritual doctrine. He held communion with mud puppies and snake doctors. He walked and knew the names of flowers, knew and identified for me: butterwort and nettle, cancer root, foxglove, shepherd's purse, sweet cicely, and enchanter's nightshade. It was a catalogue of miracles. He is the one I want to place in Galway Kinnell's poem "Saint Francis and the Sow," not Saint Francis, for my father spent all his time *reteaching me, reteaching everything he encountered, our loveliness.* Yet he did not write down his teachings (nor did Socrates), did not demand reverence, only indirectly in what became lovely after he showed it to me.

Moe-lay had so much.

I remember when Sam Cardinal died, the proprietor of the tire company my father worked for, long before my father who continued working in the same location, that had been renamed Raney Tire for the one who took possession. Such changes did not influence where bread was nor how we'd access it. Such changes did not affect the cardinals, Ohio's state birds, there all year, tenacious, named after the red robes of Roman Catholic Cardinals who, by virtue of their status, are well into ascension. We all knew bread.

Meanwhile, throughout everything we did, without our knowing it, rubber dust was settling like grains of wheat in his lungs, seeds of bread, and when he was full silo, dense as a challah loaf, he was complete, so breath left the nest. Dr. Archibald Grierson was the certifier of Moe-lay's respiratory failure: as a consequence of severe chronic obstructive pulmonary disease as a consequence of bilateral pulmonary bullae. I have a copy of his certificate of death. It is so much like my marriage license, Phi Beta Kappa certificate, three diplomas. A certificate of achievement; he has done this, he has fulfilled all the requirements, so this certificate with its official signatures and seal has been issued, granting the person named to all the rights and privileges of those similarly certified.

Best were the walks with Moe-lay to the bakery first thing Saturday mornings. In winter, the street lamps would be just going off, and holiday lights still flickered. All the shops would be closed, and in their big darkened windows, I would see our reflection. Bus after bus would pass by us, slowing down if it were raining or sleeting, but my father waved them on; we'd walk. Once we walked all the way to Fisher Body, once by the Carling brewery. Once to a refinery fire we watched from a bridge overlooking steel mills in the Flats. From the one-hundred-and-fifth block down to the fifty-fifth, the smell of the baking bread at dawn increased with each step until it became a mountain that we had to climb, getting giddy. It's a wonder that it wasn't called Everest Rye Loaf or Kilimanjaro Sourdough, but it was indeed Wonder Bread for which we trekked. I don't remember carrying the loaves home, but somehow upon our return we laid them on the table, loaf after loaf, as if we'd gone fishing or had earned special citations and awards in wheat. Where had the loaves been? Where were the shopping bags whose handles would have cut into our wrists or palms because bread is so significant it will be felt even if you are not eating it? I always know my proximity to bread.

Maybe Moe-lay entering the bakery was transformed, his arms and legs matching the baker's efforts wonder for wonder. Loaves strategically attached to my father like Popeye's spinach-sponsored muscles to Popeye. Special effects; being with him, the special effects in my life. We did have a folding metal cart in which sometimes we pushed our groceries home, but the occasion of Wonder Bread was more ritual than practical, more affirming than logical, so the bread would not have been caged even if the cage seemed to solve the problem of transport. Slice by slice perhaps we built the loaves over the course of many pilgrimages. One loaf by the end of the month. Days and days old. Straight out of the thrift store right adjacent to the bakery and the ovens where bread happened. I will never forget the first time I saw a slice turning blue, transfiguration sprouting on the white bread, furry, the start of downy plumge; it would fly away one day to heaven.

When my father named me, he said that I needed a name that had not previously existed because no one like me had previously existed, so he had a responsibility to this new presence in the world to honor it appropriately, the way that scientists name their discoveries. I therefore define this name and establish the precedent for any Thyliases to come.

So many times I was saved, by name alone, from sinking irretrievably into inferiority, from succumbing to the too easy, even if appropriate, blaming of discrimination or racism for every obstacle and failure. All black people didn't love me; all white people didn't hate me; black and white people weren't all people. So many times my name reminded me of worth, of the power of invention, language and imagination. It is a Urapé word, I once imagined, that translates according to what I need and is meant to be a name that defies abridgment or diminution. A beautiful intimidation.

To teach me, our walks always culminated with a visit to an underpass I named Echo Tunnel. He stopped talking when we reached the underpass on Elben Road and all its memory of urine. There I was instructed to say my name and when I did, it was amplified into an army whose victory was that I was anything but inferior no matter how persuasive the forces in my neighborhood, in the world.

It wasn't always necessary for my father to call me by my full first name once I understood my name's purpose, so my father also called me by a name of more simplicity and less expectation: *Rabbit*. The first time, that I can remember, when I was seven. For this selection of nickname I have no details. Occasionally, by the time I was nine, he referred to me as *The Rab*, more exalting and caught up in rabbinical regency. He seemed unable not to impart to me some authority.

But I am not now nor have I ever been rabbitlike at all. I suppose I liked bunny stories and I suppose that every spring I received a new stuffed Easter bunny, but these bunny occasions, if they existed, are not emphasized anywhere in my memory. Was it my fear of what one year was supposed to be Easter delight, a chocolate rabbit that stood, in my mind, six feet tall in the basement of the church and that I ran into sneaking down there in the dark before children were invited to witness its whacking and distribution? *Rabbit* I would be called to remind me of indiscretion.

Moe-lay never missed a nest on our walks.

I cannot know now why *Rabbit* was his preference for endearment. And there was, it seems, more witch and weasel in me than rabbit, because when I was fourteen I told him not to call me *Rabbit* anymore; I told him that I was not a *rabbit,* that it was unflattering, demeaning to call me *Rabbit,* and the moment I said it, I missed his calling me that because I knew he wouldn't; I knew for me he would do anything.

Until I was twelve and in junior high school, buying records, 45s, at Rudy's on Prinman Avenue or used jukebox records at Gray Drugstore on Nellis Road, my father bought the few records we had, and he was in charge of them, handling them by their rims or by stacking them on his fingers as if his digits were the adapter. He used Wildroot Cream Oil on his hair that, always straight, became lustrous, the sheen of a comely, chosen raven, and black like that. Even though he likely used the Wildroot in the morning, he used it again in the evening when he played his records. This was flirtation and seduction; these were love arrangements and overtures for his wife, but I didn't know that then.

Moe-lay played "I Want to Thank You, Pretty Baby," by Brook Benton, "Unforgettable," and "Wonderful World," Nat King Cole and Louis Armstrong, for my mother, "It's a Beautiful Morning," the Rascals, telling me, once I knew how, to turn up the keen, and I did turn until the knob was at its limit, but Moe-lay wanted in the music even more treble sounds that trembled as much as they did secretly when near each other even with me in the room, my fingers coaxing the knob even though it had no more keen to give.

He played "Spring" for her by Birdlegs and Pauline. "I feel that spring is coming on," the first line of the song, A-side of the 45-rpm *she* bought so that he could play it for her, infusing it with the keen. She didn't say anything; the record just appeared spontaneously one day at the top of the stack of 45s, and my father raised one eyebrow when he saw it, but asked no questions, made no comments; he just played it. My mother bought it, and I didn't hear so much as *one* hallelujah in the song! Those secular moments meant the most to her though she wouldn't admit this then or now, so I say it for her, and do for her whatever she can't do now that still needs doing, just as for Moe-lay I remain committed to the keen, my hand still on the knob, turning it a little further than was possible then, the keen so high I can't hear it, but I feel it passing through me, keen memories of his keen thinking, eggs inside a nest.

My mother believes herself now to be on heaven's doorstep; she talks more and more about what to do when she's gone. I say to her though it sounds like feeble reasoning, that she'll never be gone, that dying is not something that zaps away all evidence of your having been in the world.

—*Have you ever died before?* she asks.

—*No. Of course not, Mama.*

—*Then how do you know that dying won't be the end of me?*

—*Because it wasn't the end of my father.*

—*You can only keep him alive while you're alive. There are things I know about him that you don't know. Things that I'm taking to the grave. Things that he already took to his grave.*

—*But his ways, Mama; some of his ways are my ways.*

—*I believe you want his ways to be your ways so you can still hold on to him. But would those ways be your ways if he was still alive?*

In this conversation, she says nothing about the Lord catching her in his arms as she falls out of life. She is just scared and not especially eager to leave this world for the glory she has lived for all her life.

I do not want to be a widow. I do not want to know her incomparable loneliness.

Tale of a Sky-Blue Dress

~

Those not wise would say my parents spoiled me, but love preserves. They didn't live just for me, but they made me feel they did.
My father and I watched television together, programs my mother said
just weren't useful to her ambition of going to heaven, so she could
tolerate them (if she was through *getting that week's Sunday school lesson*),
but not *enjoy* them. Sometimes she would sit in the living room with us
and laugh at Lucy Ricardo just as you might expect she would, but she
claimed (just a little white lie) not to be paying attention so that we
could see how focused she was on her salvation. Just in case Jesus came
right then, she didn't want it to look as if she found anything other than
his words, all red in her Bible, entertaining. It would have been different
if Lucille Ball and Desi Arnaz's script had been written by King James.
But I liked it; I wanted to see it; therefore, so did she.

—*Lucy has too much of the devil in her,* my mother said, watching
her. *If she would get herself right with God, she wouldn't have to spend so
much time scheming. I'm going to be rich one day,* she continued. *Heaven is
a golden place.*

—*Don't you ever get crazy, Mama, over needing to see Peking, something
like that? I mean, some people get crazy over needing to see the moon, but me,
I have trouble believing sometimes that there's other countries on the other side
of the ocean. Sometimes I think the ocean is everything.*

—*Jesus is my travel agent. My ticket's already bought and paid for.*

—*How about a trip to the Holy Land, then? You could walk where Jesus
walked, go into the garden; if you take Daddy with you, you could do a little
kissing like what went on in that garden that night. The moon was so perfect.*

—*Your Daddy's still teaching you to blaspheme.*

—*That's in the Bible. They kissed. Bet you a King James' ransom they
kissed. But you could go there, all those places you underline in your Bible, the
cities you circle on maps.*

My father started to make sounds like a jet. *Who's going to get her on the plane?* he asked.

—*She could pretend she was getting on an angel's back.*

—*If I got on the back of an angel, I'd make that angel take me to heaven; that's really where I want to go. Heaven is a golden place.*

—*Mama, don't get on before you get your license to pilot an angel.*

Then she told me, as she'd told me many times, about the gold bricks of the streets, the twelve golden gates, the golden eyes of believers, gold tongues that could say only words of gratitude and sing only hymns out of *Gospel Pearls*. Everywhere in heaven would be the fluttering of the gold-veined wings of the angels as if the angels were dragonflies, wings that thin, invisible, the gold veins like loose strands of floating hair or strings of drying honey.

She thought she wasn't lustrous.

—*I've got heaven on my mind. It's there to stay.*

From the time that I was five, I can remember how going through the channels, my mother would linger on any program that mentioned God, and sometimes, to hear that, she'd have to catch sign-off or sign-on that included the national anthem and a prayer. I liked the test pattern and would get up early just so as not to miss it. It was a little like the painted wooden pies that taught simple fractions in second grade. It was television's most benign offering, broadcast without commentary, without commercials, without movie stars, without bias. The living room for the half hour of the test was a gallery for this temporary installation.

Otherwise for my mother, television, when it was on without any of us watching it, as it often was, just brought strangers in the house, as if our house were a public place, maybe a bus or train station; a place where there would be cordiality, maybe an exchange of names and occupations, but no expectation of remembrance or continued acquaintance.

The strangers were pleasant enough, especially the ones on "Death Valley Days"; they kept their voices at a steady volume that made it easy not to concentrate on what they were saying and they took no offense if you didn't make eye contact, yet you came to depend on the voices and the music that complemented and filled gaps in dialogue as if these were the natural and inevitable sounds and signs of life. From the TV came the sounds of inclusion, the background that was comforting in its disproving of void. Through these sounds we were connected to events and on-going existence beyond ourselves, a service any sounds that I make can provide for others who happen to hear them or the consequence of them. I can make telephones ring thousands of miles away.

My mother would have to run to change the channel before I'd see the bubbles of Lawrence Welk's champagne music or the television would be committed to that variety show that for some reason got on my mother's nerves. If I saw the bubbles, she wouldn't change the channel; she respected my delight in them, so did not pull rank. My parents never did that. My father rather liked the bubbles too, and accordions; I think he really liked accordions; I would see him many times tapping against wood or the plates just as if he were fingering an accordion's keys. He did not outright articulate a fondness for the accordion, but he became more attentive when the accordion was being played on Lawrence Welk. It was for the accordion that was regular on Lawrence Welk that my father preferred that show to Ed Sullivan, although both of us enjoyed Mr. Sullivan's resemblance to Frankenstein's monster. And it was the accordion that got us hooked for a spell on polka. Sometimes, the way he stared at our upright piano, it seemed he was trying to shrink it.

The piano had been left behind by the previous tenants. We abandoned it, as they did, when we moved from Lills. None of us could

play it. Into the night, I would pick out one-handedly the notes to
"Amazing Grace" and "My Country 'Tis of Thee" (the title is really
"America" and "God Save the Queen," but I didn't call it that), singing
softly into the keys, my lips brushing them. But there was a note, flat,
sharp or natural, for each syllable I sang; eventually I found it among
the keys that were always cool, as if they hadn't been touched. Deirdre
and her sister had piano lessons in their home; a short-haired, blue-haired
lady who wore mango lipstick taught them. Deirdre played "Drifting" so
well, even played it backward, calling it "Drafting," I was jealous, but
soon she lost interest in her lessons. My jealousy perhaps would have
encouraged her to play longer and better if she'd known about it.

We turned on the television right after dinner. After my mother
and I cleared the table, putting away leftovers and stacking the dirty
dishes, we sat back, princess and queen. No need for us to watch *Queen
for a Day*. This was the ritual for years; on Lills Drive, on Trunt Avenue.
My mother never had to wash a plate or pot or spoon or glass while
my father lived, especially not after she wounded herself on his green
coffee cup, or was it hers—they were identical. My father wouldn't let
me have dish detail either. He liked doing dishes, and sang through the
chore, a dish towel through his belt loop, a half smile at all times on
his lips, an eyebrow raised the way Leonard Nimoy as a Vulcan would
raise one eyebrow. Actually, Nimoy in the Spock years and my father
had astonishingly similar builds, and shape of face. As my father's illness
progressed, as he became more barrel-chested, his face, neck and hands
yellowed, darkened; he died light brown. I think that after my father's
death, I grew more fond of the original Star Trek reruns because it was
a way of reviving my father, placing him so far into the future, the
revival had the effect of immortality.

Doing the dishes, my father used water so hot, I was afraid for his
flesh. I thought he'd reach into the scalding soapiness, and pull out hands
and wrists stripped of their skin, which would float in the water like

the reflection of scud clouds, then would dissolve in the heat. The water turned all to steam it was so hot. His skin would be vaporized. But no, his hands came out wet and clean like the dishes that he gently wiped with the dish towel and stacked on the table. After he dried them, he would permit me to put them away. Each utensil washed received this treatment. He seemed to thank the dish for becoming clean. He seemed to thank the water for allowing the dish to clean itself in its wetness. He seemed to thank the soap for its talent. He seemed to thank the steam for its clouds that rose up from the sink to kiss his face that leaned into the empire of clouds to meet them.

Trouble was, my father began this devotion to dishes because he didn't trust me or my mother to get them clean enough; always a residue of potato or egg in the fork tines, lipstick on the rims of cups and glasses. He had the most trouble in inexpensive restaurants, wanting to inspect kitchens, wanting to see for himself that utensils weren't merely washed, but were sterilized. It embarrassed my mother and the relatives with whom we traveled, but when traveling down south, we had to stop at restaurants as we were not like those families who packed shoe boxes of cold fried chicken and such; we should have been.

I don't even think that he was paranoid about germs, not obsessive-compulsive; would not object to the intimacy of sharing a glass (he would have drunk from the goblet after my mother at the wedding, had they had a wedding)—he showed no compunction at all about tasting the tidbits offered by companion diners on their forks; the companions were family, of a similar bacterial rigging, and paranoia doesn't necessarily respect familial territory, especially the territory of in-laws. I don't think that my father was actually fanatical about hygiene; he had no gas mask in the house, did not breathe through gauze or wear rubber gloves, but clean impressed him, a thing reduced to just itself and its glowing essence. The rapture of clean.

On Saturdays, after the bakery and supermarket; after the accordions of the Polka Party televised locally from Parma (a suburb of Cleveland) during which my father and I would lose the rhythm of our dancing from laughing too hard, he and I would settle into watching several hours of science-fiction movies: *Attack of the Crab Monsters*, *Kronos*, *The Incredible Shrinking Man*, *The Giant Behemoth*, *Them!*, *The Attack of the Fifty-foot Woman*, *Amazing Colossal Man*, *Frankenstein* (the 1931 version), *Bride of Frankenstein*, *King Kong*, *Mighty Joe Young*, *Hypnotic Eye*, *Wasp Woman*, *Invasion of the Body Snatchers*, *Day of the Triffids*, *Queen of Outer Space* (featuring Zsa Zsa Gabor), *House of Wax* (featuring Vincent Price), *Day the Earth Stood Still* (featuring Michael Rennie and Patricia Neal), and *War of the Worlds* were our favorites. He used commercials as opportunities to lecture and helped me to stop believing that the large radio towers and high voltage Erector-set (that's what I always built with my set) structures that lined the countryside like an electromagnetic army would not move as I thought they would ever since *Kronos*.

My father assured me that man could not make so sophisticated a robot and that in truth, we were the power-hungry creatures. Science-fiction films of the nineteen-fifties and early sixties were mostly thin parables exposing the monsters in our mirrors, how inhuman and unethical we could become.

My father and I talked about *Kronos* for hours. It was somehow a preface to the discussion on the soul that would happen that night. This was our film. My mother's fervor just wasn't ignited by such usages of the imagination or intrigued by the boost to imagination that a dose of (pseudo) science added.

Kronos, named for the Greek god who fathered Zeus, the father of gods and men, and who himself, as Time, sprang out of Chaos and devoured his own children (anything that begins, ends), comes from outer space as a glowing disk, a typical flying saucer called an asteroid by those tracking it in the film. It crashes in the Mexican Pacific in a mushrooming splash that rivals the most notorious atomic incident. Believing that atomic incidents are inevitable and man's everlasting folly, makers of such B movies do not shirk their responsibility to warn the masses about the horrors we bring upon ourselves, engineering our own destruction. Atomic cinematic effects are usually enlargement as a form of mutation: ants, crabs, octopuses, grasshoppers, praying mantises the size of the largest dinosaurs so that man becomes David no matter that most of his life he is Goliath.

As David, man regains his status as beloved in the cosmos and God's beloved, so prevails, defeats the monster, sometimes just because there is a fortuitous shower of rain or the invading creature fails to adapt to all the conditions of earth or there is a cooperation of nations that shows for the moment the arbitrariness of politics or there is implementation of a cunning scheme that succeeds where military brute force fails. The Blob, for instance, is frozen with CO_2 after it exposes its Achilles' heel, something all mutants and extraterrestrial beings in these films conveniently have. No infallible form of life.

In fact, the use of military might often serves to enhance a monster's abilities, but the military is usually consulted and usually takes charge though ultimately generals defer to civilian scientists who in these films frequently fall in love and are sexy, often female, seldom nerdish, accessible even while the monster devastates a city—the scientist takes time to flirt and kiss.

In outer space, there were mostly fiends, mostly English-speaking fiends, before Spielberg's ET evolved. Fiends of more advanced mentality and, usually, brutality so that humanity must become humble and entirely vulnerable, defenses and offenses useless. He must be at the mercy of something greater, a greater evil, not a greater good, so that he will be encouraged, if he survives, to reroute his destiny which the film says is the greater evil, toward which he's heading at an atomic pace.

The morning after the splash, a farmer notices a metallic structure on the beach: two stacked gray cubes, building blocks suggestive of a one hundred-foot-tall intergalactic box kite. The farmer crosses himself, certain that Kronos is no gift of cosmic sculpture. Frantic, the farmer runs, screaming for the scientists who have followed the asteroid to this

Mexican beach. As they rush into their helicopter to investigate, Kronos wakes; the metallic pupa matures. A small dome head emerges and two poles so that head plus poles seem to be a set of rabbit ear antennae atop a square television that is a solid cube; no screen. A column supports this cube and separates it from the other cube. Pillar-sized cylinders form the legs that move like pistons as Kronos walks, looking for power stations, even better a nuclear power plant or two, for his lunch and supper.

Earth becomes for Kronos, and the little Kronoses to come, an atomic garden of Eden, a paradise for those who are nourished by megatons and destructive capability, the effects of thousands, at first, then millions of tons of trinitrotoluene: TNT. Cities darken as Kronos drains the power, feasts all the way to Los Angeles. Nothing, although the air force drops bombs (tasty appetizers) and both federal and state law enforcement officers shoot at it, can penetrate the dark metal. It is made of a substance not yet known to man by an intelligence not yet known to man. We are doomed.

But the lead scientist works out a theory on his blackboard as his love interest (a lab technician) and his assistant (an analog computer whiz) watch chalk reveal earth's last hope. It's still feeding time. The scientific chef cooks up some omega particles that reverse Kronos's polarity, causing autophagia—the electromagnetic creature devours himself. Too bad the scientist is savior of the atomic age only, not of subsequent ages and their revised scientific truths. What's certain is that there will be more gluttons for energy and power, for knowing whatever can be known. Another wiser Kronos might be unstoppable.

Where was the soul in that movie? my father asked. I liked his tests.

After we watched the film, he made broom straws walk for me, Brook Benton on in the background, *Boll Weevil Song,* my father singing along. No matter how many times he made them walk for me, I didn't tire of them walking just as I walked with my father.

To make broom straws walk: you need three lengths of broom straw, two lengths about one and a half inches long, and a longer length of about three inches, varying with the distance you want to make the shorter straws walk to each other; they will embrace upon meeting. The two shorter lengths are bent in half and these Vs are placed, inverted, on the longer straw, one at each end, points leaning slightly toward the center of the straddled longer straw, the inverted Vs' legs touching the surface of the table or floor on which they will walk. An end of the straddled straw is held between the thumb and first finger of each hand, elbows steady, perhaps resting on something, at a height whereby the legs of the bent straws maintain contact with the smooth surface. I have never tried this, nor did my father in my presence, on carpet or upholstery or a bed spread. Then be patient, and the bent straws will approach each other shyly. They are in no rush even though they may love each other as much as straw can love. And when some of us are children, we believe that anything can love, anything can spurn or be spurned.

As long as the straws are oriented toward the center, that is the direction in which they will move. When their points touch, they stop. Then, you can gently pull the straddled straw from under them, and they will continue to stand in their embrace. Or you may call the standing structure a pyramid or teepee as my father did. You may leave it standing there for the rest of the day, for as long as you like, as long as it survives. It is a most impermanent structure. It is not meant to last, mere minor architecture, but everything is minor in some context, so enjoy it while it's there.

Dismantling this structure is easy. A flick of the wrist. Don't let that be disturbing. Or the long straw can be reintroduced. The lovers will remember it and will straddle it. Then, separate them; put a stop to the embrace that has lasted as long as you have allowed it to last, barring interference from another living thing, be it human or other animal, or breeze or other vibration against romance. Reorient the points of the straws to the ends of the straddled straw-line and the straws will separate, walk away. Left standing, perhaps the straw pyramid or teepee will attract spiders. Or dust may accumulate under it. I do not know how long the structure may hold, but no matter how carefully you watch, no matter how good you are as parent to straw although you are not of straw yourself, the structure is fallible. One day the straws will fall as if they are Capulet and Montague on your table, everything dead about them except their love.

Besides making the straws walk, my father used them to select our watermelons. He avoided taking straws with him from home because that would have been far less theatrical. He preferred asking the produce clerk for a broom straw. An odd request I always assumed, but perhaps not; certainly the request was never denied, but invariably, my father would refuse the first straw offered. It would be somehow defective, so my father would ask to see the broom so that he could educate the clerk on the selection of a broom straw best able to detect the sweetness of a melon.

By now, other customers would gather around him. I assumed that were we in Marrakech County, all customers would be busy with their own straws, but in the north, you dispensed with the country and backwoods evidence as fast as possible, so the crowd would gather because they didn't know, or pretended not to know, about this process and were curious. My father got himself a public circle.

He'd select his straw and rub it a few times then place it on the white belly of the melon, where the melon had touched the ground and grew and, as the straw would reveal, ripened. A straw that wobbled indicated a so-so melon, one that a melon thumper would buy only to be disappointed when it was cut. Now if the seller would plug the melon, then you could be sure, but my father had a technique as reliable but without such biopsy. Generally, melons in supermarkets would not be plugged unless there was proprietor willingness to sell the plugged melon as cut melon, certainly more profitable for the store to sell by the pound instead of by the whole melon. The watermelon men who came up from Georgia and Arkansas with the stake-body trucks full of melons were so confident of the sweetness, that they would plug the melons. They knew that one miserly taste would make you buy the whole sweet thing, no matter the price demanded. They smiled and laughed, their teeth so clean you knew they were kept that way by biting into the sweet deep red flesh of Georgia melons.

We were in the supermarket, however, so we were spectacle just as my father wanted. A straw that didn't turn at all either revealed a dud of a melon or a melon diviner that didn't know his straws or his bellies. Now a straw that on contact with the melon belly turned 180 degrees or tried to do the 360, that melon you bought and rushed home to cut it open and indulge in private because the sweetness would be so intense and incredible that you would get crazy in your enjoyment; you would just totally lose yourself to the pleasure of the taste. We always took home such melons. Others in the store would ask my father to select a melon for them, and he always obliged, even offered to pay for their next melon if he failed to select the best melon they ever had. There was applause. He never had to buy a melon for anyone but ourselves. Such great melons did not even have to be cut; you inserted the knife tip and began to plunge the blade deeper when suddenly, the melon would just split by itself, the juice too red to be watermelon juice, the sweetness visible; the bigger half: the parent; smaller half: the daughter.

Tale of a Sky-Blue Dress

Perhaps we were not quite the idyllic family I imagine; after all, already in the genes was Huntington's, the disease that claims so many Sterlin. Diabetes mellitus too, courtesy of the Watkins, hypertension, heart disease, a beloved cousin would die at thirty, before I could fulfill all my promises to him, when his congested heart failed; it had been enlarging while my father's lungs were filling with rubber dust and toxic effects of Pall Malls. Those lungs were an hourglass. I ate in my first year one of his cigarette butts, a meal that returned me to Mount Sinai hospital for the pumping of my stomach. Right then my father was so motivated to quit, but nicotine owned him the way an incomprehensible hopelessness came to own some of the people around me.

If you spent most of your time on my end of Lills Drive, from the intersection of Lills and Mayfair and on toward the east, you didn't know that Lills was at the top of a hill that seemed steep to me at the time, and even steeper when Deirdre fell out her father's Chrysler going down Alyssum Drive. She was not hurt but surely should have been, her arm dragging along the asphalt.

I remember well-manicured lawns that were host to plastic flamingos and big iridescent balls, most of them pink, held by tall cement pedestals that otherwise would have been birdbaths. Lime green pedal pushers and elastic leg rompers enlivening our ring games, some that we played at the Rose of Sharon Baptist Church Vacation Bible School. There were street clubs throughout the neighborhood and club sponsored street

dances and cookouts. My father was once the president of the Lills Drive
street club; he enjoyed this civic authority so much that when we moved
to Trunt Avenue, he attempted to organize a street club there, but
nothing came of those efforts. It was by then the mid-sixties and time
to riot, although he neither looted nor burned. The Kingdom of Lills
did not predict nor usually produce dark ambition.

The day the Dorseys moved into the kingdom, I was still confined
to the house with measles. All the shades were down, the curtains
drawn, and I wore Mickey Mouse sunglasses all day. I wasn't sure what
was happening as my parents hadn't told me that the new owners of
the house would be arriving that day. From my confinement I could
hear commotion downstairs: loud voices, the sound of heavy boxes and
cargo shifting. The sound of muscles and endurance approaching limits.

War; there could be a war going on downstairs, I thought, although
I heard strain, challenge, not exactly battle, for I had seen westerns on
television, in black and white as if even tonal qualities had been negoti-
ated and choreographed. A ballet of war, a certain mildness in the
conflict, in the beauty of the Indians circling the wagons, the white
covers billowing as if the Indians would help raise the wind that would
lift the wagons and sail them away. I did what was expected of a measled
girl with a Chatty Cathy doll hearing the brutal sounds of dragged metal,
breaking wood, banged pipes; I denied that what I heard could be pain.
Chatty Cathy could talk; pull the string on her neck and she'd say: *I'm
hungry* or *Will you play with me?* or *I love you.*

A typical family arrived: Kell, the mother; Vaughn, the father;
Rhonda, the eldest; Lytta, the middle child; Trevor, the baby, the boy
still at home unlike Alonso who was gone; *he's gone* was the most anyone
ever said.

Lytta's face was round and unremarkable. A face of function, not
beauty. She was going on thirteen. She didn't speak to me the first time
I saw her up close, about a week after she moved in, but she rushed

to shake my parents' hands. They thought she was so well mannered. Right away she offered to do baby-sitting. Right away, before she knew anything about me. I was still five. In a few months, I would enter first grade. My parents thought it would be all right if Lytta worked for them. My mother laughed at Lytta's sense of enterprise. *She'll go far,* she said. But Lytta was a girl who wore a sky-blue dress of crinoline and taffeta every Sunday; the same dress, the same hope, the satin sash at the dropped waist sagging and the blue rose flat, the tulle underskirt torn and unkind to expanding teen hips by the end of the year.

Her older sister Rhonda wore glasses and usually kept her hair pulled back into a straightened ponytail, occasionally a French roll. I want to put freckles on her face, but I'm not sure that they were there; they should have been. She went to secretarial school and edited stories I wrote, but I threw her typed versions away, keeping only my handwritten originals that I hadn't intended for her to see anyway. Lytta, on the other hand, seemed somewhat offended by my pretty idea of the world. My stories mostly offered pleasing resolution no matter what peril characters encountered; Lytta questioned this optimism. She didn't try to force tragic revision, but she was bored by my writing and bored by the library books that I would read aloud to her and to Rhonda. She would say that I'd outgrow such kid stuff, but, perhaps to defy her, I continued for years to dress Skipper and Midge (Barbie's little sister and friend) in tulip and gladiola petals, so hard to stitch, lying when my mother wanted to know what happened to her flowers. It was too easy and automatic to say *stray dogs.*

Rhonda was old enough to live on her own, to spend the night with men, but I don't remember any man ever coming to her house to see her; I don't remember Rhonda and Lytta ever talking about boyfriends; I don't remember Rhonda laughing. Not that I was with them more than necessary. Small busted she was, and narrow waisted, lean calved; Rhonda should have modeled, should have done many things, but evidently she was reluctant to leave home, although, for they were an obstreperous family, from the day they moved in, I heard no evidence of solace in their apartment, saw no door opening into the land of Oz.

In the reign of Lytta, in the Kingdom of Lills, roses ringed the house on bushes the height of Lytta's thighs. And one day in the hallway, her cigarette butt still warm, she ran her fingers along those thighs, inching up the hem of her dress, to the delight of a shadow near her, just as if her fingertips were petals and this their soft season before autumn's brittle reduction, the petals crumbled in those same fingertips to powder and ash. Then the fortunate dumping of lake effect snow and the yard was a blank page on which my arms flapped furiously, a cathartic effort that succeeded only in making a cold imprint of an angel.

Going on thirteen, evil hour not on the clock, not in the elevator, not in the twenty-story building downtown, Lytta was born to two parents married to each other and owners of their garden-adorned home, two cars, one a late-model Buick and gold. I noticed the blatant normality of her family, Lytta rolling down the right rear window and sticking out her head, staring at me, as I stood immobile on the porch the day that I met her, as if to put upon me a curse as her father backed out the driveway that at that moment seemed dark as an alley.

Probable scenario: Her mother rushed to her new daughter, even if the baby cried while she was making love with her husband, and rocked that baby, said into the baby's ears, her tongue a medicine dropper, words and promises the baby could not repeat in words not even after Lytta was grown, but that influence went deep into the eardrum and from there into the brain, though baby talk does not sustain for long. Her mother with the narrow waist and slim long legs that her husband was glad, surely, to claim; all four of her babies were his.

There was a party in the basement and Lytta was there, and I am holding both party and Lytta in my hand in a photo. It was my party and my dress is barely pink and my curls are over my shoulders and down my back and it is hard to see me although I am in the center of the square. So many children crowded around three cakes, two chocolate rectangles and a round white one with coconut and candles in the center of the table. Since it is a photo, everything that was separate and three-dimensional is here one entity. As if I am flat, painted on the walls, and my hands are somehow cakes, but my eyes aren't repulsed by this deformity. Birthday girl, the cakes, fifty kids—Louis Pasteur's entire first grade—and the large girl in blue crinoline and taffeta in front of everything and so big that half of the photo is her, form one continuous object. Almost from ceiling to floor is her length, a distortion that makes her integral as a beam, the support of the scene, the icon. A mirror does this too, allows the lower half of my body to be a sink, merges my head into the cool reflection of the wall.

They sang *Happy Birthday*. Some of them said *cheese*. It was not a provocative celebration. Some just stared into the camera's flash as if to see if it were truly an evil eye. I opened the gifts in private as I always did, sitting on my Hollywood bed, the red tufted headboard making me feel privileged. I always tried to remove the pieces of tape without the decorated surface of the wrapping paper sticking to it and coming off. I liked no idea of ruin. Then I folded the gift wrap as if it were fine linen place mats and lace tablecloths that one day would be part of a dowry.

This ritual meant more to me than the birthday gifts, none of which I remember. To be honest, I really wanted to leave them wrapped, their bows neat, crisp and proper, their contents imagined, music boxes that played a different tune each day and one that I composed, or snow globes in which no amount of brutal shaking could force a blizzard; instead machine-tooled symmetrical flakes would come down like a soundless rain of white hankies from shy and lonely ladies. The un-wrapped gifts I displayed on my bed for my parents to see; one by one I picked up each present, described it, held and rubbed it until, whatever it was, it was really mine. I recall unwrapping all of my dolls, but I received dolls usually for Christmas and also from an uncle, many years later, when he was in the army and serving his tours of duty in Korea and Thailand. One of the gifts was from Lytta.

I remember Lytta's cigarettes in the hallway, the smoke forming for her an evanescent tail. My father smoked too, launching tobacco souls into the atmosphere. How full of teeth her mouth was and how absent of them her smile. I remember how she spoke to me, her contralto when she was still just twelve, how the depth would not let her whisper. Going on thirteen.

Lytta was always scratching her thighs, leaving white tracks, and scowling as she did it, cursing—the only times I heard such language; she mutilated words—until someone pointed a camera at her or until adults she either feared or respected (not many) came her way. My parents gave her money for ice cream that I did not like to watch her eat, something about her tongue, what seemed the unusual length of it, but of course, it was normal, and both her sultry voice and her breath were sweet enough for bees, even when she drank from her father's cans and bottles of malt liquor, though not to the point of drunkenness, unless that happened after my family moved away. She looked so much like, in that dress, an unpopular weed, although it grows faster and better than the showy, fragile cultivated flowers.

I would walk with her to the store on the next block; I think it was called Joe's, but whatever the delicatessen's name, it's gone now. She would talk on the way, to herself, but I could hear the rumbling. She couldn't whisper. All her talking sounded like complaint, but I'm not sure what she said; it was the tone of complaint, even if she were admiring milkweed. She walked rather fast, switching as she walked, hips involved in samba, lambada. I had to skip every few steps to keep up with her. Each time I caught up, she'd pinch me for having fallen behind her. At Joe's window she would order two cones, one chocolate for herself and one vanilla soft serve meant for me; I'd have most of it, the licks until the soft serve was even with the rim of the cone, but then Lytta would snatch the cone and finish it in two bites. Wiped her hands on my hair.

I didn't tell my parents about the pinches. The few small ladybug marks on my arms. Maybe, despite the little pain, I was just too curious about this detour from the usual path of my walking. This was new, this introduction to cruelty, so perhaps therefore exciting. I had no way of knowing where cruelty could lead. I had no words for it, for it did not yet exist for me.

Four Easters of the sky-blue dress is what I remember no matter that the memory is unreasonable. That is what I see, Lytta in that dress all the Sundays I knew her. How deforming must be the fourth year, sweet sixteen and repressed with sashes and bows, bra visible through the blue sheerness, dress unzipped because of the four years of Lytta's back expanding, the stitched waist far too high, the skirt scarcely covering the tops of the woman-rounding thighs. I make her into a profane Shirley Temple, female *Sambo, Sambette,* the curls fried into Lytta's short hair. Dancing and singing the same *Good Ship Lollipop, Bojangle* songs, for the familiarity, and the success when the music was delighting ears besides her own. Then she grows up; her body betrays its smoothness; a bar of soap that previously would slide easily from her neck to her toes, now pauses in the curves, the net of pubic hair she thereafter shaves prodigiously, disliking, I'm sure, disguises and fraud. She does not look monstrous, but pathetic; it wants to be a comic scene—most tragedy does. Yet what would she do with laughs, she who wants most to fit?

Four years of the dress meant four celebrations of my birthday. Smiles in which she did not show her teeth. Wide grins, disturbing for the way they seemed to pinch and hurt her cheeks. I remember a girl quite muscular yet trim, ideally built for gymnastics. Her face round with those apples, my cousin who studied Barbizon modeling learned to value, in her cheeks. Her hair was an angry brown, straightened hard, when it wasn't envying Shirley Temple, so that it seemed spiked. Mouth overly wide but not quite enough to be exaggeration. Nothing exceptional but her name. Perhaps like me she wanted to make an exceptional name memorable.

Lytta leaned against the house, one knee bent and the sole of the foot of the bent leg braced against the foundation. A moment that could have come out of *Porgy and Bess* or *Carmen Jones*. Part of me admired her maturity, for I was in awe of her being a teenager, neither girl nor woman. I was intrigued by how physical transition was; in just one season, her body changed so much as if under a spell, maybe one that she put on herself. Nothing I was could compare, and I couldn't imagine that what I witnessed happening to her would ever happen to me, except for this vicarious sharing. She didn't mind having a kid around.

It was Gidget and Moondoggie, but we were both girls. I thought it would be endless summer of 1960, but as her cigarette burned, she flicked the ashes into my hair. I didn't say anything when she did this, but just used my hands to rub away the ashes. This wasn't as bad, really, as bird droppings that had once landed in my hair without malice or forethought. I looked at her. I wasn't afraid to look at her. Her face was round as a moon, a plate. Saucer-faced girl. Her cheeks were so pronounced when she smiled that I could see a potential for the blowing of Satchmo. Pin-cushion cheeks. Although I saw no mercy in her face, I did not see rage either. She'd be satisfied with her reflected image; she'd have no reason not to be. It is only now that I try to impose upon her face more visible signs of unbalance and a need to inflict pain. I want her to look like a monster, but she didn't. We went inside to her dark kitchen. I didn't like to go deeper into the apartment than the kitchen.

When the big girl wanted me to see her fine pumps, beige, T-straps, taps on the narrow heels, how honored I felt. I thought of her as Dorothy Dandridge when she bent over, picked up the pumps from the box, then sat on the arm of the couch, raised her legs one at a time and slipped the pumps onto her feet as I watched from the doorway leading from kitchen to dining room. Then she stood in enhanced authority; her body elevated by heels thin and sharp as nails. She was impressive. I wanted that too, heels and inches, height, respect like that of a model, the speechlessness of those who see her, the subjugation and diminution of the beholder. And Lytta had it already; she was *alluring*—that was a word I knew from church. Same church Lytta walked to some Sundays in that dress.

While she worked, sometimes I slipped on my mother's high-heeled shoes, enjoying the noise of them on the hardwood floors, trying to sound like a typewriter and trying to intimidate every other noise. How I coveted Lytta's shoes and coveted them until I was thirteen myself, allowed to wear stockings, allowed to plan and sew with Deirdre our own Easter suits: sky-blue polka dots size of dimes on white cotton background were the blouses that buttoned all the way down the back. Deirdre and I designed the outfits, then looked for Simplicity patterns close to the original designs. Straight skirts with set-in waistbands, darts, a kick pleat in the back. Lined gabardine blazers, white with lapels of the same fabric as the blouses. Cream T-strap pumps. Twin sisters. We were in eighth grade and had learned to sew only the year before, making, in the same junior high school home economics class until Deirdre moved for eighth grade to the suburbs, aprons and mitts; mine survive deep in my mother's wooden buffet.

"Do you believe in Jesus?" Lytta asked me, empowered by the pumps, a jolting sharpness in her voice as she strutted to the kitchen, the heels clicking upon contact with dining room hardwood and kitchen linoleum. She continued to transform, not just from girl to woman, but also to beast without warning, all by changes in her voice.

"Do you want to be like Him?" The light cast her in silhouette. She sounded furious yet also seemed to be laughing, mocking. I was confused and scared. No one had ever confronted me this way, seeming to despise me so intensely and inexplicably, yet also seeming to need me. What should I say? What was the answer Lytta wanted? What was the form of surrender that would bring this episode more quickly to its finish? That was all I wanted, the ending. So I said nothing. I let the storm play out. I tried to be so quiet she'd be bored with me or tricked into thinking she was alone. My hands covered the ladybug marks on my arms.

"You know you want to be like Him," she said. How was she going to transform me? Could she really make me like Him? Why would she bother? Didn't she want to be like Him herself? The tone of her voice suggested, however, that she didn't care about Him. And then what? Could I ever be like Him enough to please her? Would I fail or would she? I didn't know anything about failure except that I didn't like the idea of it; I was raised to believe that achieving had no opposite. Lytta could not be a failure of a girl.

"Don't you know what's good for you?" Lytta asked so many questions, each one more challenging so that her voice intensified, the words spiked. It seemed both maniacal and fascinating. A compelling wickedness, something I had never seen before and had doubted although preachers insisted damnation was real. *Alluring;* the devil was *alluring,* a preacher said. This interrogation by Lytta was evidence of damnation, a revisiting of the Inquisition and Salem; Lytta was Tituba reincarnated, a Loa, Legba's mistress. I could not challenge her power, firm in the robust contralto. I was beginning to realize what she thought was good for me. At that moment, every map became a layout of a labyrinth instead of a guide from one wonder to another.

Those are nice shoes, Lytta, I whispered.

"You think I didn't hear that, but I heard you," she said angrily, the way she said almost everything.

I began to feel embarrassed by what I really was, frail and romantic, wholly optimistic. I felt insubstantial and defenseless. Trapped in my pretty idea of the world. It didn't occur to me to run or to tell my parents that Lytta was going crazy, that the dark passion in her voice was about to devour her—and me. If I dared move, Lytta would quickly overtake me, even angrier and wilder than she was now. Her eyes seemed more like cat eyes. Her veins seemed more defined in her neck and arms; they became subcutaneous ropes.

"You have to be tough," she said. "You're [expletive—she couldn't make me say her words] scrawny. The world is going to eat you up if you don't believe." Then she pulled me to the floor and proceeded to step lightly on my right palm with the heel of her fine pump. Her fine pump that she earned by killing and redeeming—through making a martyr of—the wicked witch of the east. Her fine pump that the charming Prince of Darkness returned when she lost it during their midnight rendezvous. Her fine pump that would fit anywhere she put it on me, not just my foot. Her fine pump that I had coveted, sinful child! And then Deirdre and I picked shoes so much like those a few years later; we were such good girls.

If I had to be crucified to be saved, for that had worked at least once before, then this anti-evangelist was prepared to crucify me out of a perverse love, such as the love that motivated every burning at the stake. But Lytta did not bore through my hand with her fine pump, although I expected that she would, so I was biting my tongue to offset the pain anticipated. I was silent and not even moving. I made no attempt to run as if I were indeed nailed. Then it was over. I was spared blood and gaping wounds. Spared specious stigmata. It didn't happen, and maybe I felt grateful for that, so cooperated the next time. How stupid I was; all I had to do was tell my parents or her parents and her demands would not have escalated like blackmail. Maybe I dreaded punishment, shrinking in my father's estimation until there'd be no more of the praise he fed me daily. A little vanity, a little conceit may have kept me silent.

As Lytta stood before me, she doubled, tripled, became a maniacal mountain and I shrank. It was, thinking of it now, like the scene in Disney's animated adaptation of Andersen's *Little Mermaid* in which Ursula, the octopodal sea witch, having become enraged and empowered, golden trident in her hand, squirts her inky wrath, using it as a fluid chrysalis in which she transforms, mutates, grows ever darker and vile by the second, monstrous, gargantuan, the voice deepening to thunder and drums of cannibals, until she is a living storm and a profane vision of the statue of liberty, ten times larger than and opposing what the green lady of the harbor represents.

It really did end. My lack of response may have expedited the resolution, but, no matter; it was over. I was free to return to my notebooks, my Suncrest grape pop, my jars of feathers, *The Wind in the Willows*. I got into a warm bed that night, my forehead was kissed, the sheets were tucked around me tight as bandages. My father sang. My mother hummed. Chatty Cathy said *I love you*. Spiders spun webs, pontoon bridges of silk, nets all over my room.

It is not that I was overly sheltered; I heard sirens, and I knew what they meant: disaster, medical emergency, conflagration, armed assault, imminent bomb, but the presence of horror had not before subdued romantic power. My spirit would emerge intact, weathering rages and ravages that are not as enduring as hope or the grandeur of antidote; I had dreamed myself often as the messenger with a serum, a bottle of relief. Dreams bolstered my sweet perception in the midst of darkness that was always present, a vileness skulking like Norway rats. I didn't see it, did not find in darkness a threat to tranquil perception until Lytta insisted upon such awareness, such travel in her world meant to be parallel with mine, not to intersect and converge; not to supplant the way it did. Gladys did not jump until after I knew Lytta. As if before Lytta, there was no reason to jump.

Lytta seemed consistent in her waywardness, comfortable with it, joyous because of it, and I was shocked by the constancy. I could not comprehend a maelstrom that did not relent. Her power had physical consequences, pain to which my mind was most susceptible; gradually language lost the ability to conquer, naming only the hurt while I was with her. Only when I was released from her at five o'clock in the evening could I reenter the Brigadoon, the Camelot, the places so pure they had no substance. Fortunately, I was with her for only a few hours of the workdays; never on Saturday or Sunday. Fortunately, some days she merely simmered, but those days are dim; vivid are the times she exploded with all the dazzle and aggression of lightning.

Whereas I had my root, she seemed uprooted, to live as aftermath, in her own turbulent wake. I was still five years old, absorbing as much as I could, faithful to the mystery and wonder of language and of all that I knew existed and was learning of through language, when she became my watcher, six and still faithful when I felt her fury. So hungry was I for knowledge that I made no distinction between its forms. In this naïveté, I welcomed Lytta, a girl starting to round, seemingly moving toward a more divine maturity with hips and breasts, curves of light waves and planets, curves of paths through space and time. She offered to me, a girl who had never before had to refuse anything, a gift of darkness.

Although this darkness and the radiance of the root that became my spine coexisted, I bent so that the marvelous spine seemed weak. I allowed darkness to dominate, treated it like velvet. Perhaps my encounters with Lytta seemed out of proportion because of my inexperience; her meanness provided what seemed to be an extraordinary contrast to what I'd known with the Feldmans and my parents. She was confused about what to love and what to despise, somehow concealing this confusion from all but me and her brother. And Olna.

I remember so vividly when Lytta's cousin came to visit from Indiana. A girl skinny like me but taller, browner, and with braces that I needed, still need, to correct my embarrassing upper front tooth that rests on my bottom lip when I smile, jutting out like a bad dancer in the chorus line, the only one screwing up the routine of my face now that I've disobeyed my husband and begun—what else to do when one turns forty?—the regular removal of a mustache I always loathed and long wanted to spurn but had been forbidden by my boyfriend now husband to tamper with for reasons I don't understand. Now I stash disposable razors everywhere.

Lytta's cousin Olna was shy and a picky eater too so we had reason to like each other immediately, much to Lytta's consternation. Lytta did not like our quick identification, the bond that we could use against her, so lied about what we were saying to her about each other, comments about smells and about what we put into our panties, but that was really Lytta's own behavior. She slapped me and accused me of saying things I didn't know to say, the language, the perversion I'd never heard of before. Saying, for instance, that I had threatened to turn Olna into a boy, so we could *do it,* by cutting out her tongue, molding it into a *dick* and nailing it onto Olna's private.

It could have been a great summer with Olna and we did manage a few brief trips to the playground, but Lytta would soon follow us and grab the chains of our swings, causing us to collide and fall. Sometimes, she just outright pushed us. Only a few of my skinned knees were acquired honestly. She spit into her hands to wash the dirt off our legs and faces. I didn't want to hate anybody, but I couldn't stave off hatred that contaminated and transferred my fear from her to fear of my feelings. Perhaps the hatred would have motivated me into speaking, into spitting on her as I wanted to, into stoning her, throwing bricks at her as I wanted to, into stabbing her eyes with twigs and pencils as I imagined, defenses I never executed, but I felt so guilty about what hatred allowed me to consider that the guilt became worse in my mind than anything she did to me. Afterward, I wrote about worlds lovelier than possible or desirable. She made me invent utopias. Utopias were my penance.

Perhaps I didn't tell anyone for telling would have exposed my guilt. I was Lytta's accomplice. Here I was good at something I was raised to be incapable of; in my home, there were never hostile times. My father never raised his voice, and as hard as he looked for the hundreds of miles we walked together, his eyes could find no ugliness. Mine could now. Mine were becoming particularly sensitive to ugliness and brutality. In the same field where he saw the grazing, I saw also the eventual slaughter. In the window shades where I saw the outlines of knives and pistols, he saw the outlines of fish, interesting pedestals for lamps. I wondered a few times if, since this was happening to me, I could be their real daughter, for I was exempt from grace and my parents had cornered the market on it. I didn't mean to be good at Lytta's perversion. Why couldn't my father be wrong about there being no limits to what I could do?

After all, while Lytta was perpetrator, she could not be perpetrator without a target; the target makes possible the crime; before there is a target, a recipient of the evil, it is just thought, idea, without substance; the evil is not tangible. I completed the circuit so that the evil, humiliation, and degradation could surge. And she was in charge, the babysitter; I had to obey; she had the authority to punish, the Bible-sanctioned privilege of the caregiver to chastise.

There was also magnetism of opposites involved. There had to be, as awful as it sounds, as ashamed as I am to think it, mutual attraction. She was drawn to me, but I was also drawn to her. Perhaps out of a need to define ourselves as whatever the other wasn't.

Constantly I prayed that God would stop her, but evidently she was praying for and receiving more strength to do her work well. In the clash of prayers, hers prevailed. So I found out how well I could keep secrets, pleased with myself, believing that I was the best secret-keeper on earth. I wanted to know how many I could keep; I hoped thousands, billions. I didn't want my parents to know that this too I had achieved. With them I wanted just another unmarred sunset, and another, yet another. An unspoiled, untrespassable moment. I wanted them to believe that I was the girl they thought I was. I still want them to believe it.

And the secrets were mine; all mine—how possessive I became with them. I had privileged information. Lytta didn't tell me not to tell; perhaps that's also why I didn't, as if that silence were defiance.

*   *   *

Lytta's best work was simulating pregnancy. Into her pulled-down panties, she would stuff: more balled-up panties, socks, slips, other balled-up small articles of clothing. Not under her shirt which would have been more logical. I watched her, midwife to debauchery. Even in the dimmed room, it was amazing how Lytta's panties stretched. Like the taffy I never ate that I had seen trap the hands of the one pulling it at the carnival. She stuffed as much as she could in them. As if she'd gone shopping and this was the way she carried her purchases home: between her knees. I didn't understand it and it vexed me.

Sometimes, because Lytta couldn't walk well with this load between her legs in her panties, she had me collect things from closets and bureau drawers so that she could stuff more and more, enough for nine months of growth. A tumor in progress, a keloid, not gestation. I had seen pregnant women before, aunts and strangers, so I knew something was wrong, that a normal baby did not grow between the legs in your panties as if you had defecated in them. She made me stuff the collected accessories in her panties, even gloves that I wanted to wear; it was difficult to touch, during such stuffing, only the nylon, only the cotton. But she would pinch me if I didn't stuff.

Lytta loved this game, this game that exemplified her derangement; my bully was neurotic. She waddled around the room. I tried to be as still as furniture, still as mirror. Sometimes she took off her blouse and small bra, walked around the room rubbing her breasts. Being furniture did not help then. "I'll feed you soon as the [expletive] milk comes." Perverse strip tease for me and her brother who although invited, often declined.

Alone in my room, having trouble staying asleep, I started padding my dolls' underwear too, especially Patty Playpal's, only in the dark. This was close to normal, I suppose, curiosity about the body, but perverted because I was motivated by Lytta's intention to hurt me. She liked the look of scars. Texture of scars. There was no gentleness. I know that I got the idea to make paper genitals for Ken because of what Lytta had done to me, yet when I suggested to Deirdre that we make them, she was fascinated out of a healthy curiosity, not out of the perversion that inspired it. There was a difference.

Lytta did it in the hallway and basement with older boys; I know because she made me watch them hurt each other, share Camels and Kools. It was indignifying. I didn't know that what she was doing was called sex; she called it something else. Then she'd be angry because I was there spying on her and trying to steal her man, but my stuff didn't compare to her stuff; no way could she lose him to me. She brought blood to the surface when she pinched my thighs, wound my braid into her fist tight as a tourniquet.

At night, braids undone, I slept, my hair a circle of dark daisy on the pillow. When I woke, sunbeams surrounded my bed like a tent.

Her panties stuffed and stretched into a soft cauldron between her legs, she would say that she was pregnant and that she was trying to give birth but that the birth wasn't working. A bad birth of a bad baby not even an hour old and already ungrateful, disrespectful. The baby had to be punished. "You understand that, don't you?" she would ask. Silence said yes. Piece by piece she would remove the clothes from her underwear as she reclined on the couch needing cigarettes I wouldn't get for her because I could outrun that crazed waddle. Hurting for nicotine, she would say that the only way she could get the bad baby out of her and teach it a lesson was to remove it piece by piece: an arm, a leg, the head always last and flung as hard as she could fling it, sometimes in my face.

I was watching a mother. No, it was a butcher. No, it was a magician pulling massacre from her hat. No, it was the miracle of one baby becoming twins, triplets; it was an act of mitosis, the baby divided and conquered, becoming food for five thousand hungry people; it was the wisdom of Solomon and I was not screaming as I should have been: *no; don't cut up my child; let her have him so that he can have life!* Romper

Room had me singing that *I'm a little teapot,* but I'm not a little teapot; I always knew I wasn't; I'm a little accessory to murder.

This was her favorite game and disturbed me more than any other.

My mother comes home. She sings my name to call me. I run up the stairs. This is a mother. She has a house for me. I lock the door. As I've seen in cartoons, I think about swallowing the key, but it is cold in my hand and the metal stinks, just the traces of metal on my hand from touching it. She asks about my day. I talk about school, how much I'm learning, how much I love my teacher. How I like The Princess and the Goblin. *I don't even think of Lytta. She lives in the hell my father says doesn't exist. She's going to be alone there; my father has promised me that God won't banish anyone there. My dolls are so neat sitting on my bed, it is as if they still sit in a store. I begin to think they sit on Death Row until the sun shines on them through my window and I brush their heads of dark beams. Static electricity could make their hair stick out like rays of light, radiant crowns.*

Lytta was a master of misanthropy so I did not think that the protocol of her giving birth was odd. I had few facts about birth except what Lytta was telling me, knew nothing about contractions, nothing about the noose potential of the cord, nothing about the delight of fetal movement, but I somehow knew that for no one else was birth in pieces; babies were born whole, not mutilated puzzles; there was no reconstruction possible for Lytta's lost generations of Humpty Dumpty. In the births of Lytta's vivisected stillborns, there was no cord to cut, no attachment to sever; during the pregnancy, she starved the child, did not bond, was never one with it, never housed an amniotic chrysalis. But I found in these births logic and believed that Lytta's babies, I still believe it, would be born that way. Dismembered.

Those were painful hours, but I had an antidote to them: my own room, my own notebooks. Thank God that I was already a writer and could alter fate with just a word. But still I chose surrender. Like the sacrificial lamb—such Bible stories always moved me. Miracles were married to surrender, threat, persecution. They happened at precarious moments. Often I wished to be Catholic, closer to the saints, the women floating in clouds in Fatima, Lourdes, women who were just scents and presences; you couldn't touch them, could only believe in them. Their priority was dreams. And their miracles were absolutely crucial to their own continuance. On the way to the library, I walked by the parochial school, saw girls in their plaid uniforms: junior nuns. They did not invite me inside the fence.

Blessed are the poor in spirit. . . . Blessed are those who mourn. . . . Blessed are the meek. . . . Blessed are those who are persecuted for righteousness' sake. . . . Rejoice and be glad, for your reward is great in heaven. Love your enemies and pray for those who persecute you. If anyone strikes you on the right cheek, turn to him the other also. Do not resist one who is evil. —The Gospel according to Matthew.

Lytta wanted us to fight, but Olna and I wouldn't, facing each other in the hallway, our arms limp at our sides. Mirrors. "Fight," Lytta ordered; "God [expletive], fight!" but we wouldn't. She told us that there was money in fighting and fame that she could arrange, that it was called prizefighting because it was an honor to flatten someone's nose and paint her face with her own blood. She'd been victorious in many fights. She could not lose. We did not move. We had no interest in honor, not then. Two skinny girls who wanted to go to the playground and swing despite what she'd do. We thought only of the need to push ourselves higher and higher by pumping and thereby also strengthening our legs so that we could push all the more forcefully, the swing going over the top of the iron frame, the chains that we held on to wrapping tightly around the bar, ourselves flung like test pilots from their ejection seats, or into the ocean in our capsules, in the tradition of Valentina Tereshkova, the first woman in space; rescued by the navy and given asylum in another country. We'd launch ourselves before Lytta could get there to push us out of the swings, but we did not move. Lytta spat at us, on us, and it seemed to burn; humiliation is fire.

We did not move although it would have been two against one, but what a one it was. Lytta yelled repeatedly that we were to fight. And when she was angry in a more crazed way, she forced the fight. She took my hand although I tried to freeze it, give it the weight of lead, the shock of voltage that would make her let go, but she loved the electrical pinch and gouged Olna's face with my nearly inch-long nails. I could see my hand obeying someone else's mind. I could see myself as Dr. Frankenstein's monster. No matter what message I tried to send my hand, the message was intercepted and changed. No matter that Lytta was the operator, it was my hand; I did it. The fingerprints were mine; the evidence was under my nails. It is true that I had another hand, a right hand, but it did not attempt to pry Lytta's hand from my left one; it held Olna's hand and tried in its soft touch to apologize, to console. I don't know what Olna's other hand was doing. I don't remember what Lytta was saying; my focus was on the small consolation. I saw nothing else.

My father had long nails, the look of white-tipped petals. They grew rapidly and did not break easily. I fell once while running up the steps of Doan Elementary School, playing with my cousin Mook, and my nails hit a stone step hard but did not even bend. It did no good to cut them even to play violin.

She gouged Olna's face, all five of my nails right across Olna's eyelids, deep into Olna's cheeks, puncturing Olna's lips; all superficial injuries it turned out, but they did not seem so when I caused them and found myself capable of something I thought I could not do, causing Vitamin A & D ointment and Curad strips to be all over her wrecked face, gauze thick as a sandwich. I washed my hands. Vestiges and memories of Olna's skin were under my nails for a long time. My excuse: I was just following orders. But it is a weak excuse even in this small, rather insignificant case, and even more weak, preposterous really, when offered by ex-Nazis.

I never saw Olna again, and this supervised altercation was not mentioned. Day followed this darkness, unable to do anything but follow.

We silently agreed, except for the scars that we ignored, that the fight hadn't happened, had slid into the past where we couldn't get it. Olna went home to the city of the racetrack that cars circle at risky speeds, control maintained by skill, but also by much luck. I was not punished nor even suspected. Not questioned although the fight occurred while Lytta was responsible for both of us. Olna, I knew, would hardly blame me. I don't know who, if anyone, implicated Lytta. I don't know how she explained it nor why her word was gospel. I don't know what her parents knew of her disturbing inclinations and perversions, but I don't see how Lytta could have succeeded in suppressing the magnitude of her evil, yet I succeeded in hiding it although I revealed, leaked unknowingly in adolescence, effects of that evil; I hid only the causes.

Surely Trevor must have dropped hints at dinner with his difficult family. Surely Mrs. Dorsey had doubts, maybe one day would kill herself unable to bear what her daughter had become. The parents had to know something. Surely the nature of evil is that it is uncontrollable, so how could Lytta have completely contained it except in the presence of her subordinates? There must have been signs in school, hurt inflicted there, expletives when she was called on, even when she was just supposed to respond to the roll call with *here* or *present*. How could the evidence, even if all of it were circumstantial, be so easily dismissed? Why were her antics and behavior regarded as frivolous? Cute? Just how powerful is denial?

I'd once heard Mrs. Dorsey call Lytta a tomboy to justify sassiness and arrogant gestures; she loved her and to justify that unconditional parental love needed denial, pretense: her daughter's a tomboy, will grow out of this phase; the debutante will shed her snakeskin just in time for the cotillion. But in the face of such evidence, how could denial be justified? Lytta needed to be stopped. Knowing what they had to know, maybe even participated in or witnessed or just suspected and feared, how could her parents allow her to baby-sit? So I was just a tenant, but Trevor also suffered, and he was their flesh and blood.

Thoroughly incomprehensible. Why didn't Kell call Florida, woman-to-woman, mother-to-mother?

I don't know what we were being; not ourselves. No; we were certainly not being ourselves. For self and soul are related; to be yourself is to be without pretense or anything; it is the destitute form that goes unrecognized so that my father, seeing it, could ask: *what is the soul?* To say that someone is just being herself is insufficient explanation unless I didn't mind asserting that authentic human nature is base. And I did mind, for I longed for movement toward the sublime, just to be pointed in that direction, on my way even if I didn't arrive. I still wanted to be the Goose Princess, but how could a girl survive in a world such as this as a Goose Princess? Would I not be exhorted to grow up and face the real world I freely abandoned, although it is neither the only nor the best world?

And I didn't know what we could be in the future; not ourselves. For a self is so vulnerable without the weaponry of an attitude, a silence, a little sass that behaves cosmetically; a self is so impossible in the face of so much influence. Matters of maintenance and challenges of isolation from contaminants. Everything touched me, air too, without my consent even though I welcomed air; it's just that I was not asked. Lytta did not ask. Maybe the self is sublime but in that state, naked and thin like the vision of a saint, the self is at risk the moment it is revealed. Perhaps holiness is always so close it may be grabbed, but then, sublimity may be crushed out of the self. My self was a fish, and Lytta was, among so many things, a fisherman.

This brutal ability, maybe even a need as ability matures, was within me. A new appendage, a third leg, unnatural, but functioning and altering how I'd function from then on. My root had been pushed deeper into the soil. It seemed to have been buried.

On the day that Lytta wanted to share a cigarette with me, filling me with her spirit by having me inhale her smoke, I was instructed to open my mouth to receive the lit end and heat my tongue. I opened immediately but nothing happened; I had expected a quick burn, fast pain that would end fast as the moisture of my mouth snuffed out the cigarette. I was prepared to brush furiously, as soon as my mother came home, to remove the ashes and shreds of tobacco that would be stuck between my teeth like the pulp of a rotting orange. Lytta sometimes called me *Tobacca,* a corruption of my middle name *Rebecca.* She didn't use my first name; she said I didn't need it; "[Expletive] you're nothing special," she said. Lytta smiled at that instantaneous compliance, as if it meant I was totally dominated, as if she had subsumed all of my identity. I still thought of surrender as effectively handling the situation although a therapist may have disagreed. A virus must run its course; best not to aggravate it. I tried to ignore her and her actions. I tried to overlook that I was being acted upon. After so much surrender, I misplaced what surrender was meant to safeguard. I assumed provoking her would have yielded more troubling consequences, more bestiality.

She blew smoke in my face and walked away. I did not that day taste fire. *Thank my lucky stars, their fast light.*

Even the most ordinary, the most mundane object became twisted if Lytta used it. A comb, wristwatch, a wing nut. With a nail file, she sharpened the teeth of a wide-toothed comb, and then ran it slowly through my hair, digging into the scalp to loosen any dandruff, she said, jacked in all trades. Dandruff was flakes of bad thoughts, dirty ideas. A wristwatch kept track of the games and Lytta liked anything that ticked or popped, electric blanket overheating, the anger of loud minutes. On my watch, Mickey Mouse's arms graphed the hours and minutes, taking him through contortions she wanted me to copy. Wing nut to sharpen my fingers like pencils.

Tomato juice transformed disastrously too, exploding one day all over the Dorseys's kitchen. I remember that I could not easily sleep because of an argument that I attributed to bad dream but that could have been real, a fight between Lytta's parents, she loved to arrange fights, and maybe doused her kitchen with tomato juice to provoke a fight, one parent accusing the other, no one surrendering or cleaning it up except for Rhonda getting tomato juice in her ponytail and on the lenses of her glasses. Pushing and shoving ensued, and tomato juice mingled with blood, I would imagine, based on how it sounded. The tomato juice may have been meant to sober Mr. Dorsey; he was a drinker, but I had thought his drinking sociable or medicinal, at least that's what my father said of his own Saturday rituals with Mr. Boston, but maybe more tussling went on downstairs than I was capable of imagining at that time. Maybe Mrs. Dorsey was trying to protect her daughter from her husband who in his drunkenness was molesting Lytta. Maybe Mr. Dorsey and his daughter were drunk and out of control together. Maybe Lytta had told them that she was pregnant and one or both of them, all of them, were trying to beat the devil out of her. Maybe there were unspeakable sadnesses downstairs. Maybe all the Dorseys were condemned and trapped.

So many explanations of the fracas I heard are possible, so many explanations of the tomato stains I saw. Or was it blood that I have consigned to juice so as to live more comfortably with my memories? I have a clear memory of blood that I saw a few years later with Deirdre and our mothers in a house right after a murder. It drove one of them to madness, the pulling out of all her hair; for a long time, there was nothing but stubble under the wigs. The blood was as widely dispersed and splattered as the juice in the Dorseys' kitchen. They told me it was juice between three o'clock and five o'clock while I waited for the recapper and the maid.

I had already moved away to Trunt Avenue when I saw the blood-painted walls. My mother told me it was blood; she told me I would see blood every month for most of my life, a beautiful blood. Blood didn't have to be like this. As quickly as possible, we surrendered to the bliss the event had interrupted.

There has been much confusion in my mind over the juice, for even if the thick liquid were juice, juice murals, juice tablecloths, juice rugs are not reasonable. Even if what I saw was juice, its presence remained problematic. Juice wasn't storming other kitchens. It seemed to smell of tomatoes, only to me, for a long time downstairs. No matter what floral mask was sprayed, I smelled juice while Lytta baby-sat. I sniffed so deliberately, my nose kept crinkling like a rabbit's. The countertop, linoleum, walls, curtains, and tabletop were permanently stained. And if the shadow was still present, what cast it was not really gone.

~

*P*atty Playpal was my favorite doll; she was the only one who could wear my clothes, my favorite skirt, a circle skirt that opened wider than any morning glory when I twirled, reversible skirt, red on one side, tiny red and white checks on the other. She still wears it sometimes. She was a constituent of my good life. I would serve her breakfast in her bed by my bed, calling her *Madam,* attempting a British accent. She had eyelashes I could comb, but her eyebrows were painted on, just like the eyebrows of sophisticated women who plucked theirs free of hair, then drew on thin arches.

Lytta didn't know how to play, so when she became involved with Patty, she bullied her, belittled her, threatened her in the basement. She stripped Patty naked, tossed her circle skirt on the basement floor, a squished prize-winning tomato, and had her brother rape her.

Although I did not want my doll violated, I was glad that it was happening to the doll and not to me, just as I was glad that Olna's face and not mine was scratched; glad, but guilt spoiled the gladness. I knew it was wrong. From the first foul gesture, I knew. Still, I would not have traded places with Patty or Olna. I was no hero though I had many opportunities to become one.

Trevor did not want to rape Patty so Lytta, his sister, struck him with a belt. *But he was wounded for our transgressions, he was bruised for our* iniquities; upon him was the chastisement that made us whole, and with his stripes we are healed. Isaiah 53:5 in the version authorized by King James. Trevor did not change his mind nor punch her, but complied, evidently fearing worse retribution, and failed. He told her that the doll did not have a hole. Lytta said that she could fix that. A hole was easy to install.

I was crouched in a corner not believing what was happening. Not realizing any resemblance between this foul activity and what went on in bedrooms and motels. Only four o'clock. I was trying to become furniture, lamp, lint of no use to Lytta. *God can do anything but fail.* I couldn't scream and call attention to my horror, and for Patty, I had to stay so I could tend to her wounds and resuscitate her when the torture was over. She would need me; she would trust only me. Words would not have helped. Language at last, after a most successful run, failed.

Don't worry; God will make a way out of no way. Every cloud has a silver lining—something a black child was routinely told; *dark as a storm, but white and blessable inside.* I waited to hold Patty, rock Patty, redeem the sense of touch.

Lytta got a knife. I started crying. She asked me if I would stop crying if she didn't mutilate—she used another word—Patty. I nodded. She laughed, as softly as she could, but in such a deep tone, it was a more mechanized than human sound. I needed to be invisible because there was no longer any logic as to what would detonate her, what wouldn't. I no longer knew what was safe, what was fatal. Even breathing was potentially volatile. She said that she didn't care whether or not I cried, but she did put away the knife, saying as I kept my eyes on it, that *it's only a [expletive] knife; when you're old enough, you'll get to use one at the table; your mother will put one out for you next to your [expletive] fork and [expletive] spoon. Trevor, don't you have a good knife? He goes fishing and camping with the Boy Scouts and with his father; the knife's good for just about everything, isn't it, Trevor?* Routinely, she didn't claim Trevor's father as her own. I never heard her call him *Daddy* or *Papa;* never anything like that. *Vaughn;* what a peer would use.

Patty was going to die like a saint. Then she could perform miracles and save me. Lytta said that she knew how disappointed her brother must be that he didn't get to rape—she used another word—Patty. She asked me if I had a hole. *Heifer,* she called me *Heifer; do you have a hole?*

I did not respond; Patty was saving herself, not me; of course—there was nothing else Patty could do. I was still crying but soundlessly. I had nothing to offer her but silence. She did not care; like Patty, she placed her own needs before the needs of others, perfectly normal strategy. Nearly always forgivable.

She asked her brother to see whether or not I had a hole. Or course I did, several in fact, and I wanted to cement them shut, the way I could my eyes. I didn't know exactly what to expect, but I knew it would be something wrong, abhorrent, cruel. I knew what I'd seen in the hall. I knew it would hurt, but I didn't realize for how long. I thought I might die. Surely my mother or father would be home soon, in time to interrupt, to hear me describe an ideal innocuous day in Barbie's cardboard dream house that was also in the basement, the day, the heaven I tried to conjure as Lytta proceeded with her plans. If I could just make my body as small as my voice, I could move into the dream, splash in the paper pool.

Lytta said that she could fix it if I didn't have a hole. It would not be a problem. Drill, bore, stab, and there's one, there's two, there's three additional holes. Luckily I had one. I had more than one, Lytta pointed out to her brother, so many I was the Swiss cheese made in a cat-and-mouse cartoon with the rapid fire of a machine gun at solid cheese circles; so many holes I was the Swiss cheese in the game *Farmer-in-the-Dell* standing alone; *and the cheese stands alone, the cheese stands alone; heigh-ho, the derrio, the cheese stands alone;* so many holes I was cheese that I hate enough to pick big patches of it off pizza.

Which hole do you want to try first? she asked him, urging her child to take risks. He did not express any preference and didn't even look at me. His lip quivered. I don't know whether or not Trevor was then, at eleven, noticing girls, seeking girlfriends, needing to sample the ways to kiss; had he practiced with Lytta? I wonder how Trevor survived this trauma? I wonder what happened to him? Did he recover enough from this to be tender? How long did that take? How many marriages? How many battered girlfriends? How much pedophilia?

My mother repeatedly said that God didn't put more on you than you could bear, but she would not have made such a remark had she known what was on me, had she realized what she was accusing God of doing. There were less traumatic ways to humble me. But she was right. I went home to paradise when the violation ended. I went home to her and her heavenly outlook. My father's calculations about how rich we'd be once he put his slaw on the market. Etta James coming from the record player. I fell asleep in and woke in beautiful worlds. Hominy cooking, cinnamon-and-butter-studded apples baking, coffee perking. Joy spelled out in my bowl of Alpha-Bits. When I picked up Patty and helped her sit, she too opened her eyes green as Christmas. What if I hadn't had such bolstering?

Lytta chose the hole between my legs and told Trevor to *do it* just the way she showed him or she would fix him too. *Fix* can also mean *neuter;* did Trevor know that? She did not care. He did to me what she demanded. I did nothing but surrender. It was as if he were obedient to necrophilic impulses. I tried to pretend that I was somewhere else, but wherever I went, they found me. I don't remember the details, the peculiar manipulation of the part of me parents didn't wash, that never got dirty. I don't remember how long it took, I don't remember his countenance, don't remember Lytta's reaction. I don't know why she wasn't on the basement floor, her brother straddling her, since she was the one desperate for this. After they went outside, I still did nothing. Unable to move, almost an hour with the weight still upon me. Patty and I like two corpses on the floor.

My doll who shared my skirt, my meals, my room, sometimes my pillow shared this dishonor, deepening our bond, our sisterhood. She lost with me the dignity of body; she was going to need to bathe three or four times a day as I did afterward in order to shine. She was going to stop growing as I did, held in that evil judgment, subject to evil's harsher gravity that compresses the vertebrae. Probably a good six additional inches could have been mine if the shock of Lytta hadn't stunted my growth. Held back by my own complicity. The price of the knowledge of vile encounters in the garden of the Kingdom of Lills is short, inferior stature. I can't be five feet tall unless I lie. I am the height now that I should have been the last year I knew Lytta. Height of a nine or ten-year-old at the onset of menarche. It is as if physically I can't grow past what she did. How tall could I grow in a world whose sky was on the back of a girl who didn't know how to raise the sky and get it off herself without destroying it? She loved the sky too—didn't she?—so much she wore it even after it was too small and the ruffle edging the round collar too ridiculous for blossoming womanhood. I'm barely taller than a midget, skinny, sporting facial hair even while estrogen is plentiful: a freak.

Why didn't I resist? Wouldn't resistance, no matter how small or ineffective, restore a particle of lost dignity? The person I've become would resist, but she did not then exist. She took it silently. She didn't understand that a component of surrender could be resistance. Besides, I did resist in an important way; I was able to continue the routine of my life, able to excel in Louis Pasteur school, able to walk with my father through declining streets as if we walked through ruins the contemporary equivalent of the Acropolis. I surrendered to the demands of the moment, but I didn't completely forfeit my identity. *Though I walk through the valley in the shadow of death, I fear no evil, for my father walks with me and both he and my mother sing.*

A dark cloud moved into position just above my shoulder, but there was enough sun to stave it off, burn away its vapor. This impresses me now. I was nine in my last encounter with Lytta; just nine, yet I managed to salvage my pride in my other life. I cracked but didn't break because at the root was something unbreakable. When Lytta knocked me down, I fell into the life my parents made; Br'er Rabbit hurled into the brier patch, saved instead of doomed. Saved by *Klaatu, Barata, Nicktoe;* Lawrence Welk's bubbles, "Let Me Call You Sweetheart."

I'm trying to reconstruct my last encounter in my fourth and last year with Lytta. Just as I didn't know torment was imminent, I also did not know of the imminence of its ceasing. I didn't know that her last cruelty was the last until another did not follow. These weren't daily occurrences anyway. Most of my days were trauma-free.

Lytta seldom did her baby-sitting outside, despite the big yard and front and back porches. The mulberry bushes. Perhaps the beautiful expanse of that, smell of that, bee, mosquito, and fly hum of that would have distracted her from her mission, softened her, poeticized her. She did not have trouble with priorities, but her interests were severely limited. She liked a jump rope as much as anyone else, but as whip, as lasso, as noose and bandage, thick cord around me: the spool. Wound up, I still had to jump to *Teddy Bear, Teddy Bear, turn all around; Teddy Bear, Teddy Bear, now touch the ground.* She tried to unwind me fast enough to make me spin. After just ten minutes of exposure to fresh air, we'd go inside as we did on a day with Olna.

Lytta suggested the basement because it was cool there, less humid; Lytta hated for her hair to revert to frizz and nappiness. Noticing that Olna's shirt was wrinkled, Lytta heated up the iron, fanned it in front of her face. I had not known her to be so interested in grooming; she kept wearing that blue dress. Lytta asked her if she wanted her blouse ironed, but Lytta responded to her own question by ironing Olna's shirt while it was still on Olna's back, plastered against Olna's back, not pulled away and unwrinkled by the steam without actual contact with the metal, a technique used in a pinch.

Once again I was glad that Olna was the target and not me; once again I was at the mercy of my guilt.

I was worried that she'd want me to kiss the hot sole-plate to make up for the failed attempt with the cigarette. When Patty was target, it was easier not to intervene, for Patty was a doll. Though I loved her, a dead thing. Olna was a girl, could be hurt as she was with my nails. The iron was not in my hand, but I was accomplice; my silence certainly helped Lytta burn her. Here was an opportunity to run and scream through the neighborhood, banging on doors, ringing bells, dialing the operator and asking for police, firefighters, marines; anyone with the power to subdue Lytta and lock her away from society, trying, futilely I believe, to rehabilitate her. While she was occupied with Olna, I could have run to save all of us, but I didn't. Instead, I watched. There were invisible physiological holds I can't explain. I was witness yet I reneged on that responsibility by saying nothing, by surrendering too literally to being a good witness by observing well, almost a sociopathic voyeurism. It seemed I had no ethics, but at six, at seven, at eight, surely by nine; shouldn't at least a rudimentary ethics be in place if the person is to become an ethical citizen? If it's not there by then, it probably won't ever be there.

I work hard to be an ethical being because I know how weak I am in this. I ask myself all the time just what is my responsibility to what I read and see in the news, to what I hear down the street, to the unfortunate around the world, but each time I don't act—when we don't act—*don't we all become unfortunate; doesn't it become as difficult to look at ourselves as it is already to look at the homeless, at the physically handicapped, at the catatonic, the poor, the slums? How can I pretend not to know what I know? Doesn't responsibility come with knowledge? I want to do so much that is good, but instead I write.*

She did not pull the cloth away from Olna's skin. Olna was biting her lip; if only she could be like Shadrach and Abednego, she'd feel no pain; she would not burn. *I like the Indian fire walkers; I like snake handlers.* I am praying that Lytta stop, that she be quickly satisfied, and bored with the thought of repeating this game on me: Olna's psychological double. Lytta was burning Olna's back. Olna had no pubic hair for Lytta to iron—she checked—I had none either—that was why she ironed Olna's back instead, but she didn't seem much interested in backs, flat and neutral, prototype of the trampoline—great if walking on the back were not actually therapeutic. Three or four strokes with the iron and she was finished, but somehow she burned herself, sucked her thumb, ran cool water from the basement sink on it and forgot why she'd asked me to come. That was the last incident in which I was involved with Lytta. Enough to mark me, but not quite enough to destroy me.

I don't know what impact Lytta had on Olna's life. My family moved away, but Olna and Lytta were linked by blood, would suffer family reunions, eulogies, and gift exchanges together. Olna would know the fate of her first cousin, might not reject her liver or bone marrow if she needed it. Well; nor would I.

Each time with Lytta, something vile transpired. It was so agonizing living two lives, the one sweet as if I knew nothing of sex let alone of sexual perversity, the other wanton. The silence itself hurt as the vileness, in having no outlet, increased its grip on my thinking and my feelings. It got to the point where I lost the ability to speak of the violation although I wanted to free myself of it. Since I had surrendered to it, it owned part of me. I made myself subordinate to it; I was too young to deal with this on my own and also too immature to realize I had to ask for help.

Besides, I liked doing things on my own; didn't like to be told, as if an activity were ruined if the idea did not originate with me. I wanted to create things, invent, not merely follow. I thought parrots were the most awful birds because, as far as I knew, they could produce only echoes. That would be the worst punishment for me, reincarnation as a parrot; brimming with ideas and no way to express them. I liked to figure things out, convinced that given enough time and the right circumstances, I could figure out anything. But I no longer knew how to speak and assert my own ideas; I no longer had my own ideas as I surrendered further and further to what happened with Lytta. I wasn't able to figure it out. I stopped juggling my perspectives.

It is unbelievable to me now that my parents did not notice my turmoil. I worked hard to suppress what happened, and apparently I was successful. Lytta was a confined terror. Only in her domain could she hurt me. It was only two hours a day that I saw her. Just one hundred and twenty minutes. Not really much of an ordeal; I knew when it would end and when it would begin. I could prepare for it. It was nothing like the long-suffering of the imprisoned and enslaved. I had no barbed wire or shackles. It was mostly my outlook and my writing that began to change. The way I saw the world. The way I interpreted what the world saw in me. Around my parents, I tried to behave as I always had, for they did not change. They had stability, and everything they had, I knew they would give me. I looked at them and tried to fall into the lovely rhythm of their breaths.

All along I wanted to be helped and saved, but I couldn't initiate the saving unless it was there for me to surrender to it; I was too wounded, but because I wanted it, whenever chances for it appeared, even crackpot chances that actually further condemned me, I seized them.

I guess we cannot save ourselves, but when there is a savior, we must help the savior; a savior is not necessarily strong, just willing to assist. We have to have some idea, however vague, of the assistance needed or we may not recognize nor take advantage of the help. When we're in the quicksand, sometimes a rope is offered, a serpent is offered, but if we hang on to it, we might be extricated from a worse fate of total loss. Yes; we must let go of the serpent, but only after, though it's biting us, it has pulled us out of the quicksand to solid ground. Then we crawl. One day with practice we may walk, but it feels so good just to crawl.

The Butterfly Prize

While I am with Lytta, my husband is growing up in Dunson, Illinois; he is eleven when I meet her; he is fifteen the last time I see her. We are being shaped, without our knowing it, in those years and the years surrounding those, into man and woman who can benefit from each other's company and abilities. I am growing in the idylls of surrender, sacrificing to a numinous ideal I don't yet comprehend.

Wesley is breathing peculiarities in his air, stench of stockyards and meat-packing house; he is able to visualize what happens to lamb and veal without having to slaughter them himself; it smells as awful as it is; also smells somehow necessary. For a time, he cannot eat chicken. He sees his mother raise chickens and wring their necks. He sees that he can do this too, although he refuses, continues to refuse when the fried pieces are passed around the table. He can imagine intestines on the floor, hip boots because of the depth of blood, intestines hacked into segments the length of caterpillars.

He begins to earn his own money, a paper route, flyer distribution, collecting coupons for the premiums, busboy and dishwasher in a roach-infested hotel. Even with this income, his family has nothing. All they own is their single-family home, demolished years later for urban renewal, displacing a sibling, her kids, an aunt and brother; the neighborhood had become a slum.

These are the years in which he discovers girls, holds their hands, experiences their lips, notices as one by one they begin to wear bras and stockings. These are the years that he goes to the neighborhood center, performs in plays, learns to play chess with a proficiency renowned in the center, beats the director at least once. As soon as he's old enough, the day of high school graduation, he enlists in the air force so that he'll have to go above the clouds; the world is not in Dunson.

He knows a panic unlike mine, one that makes him unwilling to walk through the woods for fear of the caterpillars climbing down from the trees on sticky silken strands. Creeping intestines. In his yard in Dunson was what he calls a caterpillar tree, but that was really probably a crack willow or pignut hickory whose male flowers hung in disturbing cascades of furry catkins fulfilling a rite of spring, complicating the meaning of Easter when he'd have to walk to Sunday school, without, I think, his mother who had custody of all nine of them, recite his Bible verse and come home, the caterpillars dangling and threatening him with something more terrible than fundamentalist damnation in the immediacy and the likelihood of a caterpillar down his back, under his shirt, eating away his skin until he would look like my Uncle Jack who I saw when cancer had consumed his chest, throat, and face; he was open and ravaged. So too was my mother-in-law Delfa consumed, metastasized cancer in the breast, mouth, and brain. The kind of ragged, merciless, and destructive eating that caterpillars do just to become, some of them, unnecessary and still unglamorous gypsy moths.

Caterpillars are something my husband fears and loathes no matter the butterfly prize. The furriness irks him and awakens brutal abilities; he changes in their presence, even in the presence of cats, mammoth caterpillars to him, his demons; he changes into someone I fear although I'm still, like a moth, drawn to him.

This past summer we walked late after attending a program of modern dance, my arm linked in his, our noses making us taste the deep scent of dogwood. The street lamp cast leaf shadows narrow like clusters of caterpillars. I held his hand and remembered years ago in our relationship his dousing of a caterpillar in his sister's yard with charcoal lighter fluid, then his striking of the match. It was sinister and it moved him.

I remembered how grateful his sister was and how she confirmed that Delfa could not stand them either, especially the woolly bears and tufted tussock worms. The tussocks wore those pickaninny wild unplaited hair bunches. They became a nuisance on the porch right after the divorce of Wesley's mother and father when he was so young that he can't recall them ever kissing, just fussing.

On another occasion, he resorted to simple impaling of the caterpillar; there was not the reverence fire automatically invokes. This seemed purer perversion. Loathing is more motivating than is admiring. It held his attention for an hour whereas in galleries, we move by photographs that touch us after viewing them less than a minute. When purging seems mandated, an urgency evolves to which it is easy (necessary) to surrender.

We share disgust for tomato worms, their hooked heads, their green bright as nausea. I had to pick these off the tomato plants I raised the two summers of my school garden. I would put on my rubber boots and stomp them. It had to be done for the sake of the tomatoes although eating tomatoes caused my face to swell and a red rash to erupt, whereas tomato worms weren't to be directly digested at all; still I felt that I was serving my community, and my father who loved green tomatoes, and when my garden was inspected, required for the certificate, the garden was praised. I hosed tomato worm guts off the driveway at the same time that I hosed maggots out of aluminum garbage cans.

My husband was burned in his infancy with an iron by a sibling who had hoped for four years to be an only child. The scar is a smooth starved prairie on Wesley's leg, a landing strip for those occasions that bring him down. He was inspired, and jumped when the hot silver soleplate sizzled on his leg. No hair grows there.

As soon as he was able, in a few years, as soon as my husband knew to try it, he climbed a roof, was up as high as the terrifying branches, then flew down, a skinny superman landing mostly unhurt in the grass, glass, and leaves, the blood loss minimal, much less than the Red Cross would take, the scar from the gash now the length and width of a healthy glossy caterpillar. No hair grows there either.

At night his sleep was cushioned by music filtering in from the American Legion next door and dreams of new wardrobes from rummage sales and Goodwill, holiday food baskets delivered by the elders of the church. His was no private destitution. Dreams, this puny boy, of the strength to endure the verbal excesses of bullies who loved to deride his overwhelming depth of dark complexion by calling him *Smut*. He did not have his own room. At times he felt cramped—was it two, three to a twin bed?—like a caterpillar.

Wesley did not know to quote Primo Levi who practically justifies my husband's contempt for caterpillars. Levi quoting Dante says that caterpillars are "insects in default."[1] Levi goes on in this essay to pronounce them

> *by definition ugly: clumsy, slow, bumbling, voracious, hairy, obtuse; they are in turn symbolic, the symbol of what is crude, unfinished, an unattained perfection.*

This is a definition of Lytta also. But this tragedy is countered with Levi's further comments about an astonishing emergence:

> *The caterpillar, which hangs in the aerial and temporary tomb of the cocoon, changes into the inert chrysalis, and then comes out into the light in the perfect shape of the butterfly: the wings are still inept, weak, like crumpled tissue paper, but in a few instants they strengthen, stretch, and the newly born lifts in flight.*

....
[1]Primo Levi, "Butterflies," *Other People's Trades,* trans. Raymond Rosenthal (New York: Summit Books, 1989), p. 18.

The acquired "transparent and veined wings" are no accident; there is a butterfly root of which the larva or caterpillar is almost entirely made. A moving root, traveling root that in surveying the environment becomes the winged product of second birth's education, the entire fund of information. By entering a kind of tomb, as Levi calls it, the caterpillar symbolically overcomes the flaws and inadequacies of its life; it learns from its inadequacies how to improve itself, how to transcend its identity by killing the old self. With the former self dead, there is no chance that the butterfly revert, suffer relapse, succumb to old temptations. The language that defines caterpillar does not define well butterfly or moth.

There is such hope here: a foul thing, caterpillar that must crawl through muck, dirty insect, low-life bullet of scum, emerges from its time as chrysalis with wings diaphanous as glory, proof that something born low and with nothing can earn wings so that it may not be differentiated from angels.

Wesley and I were en route to each other; we were already, in 1960, 1961, 1962, 1963, making the decisions that would bring us together as if that were the reason we made them.

A Thousand Doors

$\mathscr{I}$ learned early that paradise had a zone, and that to go outside it—to become part of the world—would be to leave the limits of its effectiveness. Though restricted to its zones, paradise didn't settle in just one spot, however; there were kiosks and outposts of paradise throughout the world, most unmarked, most stumbled into, but everywhere so that one could travel all of one's years among them; a network like the Underground Railroad. Louis Pasteur school was such an outpost. But there were times that I was not in one of the outposts, when I was between kiosks; when I had left one and was desperate to locate another. I needed to learn to go into the world without losing faith. I needed to be able to see things, meet challenges and confrontations without losing myself. But I wasn't good at this time between kiosks, and I didn't want to disappoint or distress my parents, so I left it as if everything came easy for me. *A beautiful day in the neighborhood.*

The world that my parents worked so diligently to beautify was the world that I struggled to maintain. Out of respect for their life's work, I wanted them to be happy and oblivious to the brutality I experienced, for they had overcome brutality of their own, horrors in the south. They had earned and deserved respite from strife. They worked doggedly, polishing each other, loving, until they restored a gleaming able to penetrate darkness, a beam like a silvery shadow against a blackened sky, against the majority of space. The darker the circumstances, the less intense the light need be in order to be seen and make a difference. A feeble light can seem remarkable, subversive, rebellious. I would be lost without the courageousness of a small light, of an illuminated recapper and maid. Would I dim this?

More than anything, I wanted my parents to be proud of me. I didn't want them to have to regret my birth, to shuffle in public out of shame for their disgraceful contribution to life. They were somehow ultimately responsible for anything I did or failed to do. They were defined by me as the Dorseys were defined by Lytta. Lytta's mother, Lytta's father, Lytta's sister, Lytta's brothers, Lytta's cousin—Lytta is always the reference point. They are important to me only because of their relation to Lytta. I didn't want my parents to question their years of devotion to their daughter, giving me more than they could comfortably afford, denying themselves trinkets and entertainment, stylish fashions, sophisticated meals, so that their earnings and time could be lavished on me.

What a chance they were taking with these investments. What could be worse than the ungratefulness of a child so indulged? They gave me their lives; in making me the center, they subordinated themselves to orbit, submitted to my gravity. It wasn't my life alone; they shared it. If I hurt, so would they; if I succeeded, they did too. It seemed reasonable that pride would be wrecked if they knew of my strife. What would have been the point of making them suffer also?

The idea is to reduce suffering in the world, not multiply it—three suffering people where there'd been only one? That is neither rational nor useful. And after all they'd built for me, I owed them commitment to their architecture; I would not be the one to demolish their lives. The fortress must not be weakened or it cannot be a fortress. So I at home with them lived out my fantasy life, my dream world, and they encouraged me so that I believed the dream could be superimposed on the other world, suffocating it, causing it to shrivel and disintegrate.

Somehow, my parents knowing about Lytta and other incidents, would have forced me to confront inadequacies in myself that I wasn't ready to admit to; in order to live comfortably with myself, I needed the infallible image that my parents provided. They were accomplices in denial; with their help and approval, it was easy. Frankly, I didn't want to admit to myself that there was something important I wasn't good at, something important I could not do, whereas now, I am mostly comforted by limitations, glad I can bypass some good opportunities. But then, failure was new. Intimidation was new. Lewdness was new. Dissolute interpretations were new. I could be, if I tried hard enough, good at denying Lytta, good at pretending she did not affect my life, good at sparing my parents unnecessary heartache. All the while, however, I didn't like my acquiescence to that girl; I despised that frailty so I logically preferred my illusion of invincibility; I was proud of my lie.

In notebooks, I wrote Lytta out of my life by not acknowledging her. However, I should have acknowledged these things; we don't need saints so badly that girls must always surrender. It was easier, for many reasons, not to acknowledge misery, easier to treat Lytta like the night that unfailingly gives way to day even though day too wanes. And I surrendered for years, long after Lytta was no longer the one I empowered; in all relationships, I surrendered.

Anyway, since fighting would not eliminate evil, I needed my energy for those things that could be saved and changed. As I walked with my father, I learned to submit to my senses, to be open and receptive, observant. Absorb, take it all in, internalize the world and then think, meditate, draw conclusions, comment, interpret, understand, prepare for epiphany, the great unfolding. See it all as well as I can; my words are only as good as my vision. Not seeing well is like not seeing at all. Therefore, don't run from Lytta; know her well so that her traps become obvious and ineffective. Surrender to knowledge and profit from surrendering. Know some things that those who do not surrender cannot know.

But I made no distinctions between the forms of surrender.

One day there was no torment from Lytta, and the next day there was. In remembering, it seems that abrupt. I can't isolate the moment of its beginning. All I know is that there was a time that preceded the advent of torment. A minute. A second. Without provocation, it started. It had a genesis. But I don't even know how it started, how I could allow it, but that's the question: how is evil allowed, even a small evil such as Lytta?

I will always be linked to this girl (*girl* I say, as if she is imprisoned by those days), but without despising what is on the other end of the chain. Each day is an additional link, a step from her, but the chain remains. Its weight diminishes without ever fully disappearing. Only Huntington's or milder senility could permit my forgetting her. It was an illusion that Lytta was powerful, and the illusion was mine. Because of her, I am left with a need to make sense of humanity's defects and pathologies. But without anger. A virus does what virus does; it is entirely consistent with its identity—of what use would be anger against such authenticity? How, then, to live with these pathologies without succumbing to them, assuming they can't be changed?

Had I not known her, my writing would surely have some other thematic preoccupation. I don't think it is necessary to recount the evil just to say I too have been wounded, for wounding and healing are part of the circle; they happen to all. For its pattern, this life is not unique. Certainly Lytta also is not unique, although I speak here as if she is aberrant. But there are so many like her that the numbers suggest normalcy even though such people of ill will are outnumbered by the compassionate. I believe this, without the benefit of statistical validation to support my belief.

My pained childhood and adolescence were not the fault of Lytta, for I reacted as I did because of my tendency to surrender; it could have been good surrender, purifying sacrifice, but with Lytta, friendships, and men after Lytta, was not. Perhaps I was biologically predisposed to respond through surrender. I had been surrendering throughout my short life, but the consequences when I surrendered to Lytta were painful instead of rewarding such as the rewards of surrendering to good books and the mica and quartz in my path. Still I must ask what sustains evil? Still I must wonder if evil is entirely the product of surrender?

Why isn't evil refused the way my ninth-grade class refused Carla, replacing sandwiches in her brown bags with soap and deodorant? More soap and deodorant for Christmas. Why isn't it rejected the way Kally had to reject me in order to lock me inside our shared locker in seventh grade? Kally who was ostracized herself for raising her desk every few minutes in science class to bite from her pork chop sandwich in which grease congealed as thickly as the unbrushed gobs of it in her hair. Evil could have been banned, but surrender, not apathy, encouraged it.

How did surrender begin? Didn't the elements have to surrender to each other to make the compounds? Didn't the amino acids have to surrender and compromise in order to make spirals and chains that make life? Doesn't the sperm have to surrender to the egg, the uterine wall to the implantation? Isn't surrender the root?

I hope there were no signs or warnings that Lytta was about to erupt. For if there were, then there could have been intervention also. I could have been whisked out of the path of the lava flow, so far away I would have felt no heat, no shaking ground. And I, such a good observer then, surely would have seen whatever signs there were, allowing me to lock that door before anything awful happened, not after. This is why I ask so urgently *how;* I'm hoping it cannot be explained, could not have been prevented, that I was not a little surrendering fool.

I don't hold my parents responsible; some things aren't found if no one seeks them. They were looking for other things, mostly how to maintain my happiness and make me recognize some splendor because they knew what was coming, adolescence and maturity, and they hoped disillusionment was not inevitable. If the world is first made splendid, then that is the kind of world the inhabitants of splendor will remember and devote themselves to rebuilding. Each time, as with the trinity of little pigs, using materials more able to withstand assault so that by the time splendor has the stamina of bricks, the edifice is impervious. I appreciate my parents' noninterference. I am glad that they desired to do no harm. They believed in me and I reciprocated the belief.

Thylias is another survivor of fire. Who would I be if I could not say this? What purpose would my life have?

The first day of Lyttanic agony probably began with Alpha-Bits and no limits to what was on the horizon. I expected the day to be ordinary as indeed it was, behaving as days do. When transgression is going to happen, the sky does not blacken in warning, protest, or solidarity, sinking so low there's no misunderstanding of the wrong, the magnitude of the coming violation. If it blackens, that is coincidence, electrical or magnetic disturbance independent of the imminent harm. There is oblivion in nature, no respect of the human condition. There is perspective. The sun has shined on days of sudden infant death syndrome, gassings, and missiles; days of hunger, espionage, and murder, days of migrant workers tramping for dimes and nickels in sprayed fields. Days with no mercy at all entering the myriad sweat shops. The sun has shined. Someone has won the lottery. Someone has asked for relief; a mercy killing has been mourned, protested, but finally understood.

An anencephalic girl has continued oblivious to media fuss, the miracle her mother fasted over, the God her mother implored to give the girl consciousness, awareness of pain by placing a brain in her empty, flat head. How overwhelming it seems. How difficult to see the mother singing happy birthday to a roboticized doll. How firm the mother's faith, to which she wholly surrendered, that a brain would be there in the morning, morning after morning for three years; faith that I admired, found beautiful if obsessive, and hoped would not crack. But of course would crack because that miracle was not going to happen despite the sweet scent of chrysanthemums that the mother trusted near the end to be a sign from God, an angelic vapor to enter the girl's nostrils and travel to her skull to take root and flower into twin mums of cerebrum. I am enriched for having seen such implausible faith.

The scarecrow of Oz could sing and dance, like happy fictional darkies, but could not know what the dance meant, could not know how degrading it was to be told *Dance, boy; dance!* and then comply. Not that he isn't a fabulous dancer. He didn't need a brain to move that way. But she does. To know even her mother's extreme and desperate love. No meaning without a brain. No dignity, no justice. Nothing.

Despite the respirator, the girl's brainless body stopped functioning after three years and could be buried instead of museumed in the hospital. Grief is local and eventually overcome, whether or not there are sympathizers. You can't resist surrendering to grief, but grief releases you one day or another. It begins to recede, practically from the moment of giving in to it, although some giving in results in drowning. So on the day of my troubling surrender, I'm sure that I bathed and fed my dolls, kissed them, gave them dreams. It's likely that I played jacks with Stellica, the girl across the street who was the best friend, besides Deirdre, I ever had, and mine alone. That night, for we could do this, perhaps we signaled to each other with flashlights and simultaneously turned off the lamps in our rooms. But inside this frame of jacks and signal, there was confrontation that Lytta instigated and to which I surrendered. I'm sure I didn't know then what torment was, but I surrendered to it anyway, according to my nature.

For sake of maintaining even a flawed paradise, I must say that I did not ever allow Lytta into our apartment, not even via my dreams, for it was inviolable space that she could not trespass. If I brought any of Lytta inside with me, it was only the wholesome part of her, a scrubbed form whose bubble gum seemed a pearl balanced on her lips. The rest of her was consigned to shadow that my shoes held down outside the kitchen door, their memory of my weight pressing hard.

How very strange, perhaps inaccurate; obviously Lytta, who knew how to pick locks, any time could enter the apartment of her parents' tenants; for instance, sometimes Rhonda collected rent and Lytta certainly could have accompanied her although I have no memory of that. She provided the baby-sitting service downstairs where she lived. And my annual parties were in the basement. There also must have been occasions when one of the Dorseys came upstairs needing an egg, salt, or aspirin. I just don't remember such neighborly requests ever being made. It is really as if something prevented Lytta from stepping through the doorway, as if she feared the consequences and judgments somehow inescapable in my apartment although nowhere else. But that is too convenient; I do not believe that evil, if it exists at all or separately from its opposite, is so obedient to such division; more logically, Lytta did come into my apartment, but I have deliberately forgotten the visit. Obviously since my parents were also home it was as if she were not there. Not the Lytta of malicious intimacy withheld for private audience with youth and innocence.

This is certain: the version of Lytta I knew never set foot in our apartment. While the other Lytta was there, assuming that at least once she came in, she was temporarily redeemed and relieved of what must have been such an unnatural burden to torment me, her younger brother, and who knows who else, children in her way on her hurried walk to school; strangers sharing a bus stop, people on elevators, behind her in line, cashiers accepting in their palms money from her and having their lifelines accidentally scratched.

Once, she cut a man.

For the sake of romance, I want to keep our apartment sacred. On behalf of the numinous, I want a kiosk so wholesome and affirming that Lytta is intimidated, that Lytta defers to goodness, helpless beside it. That she surrenders to something less injurious—for I was not the only one damaged; so was she. If I place her inside our apartment, then there was no safety, no haven, no romance, no chance for those who would not rage and riot, no chance for those fond of contemplation, driven by the golden shimmer of waning day on a river most look away from, avoiding glare, a small bright hurting in their eyes. There was truly something stronger than her if, like the vampire touched by holy water or touched by just the shadow of a cross improvised from desecrated bones, Lytta shrank and cringed just seeing our door, hearing our laughter the depth of wood away, knowing how the cards in our hands, whether the game was called hearts, crazy eights, or old maid, spread like a peacock's tail, a most amazing tiara of the rump.

I do not understand how such a girl evolves, how the world tolerates such ugliness, afraid to call it that as if ugliness has rights that must be protected. I do not understand how she would go about performing the rituals and daily ablutions that I do, brushing teeth and hair, smiling into mirrors, applying lipstick and mascara until satisfied with our faces, dabbing on the same cologne, White Linen this year, in the same strategic spots, and even adding still more refined sugar, never lemon, to our tea while others at the table stare an inquiry both about our awareness of the repetition of spooning that my left and her right hands are locked into, and about our problems with sweet taste, the disaster with diabetes foretold. Perhaps we have used, still use—she would not be too old— the same brand of tampon; maybe our cycles are synchronized, but I would hope not though I know both sides of war bleed. And is it true that I would not be this writer if not for Lytta? I am not ready to admit to her necessity in my life. Good fortune that she brought me.

It was like this: *While she's near, you smell Lytta. Despite an abundance of cinnamon, assault of a skunk's assault, Lytta rises above it, the rising of cream, rising of fat in the jar full of oil in which meat has cooked. Your nose becomes so full of her pungency, it is Lytta's nose; it can't be your nose if she occupies it and displaces your olfactory preferences. You are so afraid, your nose congested that way with rough spice, of becoming her, because now you know how. Had she, mentor in a nose, not been there, you would have no idea of this path the scent is cutting, pulling you along behind it. You have no problem; you customarily walk behind your nose, and it still looks like your nose, is still on your face, is still inhaling. You aren't gasping for breath. Lytta is sustaining you, revising your respiratory system so that in order to live, you need her in your nose.*

What causes the behavior of demons to more closely match what I, what anyone not demonic, would have demonology be than what demons might want for themselves? Self-perception and definition may be transformed; it is not a scourge any more to be black. My attitude and understanding of demons has not been derived from conversations with demons, but from musings about them, from the ideas of demon denouncers. The demons that speak in films (and in history) are horrible and have offended humanity in unforgivable ways. They are present merely to be exorcised and loathed, to be overcome, to allow a triumph for humanity, the sweetest root, but if demons permit themselves to be such a convenience for the establishment of the glory of humanity, then demons are perpetrating benevolence and sacrifice; they are not then purveying evil.

Soon after we moved, Lytta was leader of a gang, adolescent proud of having stolen and stripped forty cars.

⌒

In my memory Mrs. Kell Dorsey is a gypsy. Her face was dark, sepia with fine, fine Ethiopian features. I recall that she wore her hair always loose and it hung just below her shoulders and was silky, many strands gray, but thin black strands still dominant. She had a silver-rimmed tooth right in front and her eyes were just slightly whiter than her teeth. What a beautiful woman she was, even down to feet in which the sepia seemed as liquid as it did in her face. She wore scarves and loose, thin, long skirts and it seems that all of these were some shade of terra-cotta. Of all the Dorseys, hers is the voice I do not remember; maybe she spoke so softly it was all whispers which don't really vary from person to person. I can remember some of what she said, but not how her voice sounded. I see a smile when I think of her though not a wide one; I think it was just a peculiarity in the way she breathed, opening her mouth as if maybe her nostrils could not pull in enough air, but seeming to smile constantly as a result of breathing. And maybe for all the eating of air, she could not bother with speaking and maybe if she had spoken, it would have been just to announce that she had such a taste for some air.

This is how I remember her, someone distinct from her family, unlike her family, more deeply complexioned than any of them. She died on my birthday; I think on my seventh. The cause of her death was not shared with me, but I have long assumed cancer or, when I was much younger, that her face got stuck in a fragrant pillow when her nose would not let go of the smell. Death is a floral experience; bouquets, even of weddings, have short lives, and flowers position them- selves around coffins and graves. I did not mind leaning over my dead father and smelling gardenias, placing a lock of my hair and a rosebud in his hand. Kell Dorsey's was not an expected death, at least not expected by me.

The day before, I remember her bending in the kitchen, perhaps reaching into a bin of potatoes that I'd seen her reach into several times, the scarf sliding off her hair that perhaps she kept covered because her hair shined and the attention the shine would command would have embarrassed her, but she delighted in her gold earring dangling. Hair radiant like Saint Catherine of Siena's but darkly. Yes, it was dangle, dangle, smile, smile, dangle, smile until Kell was upright and handing something to me. Not a potato I don't think. Maybe she extended to me just her hand. A note to be read in the event of her death. The next day, she was dead and my birthday party proceeded and Lytta wore her blue dress. It was not, I don't think, the year of the blizzard (milder than the one in 1954 but still a respectable storm) and power failure when my party's ice cream was buried in the snow on the front porch. That likely happened another year.

Logically, Kell Dorsey was not proud of Lytta; Lytta excelled in deviancy. Kell Dorsey was not proud of her daughter; Kell Dorsey probably died believing she had failed her flesh and blood. Kell Dorsey, the sepia mother of terra-cotta scarves and skirts, did not lead her daughter to destructiveness, but that is where Lytta went. How hurt Kell must have been in her solitude. I can't imagine having to mother Lytta. How did she bear all her regret? What else did she suffer? Rhonda did not accompany Lytta either. Whenever they worked together, I was spared. I could tell that Rhonda preferred me to her own sister; she gently combed my hair while I read to her.

I did not go to Kell Dorsey's funeral and I'm not sure why not. Perhaps hers would have been my first official funeral, and my parents thought I would be shocked and unable to still see beauty. But a corpse was no more dead than my dolls. Than I was with Trevor.

Sometimes I say when I'm feeling particularly tired that I'm dead. My three-year-old asks me if that means I will have to get into the coffin. Last summer was his first funeral, his first viewing of someone embalmed and about to be buried in her best, blue it was, chiffon dress. He touched Belvia, kissed her cheek, my father's sibling dead before him, her face beautiful, thin nose, hair long and gray, her eyes closed to her own Huntington's. He watched the lid close and it was no different than it looks when the piano lid shuts, the keys hidden but still capable of music. He watched the pallbearers move with the silver box from the church with ease followed by women carrying the many pots of flowers, all of these placed around the coffin in the hearse. He followed the coffin, so intrigued and asked again and again if the coffin would open, if it were like a jack-in-the-box, if she would stop being dead long enough to speak to him and hug him, if she really wanted to be by herself, if Daddy and I would get in a coffin just to be alone, if there was a way she could taste a piece of the chocolate Egypt cake he had made. My eight-year-old was more interested in stopping the heaving of bereaved shoulders, his large hands firmly on them as he made his way through the pews. Dennis always designates himself comforter. Ansted knows already in his three-year-old way of knowing that death is a season, and that everything dies. I have not been able to tell him what he wants to know about where it is that death takes you even though death is everywhere; the minutes die. He says that he wants us to die together.

—*Mommy, I will die with you.*

—*Mommy doesn't want you to do that.*

—*Don't you love me?*

—*Yes, yes! More than the stars.*

—*I love you more than the moon, more than the plants, more than the rivers.*

—*More than the colors, more than the sweet juice of our breakfast, more than the dolphins and the roaring in the conch shell.*

—*More than the world.*

—*More than the universe.*

—*More than anything—so we must die together.*

—*I want you to live forever. Long, long after I'm gone.*

—*I can't live forever. I have to die, Mommy. I just have to. Everybody is going to die.*

I had seen death occur right before me by the time of Kell Dorsey's funeral, but no one knew this. I was outdoors playing, hiding in bushes and I could see, through branches and berries, other kids playing in a side yard where some people in the neighborhood dumped things. Three boys and a box. One boy was badly hurt (and brain damaged, eventually died) after two other boys accidentally hammered nails into his head by jumping on the box he was inside. There was much variety in his wails and gasps until his silence dominated. The noise did not bother anyone. It was summer. Windows were open. There were few if any air conditioners on Lills. The street was becoming increasingly noisy anyway. Kids played tag, war, cowboys and Indians, house—all those games were noisy. But through all the companion sounds, I could hear these three boys plainly. No one yelled from their windows for these boys to lower their voices.

Although Lytta was not present, it looked so much like an activity she would engineer. I remembered how not long ago she had wanted to hammer her heels into my hands and wrists. I could look at the houses on Lills and have no way to discern the safe houses from the unsafe; it was possible that there was no safe place to go. Which were the kiosks?

I also knew that such events might not happen if I weren't there, that they happened somehow for me, that I attracted them, helped draw out evil the way isopropyl alcohol draws out swelling and brings a pimple to a head. I was designated witness somehow because of Lytta who made it possible for me to see such things.

I heard distortion of sounds at first human, but these quickly transformed into something, accompanied by those harsh visuals, unrecognizable. But it was not as difficult to listen to agony as I had hoped and believed; nor was I terrified by the proximity of death nor shocked by how easily play and exuberance became maliciousness although nothing that the jumping boys were doing changed. They were still playing, laughing; screams of delight and paroxysms of pain mixing seamlessly and then transforming brutishly. They were ignorant of their concurrent identities of boys and assailants, how one identity furthered the other.

They played in a wooden box, an enormous crate from which nails protruded into the open space, into the clubhouse, the hideaway where the boys thought of manhood and the best ways to get to it. The wooden lodge that maybe later in the summer they would have painted and named, the boy inside the box perhaps voted secretary or treasurer. They didn't know about the nails but did not relent when the boy's screams changed. Something that began innocently became deliberate. I watched and made no effort to intervene; a girl wasn't welcome anyway, and I had no real proof of malfeasance. Once when I thought I had it, proof had turned out to be only juice. I surrendered to what already had momentum; I was at rest. I considered that I did not know what fate the box held nor how many Houdini's had been born. I wanted anything I saw or did to be innocent, so held on to a possibility of innocence long after innocence's demise. It was that way with Lytta; I entered each encounter with her hopeful that her heart had been cleansed.

Perhaps I was the one who first noticed it was not possible to play anymore. Perhaps I was the one who first saw the boy's blood and wondered why fresh-let blood had no smell. From the bush, I continued to watch as the game crossed the threshold of spite; once blood asserted itself, the jumping seemed hateful, deliberate, more forceful as if it was then important to deliver the wounded boy to death efficiently with no possibility of his returning to life, friends, and revenge. The sight of blood seemed to make them want their former friend to die.

Did I somehow want to have this example of death, to witness the transition from life to death, using that transition as a model for all others? Why wasn't I frightened by how easily my silence defended curiosity even after curiosity turned sadistic and cruel? I chose not to interfere with a natural process taking place. An innocent German civilian. I lacked the courage of Gretel in front of the hot oven; there was a chance—and because of Lytta it did not seem a remote chance anymore—that approaching them, warning them of the presence of the boy bleeding inside their hard trampoline, I would be shoved into the prison of the game with the boy, martyrs together but for no cause that would allow our deaths to be venerated.

I chose to let the events unfold, naïve, not because I was six, but more naïve than many six-year-olds in my belief that imagination had depth so was a suitable replacement for reality. Reality was formed by belief, not by events; I didn't believe the boys were jumping and becoming hammers sealing a coffin. I saw such horror because my eyes had been corrupted and tricked into seeing a mirage that tempted me to accept that this was the way it was meant to be, as if fate had shared with me a secret. The boy had had what we all will have: a beginning, a middle, and an ending, his perhaps far more harsh than other beginnings, middles, and endings, but he was not deprived of them. Fate was fair. Fate did not juggle. What pitiful rationalization. Entirely without depth. How did I believe it?

I did not make a report about the boys. I feigned new shock when I overheard the neighborhood talk, my ears covered by white gloves as I walked home from church. Shock although in school we'd been introduced to pollination and the many ways, often sexual, in which pollen and seeds were distributed, and I knew what kind of seed had landed in my innocence, and I knew what was growing; I knew that what was happening was what had happened to Kay in Hans Christian Andersen's "Snow Queen"; a piece of that mirror that transforms perception ugly, distorts grotesquely had landed in me too, a determined seed. But in that blissful apartment, I snipped off the sprout every day. On television, I watched *The Bad Seed,* but didn't enjoy a human monster, a little girl—my age—who could kill.

I did not go to Kell Dorsey's funeral though she had died on my birthday and had been the most extraordinary sepia I'd ever seen.

It was so easy to escape that I wonder why I did not do so more often, why I did not become more reclusive, why I did not go into hiding in our nest of an apartment. So much could have been avoided that way, and some heinous events perhaps, my child self reasoned, would not have happened had I not been there, a required witness though unwilling and not a good one; while I remember faithfully what I saw, deliberate and accidental acts of violence and self-defense, I did nothing but house the details, allow them full access to my gut and center where like snakes and worms they wound themselves through every intestinal avenue so that there was no direction I could pursue without taking with me the snakes. My thinking seemed clear enough, but the placement of these details in my gut and center helped them conspire with gravity against my desire to soar. They held me down, hardening, stones I could not pass. In time, I came to depend upon the snakes as guides and as the lengths of cord and ribbon to lead me out of labyrinths the snakes themselves made. In time, even my writing surrendered to darkness, and then I had no way out that I could recognize. After witnessing some crime, I went inside, and closed and locked the door to bliss. Washed my hands.

I did not juggle well the sublime and the profane, the shifting from one to the other.

While again walking to the library on Plummer Avenue, near Everlasting Baptist Church, I noticed a boy riding his bike close to the curb. I was nearly seven, allowed to walk to the library alone, mostly on Saturdays, but I went there after school until almost five, some afternoons, so as to avoid Lytta. In books I traveled to the distance from which her world, already lifeless, existed just as posthumous glow, a star already dead, only its last light left. Sometimes, she came to get me, calling me a bad girl in front of librarians I loved, saying I knew that I was supposed to come straight home from school. She was right; I was disobedient, but she didn't tell on me to my parents. This day, she didn't come for me.

The boy must have seen me although I tried not to look at him directly, but he knew I could see him slyly, peripheral vision, being a few years older and experienced as he was either allowed or else was giving himself permission to ride in the street. I was restricted to riding on the sidewalk, had training wheels until I was nine and Deirdre let go of the rear fender; I continued to ride, believing that she still held on to it. I was glad for the sidewalk restriction because I loved so much the sound of the bell on the handlebars. It sounded, I fancied, like the voice of the emperor's mechanical nightingale in Andersen's story.

Showing off, the boy veered away from the curb, further into the street, when he took his hands off the handlebars, but he was not apparently in danger and when I seemed to be smiling although I really wasn't, he was satisfied, put his hands back on the handlebars and pedaled harder, ahead of me by a few yards just as a truck rounded the curve and hit him, crushed him, flattened him, right in front of Menden City Hospital. No better place for an accident, I thought. The doctors could just come running and save him on the spot. Or the Everlasting deacons could pray for his resurrection. But no chance of that. He was dead. There was merger already of his pink bubblegum and brain. The truck could have had tires my father had recapped, the treads full of skin, bone, hair, tooth, blood. I saw the split second that separates life from death. I saw the suddenness, how the boy had no opportunity for a last request. Convicted killers have the privilege of last request, meal, but not this boy. I didn't know what was expected of me. I didn't know how to resuscitate him. I didn't know how to administer the last rites. I didn't know.

How mangled his body was, yet I was not perturbed. Death demanded no action. It couldn't be undone. He didn't say anything as it happened. He made no sound. No angel came to snatch him, and I hoped for a glimpse of his soul. After a while, the blood stopped flowing. The pools of it were like melted flowers. There wasn't as much as I expected. Who was he? Someone asked if he were my brother.

The truck driver was distraught, frantic, apologetic. As a crowd gathered, the driver started to pick up the body, but someone yelled that the boy shouldn't be moved. Someone else—it should have been me, but the first one on the scene was immobilized—ran toward the hospital, screaming emergency, voice as siren. I kept looking at the boy as if looking would give me his name. I wanted to know his name. Immediately I thought of *Lazarus,* and I started to call him that; my tongue tasted only the first syllable before I was pushed out of the way in favor of adults and doctors.

Minutes ago, I could have spoken to him and asked him to walk with me. I missed my chance to intervene. I contributed to the accident. I assisted the wrong force. I saw it happen anew every day, could see little else, and wondered whether or not the world must become less beautiful for others as it became for me because of this vehicular killing. How had the whole world, not just mine, been changed? Surely this event must change it! Wasn't this event truly extraordinary? What kind of world would not change when it suffers a loss? What was my duty now that I knew what had happened? What was the responsibility of the witness? I looked again for evidence of his soul, but still didn't see any.

This acknowledgment cannot help him, but it is all that I can do, and more than I did then. I just said that the truck hit him, but even the last person on the scene could surmise that. I told no one the extent of what I'd seen, opting to blend into the crowd, slip into the library, read more fairy tales and Laura Ingalls Wilder. By the time I walked home, toward a blue dress waiting, the crowd had dispersed, the body had been removed, the truck driver released; just some bloody smears on the asphalt.

So my life begins to unravel after the stunning magic of the Feldmans, a mystical couple that no one remembers. I say, and it is true, that my life's first years were idyllic. Despite the stark contrast of Lytta and the tragedies I witnessed, I could still smell flowers and visit Echo Tunnel. I could write all night in Urapé passages as soothing as Psalms— more so, for my passages had no war. The life of the pendulum, swinging widely, as far from horror as possible so that visible is only the pasture, and then back again so that the only activity is cruelty, and stuck there when the mechanism ceases to fluctuate, when the shadow is so immense, it takes more than a decade to complete the eclipse. What happened to me? I was an insecure little girl eager to lose herself to books again and again. I visited little houses, castles, retreats, monasteries, submarines, Alpha Centauri, huts, and cottages where there were hammocks and canoes for the souls that needed them. I wrote about methods of transportation because I needed to flee. A tremendous need was forming for faith that the world would reveal to me a sacred purpose for what I witnessed. Once I learned it, every new concept would become easy and open a thousand additional doors. Knowledge would take me so far that I'd never get back to Lytta and the Kingdom of Lills; I would not live long enough. That is how I came to understand eternity, as the opening of the first door.

~ Mook Season

During seven months of my last year in the reign of Lytta in the Kingdom of Lills, my Aunt Essell, her son Leland, most often called "Mook," and occasionally his father, Leland Sr., most often called "Jack," lived with us. While between eviction and employment, living off complicated and hurting love, repaired every night only to come unglued in the morning. All they could do was surrender to it. It was a family ripe for violence, yet there wasn't any. They were urban, low-income exceptions from whom I learned much; there was stamina and conviction for me to witness; there was defiance of their extreme bad luck and their social chaos. All was survived and endured impressively, without bitterness. Not once did they designate a scapegoat, not even when their frustration was most intense. Somehow they were fortified by their struggle, using it as a springboard into a hope that became palpable as their dependence on hope increased. When my blue-collar parents permitted them to live with us, they were giving me, they didn't know, respite from Lytta's torment.

I had to give up my room just before my eighth Christmas. The three of them took over my rear bedroom and the adjoining room, took over my view of mulberry bushes, my watching icicles turn crystal when the sun was angled just right, and diminishing drop by drop, so slowly, a drop would land on an evergreen needle then roll off gently before the next drop arrived. The drops were as slow and graceful as the pearl drifting to the bottom of the bottle of Prell.

Mook didn't think much of Lytta when he first saw her that winter. He didn't even notice her dress; it was as if he couldn't see it although I would jab him in his ribs and tell him to look at how silly that girl looked in that blue dress. It didn't interest him. He was almost six years old, but he was as big as Lytta, on his way to his eventual three hundred pounds. They sized each other up when they met in the hall, and Lytta was first to back down. Immediately I knew that I had a bodyguard. I stuck out my tongue at her, said *neh-neh-neh-neh-neh,* and ran, never out of Mook's shadow. She didn't touch me, did nothing but smirk while he was there. He was her equal so she didn't even speak to him. In fact, Rhonda assisted every afternoon now, since Lytta was not experienced enough to care for two children, one of them a big boy; we would have been too much for her to handle alone.

Jack and Essell were the first ones of their families to head north of Nashville, settling first in Connecticut, near mountains just as they had lived in the mountains in Tennessee. Maybe Essell was inspired simply and forcefully by the trains that cut through their yard on Ailanthus Street, their steam that was a dream cloud in which she could better idealize whatever the elegant fog of travel helped into loveliness and importance by wrapping shoulders of Bergman and Bogart. She wanted to move, and her young husband then would do anything to please her, for that was his pleasure too.

Maybe in the steam of train and passion, Essell saw all there was to do in this life before, she did not know this, the advent of: congestive problems of her heart, death of an alcoholic spouse, hypertension, insulin-dependent diabetes, amputations of both her legs above the knee, a good hundred pounds each, her last years in a wheelchair, the house overrun with roaches but, thank God, she was its owner a full year before dying. She endured such things with her second husband, eventually endured him too who was Jack Sprat skinny all his life and the very definition of dark complexion, his mouth full of obscenities that spewed rhythmically so that it was soothing to listen to although it was also the source of some of Essell's personal disgrace and shame, especially when I was there and she was caught between what to her were the extremes: profanity and college, yet Milton allowed her son, the amazing mass of him, to be his only child, asking of her only: beer rights, his vocabulary, opportunities to dance as only the skinny can: slew-footed, swinging and bopping, a jitterbug until his last day, last hour in the twitching and palpitations.

Essell was a yellow-skinned girl, took after her father Curtis; Jack was mixed, a black parent, a white one who dominated Jack's appearance. Everything was smooth until he became a VO man. He went to bars after work, eventually instead of work; missed the Soul Circle— didn't even know that Moe-lay ran one in the kitchen. Their son Mook had reason to be troubled yet wasn't. Being so big, he had an imposing presence that well supported a curiosity we shared, his slightly more vulgar than mine.

Aunt Essell smoked Camels heavily when home; I'm assuming that when she cooked for budget hotels, then years later for schools and nursing homes, the cigarettes were not dangling from her mouth, grotesque, I thought, but the balancing intriguing. When cigarettes weren't dangling, she was so beautiful. There's a photograph of a three-quarter study of her head and shoulders, the short hair with Ss of gray is so gently waved it looks like a moment in the glissando of a harp. Her eyeglasses are perched like something winged unafraid to light there, although the human face is usually avoided by, say, butterflies.

She knew how to cook the contents of tubs labeled *chitterlings* that were called *chit'lings,* that are good, Aunt Essell once observed, with hot sauce, but she could not tempt me. She remarked how those women in the nursing home wanted her to cook chit'lings all the time; they never tasted any like hers or perhaps any at all before hers. She said she didn't even mind cleaning them as long as she didn't have to clean them every day. She was used to fresh meat for dinner, meat alive just minutes before going in the pot. I wanted Aunt Essell's pies and biscuits, but only my mother's potato salad because my mother mashed her potatoes first, disliked the chunks her sister and most everyone else thought had to be there or it wasn't really salad. I watched my aunt skin spare ribs, pulling from the slab a single continuous membrane certainly indigestible, and watched her debone fish that she always bought fresh, chop off the heads that I set like votive candles into paper cups before they were disposed of or fed to animals—cats frequented her yard, mostly a black one I called Tilmance; watched her wash turnip and mustard greens, dunking handfuls in a sink of ice water, from which the greens emerged more vibrant; so beautiful, my aunt in the kitchen.

While she was gone to work—she left late in the afternoon for the dinner shift, leaving Mook and me alone for only an hour until one of my parents arrived—Mook would examine the cigarettes she had at home everywhere, in pockets of dusters and housedresses, purses, some- times even in slippers, pink with a puff across the instep. He never attempted to smoke them although he had access to matches as a book of them were placed with every stashed pack of Camels. Instead, we cut up the cigarettes into inch worms or split them open and emptied the tobacco into the shoe-box toilets of Sleepy Eyes and Mary, two of my dolls. They did everything that I did.

The cigarettes were the needles that gave us penicillin and brought us back from death. They were lenses of microscopes, long lenses for powerful magnification. Cigarettes side by side were: conveyor belts, rafts, and fences, a mouth organ when stitched together with thread. Mook did enjoy the matches, however, more than he enjoyed expanding the alternative culture of cigarettes. He kept a book in his hand even when holding them interfered with his doing something he preferred to the holding of matches. He liked the smell of the burnt-out match stick and there was only one way to solicit the smell. Eventually it was unsatisfying to strike match after match letting the flame die before a purpose had been given to the flame. He didn't want to waste the fire but I thought that just seeing the light was grand although it was my seeing, not the seeing of Mook. I did not intervene; after all, there was the small grandeur of harmless burning, and there was the spiritual fire in his fat fingers, even when he approached the curtains in the room farthest back and ignited them just as if his conviction, his religion required of him this ignition. Most of all, I was afraid of the fire, becoming a hot extension of his fingers.

The curtains were of a fabric that burned slowly; beads of fire climbed, it seemed, individual threads. Someone, not me, snatched down the curtains and clapped out the fire, snuffed out the hallelujah that I thought would explode when the beads reached the valance at the top. A parent must have come home. A parent must have been the one who pried the book of matches from Mook's grip. This happened; I remember the hands, but not whose hands they were. Maybe Rhonda looking in on us just in time.

On my birthday, Mook and I threw snowballs at Lytta from the upstairs back porch. His aim was as sure as my luck. I expected her to say something similar to what the Wicked Witch of the West says: *I'm melting, melting. How could such a sweet little girl ruin my beautiful wickedness?*

Smell mattered to Mook. When the matches and Camels were locked away or hidden better, Mook started sniffing his mother's girdles and cardamom, the asafetida parents thought we couldn't reach.

It was also smell that sometimes provoked the most concern. Smell of the needle cutting too deeply into the grooves of Ray Charles and the Raelets singing: *Hit the road Jack,* over and over again, my aunt playing the record most when Jack wasn't there, so that she attempted to celebrate his departure. But from time to time he staggered in, weighed down with those Jack smells that were too overpowering to sleep with the way they infiltrated dreams within the radius all of us were in. The smell of Jack helpless, his wife upset, disgusted, complaining about the helplessness of both of them, disparate helplessnesses whose timing coincided. Jack doubled up as helixes of his helplessness spiraled into him, replaced his DNA.

In the hospital, doctors, affected by the helplessness, helped my aunt prepare for Jack's end, that her disgust had claimed for months to want but that the rest of her did not. The smell of that room. April. Mook's birthday. The smell of the chlorine into which it now seemed she was dunking: her life ice cold, the greens. Mook who was there every day to say good-bye to what he barely knew, the suffering of a man who looked like most artistic hopes for Jesus. The skin cancer ate his face and neck, part of his chest, a corrosive and abrasive hunger. But how can there possibly be a benign eating? How can eating not transform what is eaten? What is the manner of biting, chewing, swallowing, and digesting that will not destroy? And there will be some sort of waste; after the eater has gotten sustenance from the meal, anything left is eliminated. Then there may come along some scavenger who picks through the delicious waste.

There were holes, nothing but holes in Jack, an emptying of his physiological privacy, as if the world that saw him comprised only surgeons, primary care physicians specializing in internal medicine who needed to have a look inside. Lovely rot. His right cheek was eaten away. Cancer had been with him as long as Essell had, but she did not know, could not detect a foul and vulgar presence, and when she did, she called it something else: his depravity, his vileness, his worthlessness distilled and in a bottle. What were her options? She'd had no prior experience with lingering evil; it was swift when it caused the death of her father. She showed Jack no mercy, conspiring with liquor that also showed no mercy. But she didn't leave him, always readmitted him into those back rooms, into her bed next to the heart from which he never left. She wanted him to want more and to handle his disappointment with sobriety; it was fine to be a poor man, to drive a school bus, but not to be a lush unable to stand tall, instead staggering, practically on all fours, practically a beast. How she missed him; he was gone, his drunkenness buried, and still her nights were teary, a vodka running down her cheeks, breaking in the fall from chin to ample bosom in my room.

Mook was six years old and recently fatherless in that fifth month in my room when he wanted to play a Barbie board game with me and I would not let him. *You are a boy, Mook; you cannot play.* Instead, I shared with him my chicken pox. Mook watched Jungle Larry and Captain Kangaroo with me and for his birthday received a doll (he was destroying the Thumbelina and Kissy dolls I'd gotten for Christmas), Jungle Larry safari equipment, and a map of Africa that I gave him ON LOAN ONLY, I wrote on the gift wrap. Thumbelina became a white chimpanzee the map led us to, that we were determined to raise as a human.

Mook's baby doll was not long for this world, her hair going first, Mook yanking it instead of combing it, Mook dragging her through the mud as if she were a secret weapon, a version of Trojan horse and from her mouth would crawl inch-high plastic soldiers. Mook had his doll and still wanted to play the game. *You are still a boy, Mook; you cannot play.* But he wanted to badly. His life began to depend on playing that game that certainly I would not permit him to win even if I ever decided that he could play. Mook begged me. I have always remembered this because the time would come when boys would not beg, would not have to beg because I learned not to say what had been so easy to say to Mook: *you cannot play.* And Mook acquiesced to my authority, to my proficiency with words: *You cannot play.*

He would watch me sit the dolls around the board, watch me speak for them, and move their markers, watch me claim the universe of the game, watched his own exclusion, and I would not amend the language; not in three years had playing given me such power. I was getting back at Lytta through Mook, dear Mook.

One day, I don't know what had changed, I told him that he could play but only if he let me call him *Alice,* but I could not call him *Alice* unless he wore a dress and had ribbons in his hair. I had in mind Lytta's tattered blue dress. After he wore it, I envisioned him burning it for me, but I couldn't think of a way to get it. None of my dresses would fit him, but my mother's did and I shortened it by tying a sash around his waist. I parted his hair down the middle, applied West Indies Hair Grower to make his wavy brown hair shine like the hair of a good, well-groomed Alice who wore taps on her patent leather shoes and ruffled socks that matched the ribbons. Alice played the game all day that day and thought that she had won something although she did not again play, did not again suffer ribbons or tea sets. Whatever the advantages of that superficial femininity, he had it for a day. In first grade he read, as I had a few years before, *Alice and Jerry* books, perhaps with more sympathy for Alice's life of *run, play, look, see, jump,* and *stop: See Alice. See Alice run. Run, Alice; run.* But did she run to catch up with Wilma Rudolph?

Eventually, when he was thirteen, something needed exorcising from Mook, something that was not named by doctors those weeks he spent in St. Luke's Hospital, something that had made him incendiary and needing to interpret the world through flame. Perhaps there is no word to name something so ugly. In not having a name for it, perhaps it cannot be called by accident into active duty again. It was a discharge that gushed green and thick from most of his orifices, most profusely from his mouth, nose, eyes. There was no stopping the green avalanche of it, horror of it, smell of it; Mook in isolation, red notice of toxicity on his hospital room door. This to inform those who loved him so much we could not stay away that we were at risk with that love, that our safety could not be assured, although of course safety never can be assured. We saw it happen, this green purging that was ceaseless, that filled bottle after bottle, kidney-shaped dish after kidney-shaped dish and was then studied or disposed of with other hazardous waste. Otherwise, between the flowing, Mook could speak, eat, but certainly he could not go to school, certainly his plastic utensils were discarded and his sheets sterilized, perhaps burned. I remember being gloved, gowned, and masked to visit him, and with all that cover, I still was not permitted to touch him behind his plastic tent. The malevolent agent was never named to me; I still don't know the toxin, but certainly it is right to say that this thirteen-year-old boy was emptied of malice and discouragement.

He left the hospital pronounced cured by the doctors. And he was cured indeed; despite the loss of his father, despite a stepfather who, no matter the love, was also a drunkard; despite the poverty he knew always, after moving away from the possibilities in the circles around which as a toddler he steered his intimidating tricycle—an adult would need a ladder to mount it; despite his depressed neighborhoods, his limited academic success, Mook never himself became a drinker or a smoker; Mook never himself attempted any substance abuse, never lost a faith in life's preciousness, and although he did father three children out of wedlock, they were by one woman who moved in with Mook's family, to the delight of his mother who was glad to help raise her grandchildren.

In this life, I can find much inspiration; our social circumstances do not have to rule us nor force us into bleak outlooks. Mook had something else more persuasive that kept him able to feed on sunsets, a drive to the lake, the casting of his line into the water from rocks that when wet looked as vivid as diving dolphins and whales. He perhaps should have been more discouraged, but such things still meant something to him. A late afternoon of doo-wop like an eternal flame.

The Saturdays he was with us, Mook sat in the informal spiritual circle; it expanded to encompass him. He was unusually kind, amazingly, some would say, avoided the crime and immorality increasingly prevalent where he lived, evaded the degeneration around him, in it but not of it. He never submitted to a pervasive disillusionment that can precede lawlessness. I have heard that he and the mother of his children had a volatile relationship; the words were explosive, perhaps there was also undue reciprocal (they were both big) physical aggression. I have heard that they were not compatible, that Mook planned to end their relation-

ship and move on to another young woman who like himself had dreams
and hope, who was not lazy in regarding her life, who was generous
and compassionate. But this young mother of Mook's children so heavily
criticized ten years ago is praised now, regarded as a model single mother
who provides impressive foster care for at-risk children. She is the only
link to the children of Mook. And like Mook, they are so calm, like
the ideal model of monks; it is eerie sometimes to see them, for the
impossibility of their attitude, two of them teenagers and at home in
poverty without problem, total disinterest in rebellion, even enthusiastically carrying their mother's foster babies, the diapers, the bottles; and
the way they whisper, refuse to project their voices—so eerie sometimes,
the serpent whispering in Eve's ear.

But it's not *that* this time, it's extreme goodness, and it's still scary.

I loved to hear Mook sing as he worked on cars, an excellent
mechanic, as good as his uncles who had held automotive jobs all their
adult lives. Mook learned on his own. Mook who could never write
successfully an academic paper so I wrote them all, and he graduated
from John Hay High School on time as did the following year the young
woman, then pregnant with his first child, after I wrote essays for her.

In 1987 while I was stranded in Brockville, Ontario, my car suddenly
needing a torque converter, Mook died, a massive heart attack while he
was driving to work. The only warning, obviously not regarded as such,
was twenty-four hours worth of heartburn; it did not let him sleep on
his last night. He slumped across the wheel, the horn blaring until
paramedics, who arrived as fast as a miracle, moved his large body away
from the wheel, pulled him, nearly dead, from the car as he mumbled for
them to call his father, tell him what happened. *Call Tee-Tee,* my mother.

Mook, who was at least one hundred pounds overweight from the
time he was ten, was gone, and with him a remarkable tenor that the

world never got to hear. He was thirty years old. Mook was gone exactly one year after his mother, and we kept saying when we, my mother and I, did not know what to say, that it was a blessing that she went first, because if she hadn't, the loss of Mook would have killed her. And I was there for Mook when his mother died just as he had been there for me a few years earlier when Moe-lay died, and we felt more like siblings than ever before, and we sang together: his tenor, my soprano. And at his funeral, it was my soprano alone though in my mind I could hear the supplemental depth of his tenor accompaniment on *Soon ah will be done wid de troubles of de world.* At Moe-lay's funeral I sang *Deep River,* Mook sitting in a pew silently mouthing the words.

The ideal woman of Mook's affection came into Blessed Messiah Baptist Church right after my solo, just before Mook's casket was closed and the pallbearers, Mook's uncles and friends, carried him to his interment. She placed a single rose in his casket, kissed his cheek, and left, a black lace mantilla flowing like a bridal train.

When Moe-lay died, Leland and his girlfriend brought covered dishes and stayed with us through the night, only the girlfriend sleeping. The preacher who officiated at my wedding, and now battles prostate cancer, stayed many hours too, allowing us to borrow folding chairs from the church. Many were the consolers and all the consolers brought food as if we could fill what was missing with food, as if their best culinary efforts could sustain. Despite the inadequate ability of food to soothe, we would have been lost without those gestures: the act of giving, the attempt to nourish the parts of ourselves we were most likely to neglect as grief redefined us; this encouraged us, began to lift us. We continued elevated in our lives, believing there was nothing left that could ground us. We continued our desperate rising, the root having given rise to a beanstalk, access to a superior kingdom with a singing harp and a good-sized goose.

Twenty-six Keys

School served to reinforce each day as affirming; I didn't need Mook to be confident there. Louis Pasteur Elementary School was one of the kiosks of paradise in which I sought refuge. I wasn't asked to study Lytta there, only what was more important. It was the place that offered me the profundity I craved, each semester expanding concentrically, the universe enlarging as my mind did, so that my knowledge of it never actually increased; in fact, its expansion rendered me practically invisible so that I could explore undetected, without upsetting the natural progress of events. That which is unseen is also unmolested.

What I loved to do was demanded of me at school. It was my natural habitat where language swelled and swirled cyclonically, careened and dazzled as words made sense of concepts and allowed me to put them into practice, linking everything, the roads infinite, the destinations accessed by those roads infinite. School gave me an idea of what was possible for myself, transformed my dreams, challenged me in ways that increased my delight; I raced through my classes, eager for something to learn, something else to enact and embrace; I wanted to be full yet never was, despite how ravenous I was for books and everything they contained.

It was pure gluttony that drove me to succeed in school. Gluttony and a desire to overcome Lytta. There were no boundaries; I could not be contained; my growth in school was unchecked, unruly, unstoppable. I too had in me wildness. There was nothing more marvelous. School made me feel invincible.

When I began kindergarten, I was ready with an impressive juvenile library in my room; hundreds of books, one each week since I was a year old; now, in kindergarten, I was getting a library card and printing my name on a tracking card in the back of each book I borrowed; I surely signed all the books in the children's room, taking home seven, eight books at a time. Of my own books, the first to have lasting importance to me was *When They Were Girls,* a perfect square, as I recall, five inches by five inches, in my possession when I was six.

I drew so much life from that book. *When They Were Girls* was about the childhoods of great women; their lives when they were like me. I used to rub the dark green cloth cover that distinguished it from the glossy cardboard covers of most of my juvenile books. It was not one of the *Little House* books or the Bobsey Twins books that I bought at the drugstore or at Woolworth's. Most likely it was a gift from one of the women my mother worked for, and I was meant, as I indeed was, to be encouraged by the mostly unspectacular beginnings of women who later became influential and autonomous. But since the women did not reconfigure their early lives themselves, certain dreams and thoughts, certain subjective and personal nuances were absent. And these distillations of experience into memory are what most interest me for their truth of how life is felt and perceived, for their revelation of the relationship with facts and not just facts themselves. It was a book written by someone who compiled facts, brief generalized chronologies, but who did not include the woman's own interpretation of her life, not the transformation of detail and subtlety into her daily poetry. The actual language of their lives was not there.

Even so, the facts themselves were stunning. In the book I found two mentors: Susan B. Anthony and Saint Maria Goretti. The book introduced me to many possibilities. I didn't think for one minute that little white girls and little black girls couldn't aspire to the same destiny and success. It didn't matter what culture the girls represented; I thought all girls shared something and that we were heading, all smiles and braids, to vast opportunities that we were free to imagine and reimagine. Nothing had told me otherwise. In my childhood, I was: Marie Curie, Sacajawea, Amelia Earhart, Sojourner Truth, Annie Oakley, Maria Goeppart Mayer, Margaret Mead, and Madam C. J. Walker. I still had Mrs. Feldman's gold pen to help me write these aliases.

A black silhouette of a girl, perhaps a swing also in silhouette, was on the dark green cover just above the title, *When They Were Girls.* I recall that I read this book in the Kingdom of Lills while everyone else slept, and I reread it until I nearly had it memorized. I was greedy in private, licking my lips, belching my own poems. I slept with words; I dreamed words, all night turning pages in a book my dream wrote.

It was not the kind of book my parents, especially my father who bought most of them, usually bought for me. He preferred to indulge me with science. That is why I assume the book was a gift, perhaps appearing magically on my bed just because I needed such a book, a breakthrough as significant in my life as the blue-glowing radium of Marie Curie. Placed in my hands by the spirit of some great but unknown woman writer of the past intervening in my life early so that I commit myself to ambition soon enough to be able to achieve generously in my allotted time.

Most books came into my life without mystery; I remember being invited to sit in during the salesman's visit to peddle the *World Book Encyclopedia.* Perhaps my parents' invitation tipped off the astute salesman who, as I recall, sold the entire set the moment he said that any child would benefit and see improved marks in school, but for a bright child (nod in my direction), the books would be indispensable in helping her realize her potential. My father had great faith in my potential. Between 1962 and 1971—my last year of high school—the set was supplemented and kept current with two annual volumes, the *Year Book* and *Science Year,* once it was introduced, both fully indexed.

Before I could read words, I read images; my father began taking me for those long walks in the city before I was two, down busy streets with cars switching lanes like insects seeking the headiest perfume, manhole covers like gigantic buttons fastening the streets, steam pouring out of grates like underground dreams getting a chance, and somehow we also managed to traverse the least urban margins: culverts, fields, large yards with sunflowers and trellised vines, laundry on ropes tied between trees. The city's system of metroparks in the Emerald Necklace. Where hadn't we walked by the time I was ten? No doubt we covered the miles to South Dakota although we traversed only local terrain, never tiring of it nor getting lost. He was the one who first taught me *igneous, sedimentary, metamorphic.* I could read those words in the texture and structure of rocks. During his seven months on Lills, Mook didn't come with us.

After substantial rain, there'd be additional creeks in the sunken and drainage areas of parks; in these I launched boats that were Moe-lay's empty cellophane-wrapped Pall Mall packages. Or I launched them in our driveway's pool that formed when the drain in the center clogged with leaves, twigs, and litter. Dressed like the Morton salt girl, in a yellow rain coat, bright rubber boots, and holding a red umbrella, I would take sticks and unclog the drain, mesmerized by the muddy whirlpool as the water whooshed.

Mrs. Feldman would watch me from the window, shaking excess rain from my umbrella when I came in, giving me a towel for my feet; I was a vigorous splasher. When I was five, six, and seven, I was still splashing, but now Lytta watched me from the same window and didn't come out in the rain.

Returning from the walks with my father, I always had a new Golden storybook from the drugstore or, by the time I was seven, a new volume in the Golden Library of Knowledge: *White Wilderness; Polar Regions; Automobiles; Submarines; Engines; Energy and Power; Mathematics; Vision; How, Why and What We See; The Body in Action; The Moon; The Planets; The Sun.* I still have these books, and they are still useful; solar eclipses predicted through the year 2000.

Although I preferred books, I did have toys. On Christmas, dolls like Little Miss Echo, Kissy, Thumbelina, Chatty Cathy, and Tiny Tears arrived with rockets, helicopters, trucks, Greyhound buses, trains, airplanes, bulldozers, and submarines. These I first pulled from the cardboard box when it had arrived, roughly handled, from Sears in late summer: the new Barbie, Skipper, or Midge doll, new wrecker with foam ball officially nine months later when I'd be convincingly surprised and grateful to see them under the tree; luckily my parents did not dust them for my fingerprints.

This in no way means that I did not believe in Santa Claus. Something about the red suit, the chimney entrance without his getting sooty, and the sack of toys was irresistible. He had the power of angels and saints, which he was originally, as Saint Nicholas, as Kris Kringle, corruption of German, I believe, words for Christ Child. A sacred, holy image dressed in red like a devil.

At my house, Santa ate a piece of coconut cake and I was glad that he liked what I liked what with our being so different and his being of the jolly culture of self-abnegation. My mother used Baker's angel flake coconut in the blue can exclusively. The shredded coconut was so moist it stuck to her fingers and whatever she touched. Santa was an idea that comforted me and I never thought about his reality, never needed to see Santa emerge head or foot first from the chimney, and did not think it problematic for someone of his ability to enter through a chimney even when we moved to Trunt Avenue and no longer had a fireplace. For me it was far more interesting that he didn't bother with the door or window that all houses and apartments would have. I liked that he proved there was other access, other ways in, other ways out, and possible to travel the world with a sack of inexhaustible supply yet no weight, no burden—entirely in the cover of darkness, that treachery, without ever being robbed.

I knew that toys were not equally distributed, that some belief systems forbade him, but those in my city who woke only to promises nevertheless wrote to him asking for Christmas miracles because they believed in him. If there were no or few toys, their own naughtiness could explain it; never mind that affluent naughty ones were rewarded and less affluent naughty ones, like me, were too; still, there was that naughty comfort. Some who wrote to Santa had not written before to God, although Santa is really an extension of the idea that God is love. Santa's image, however, was more consistent; he was a beautiful concept, a splendid idea whose implementation was imperfect. As a Brownie, I sang Christmas carols in a department store. As a member of the school chorus, I sang at the County Workhouse, for those who'd be incarcerated for the holidays. With the hat on my head, I looked like an elf, one of Santa's freakish angels.

But I knew that my parents worked into the night assembling and arranging the gifts under the tree so that when I woke I would find in the living room a kingdom of delight that the Golden Library of Knowledge was forbidden to reveal, a kingdom that *Energy and Power* could not explain. The best gift of the day was the inexplicable and the numinous.

Because of Mook's gifts on his Christmas with us, I assume that it would have been the same had I been a boy, gifts of that doll whose arms coming together made her mouth pucker and the plane with a compartment that opened to release missiles or, depending on my mood, to accept on tethers those needing rescue; the rocket that came apart in stages, the fashion dolls whose torsos could be turned backward on their legs, their feet that could not be unmolded proving the different evolution of dolls and women. As I was all curiosity, I had the right father.

I was so busy learning that I was not aware of my plainness, the unflattering way in which my hair hung of its own accord in crinkles and waves, often braids, a density of hair too great for such a narrow face, for which the eyes also were too large, the mouth too conspicuous, the forehead too high and prominent to ever appear without bangs. Yet cliffs that offer spectacular, breathtaking views jut out just that way. My parents treated me as if I comprised loveliness upon loveliness. Breathtak-

ing view after breathtaking view. I was treated the same way in school
by teachers like Mrs. Stupak, Miss Porter, Miss Matthews, and Mrs.
Bullock, all women, all from Louis Pasteur Elementary School, all nurturing; they allowed children to flourish, gave us the room to grow
and blossom unfettered in such an intensity of light, intensity of books
and experiments.

Consider the Day of Seeds when we held seeds (something I'd done
prior to school with my father) and warmed them almost to incuba-
tion and sprouting with our hands, drew seeds, studied seeds under magni-
fying glasses, tasted seeds, traced seeds, guessed from whatever proper-
ties of the seeds we could discern just what kind of vegetable, flower,
or tree would grow; glued and painted into brooches the ones we did
not plant. Those teachers spoiled us, supplementing the requirements
the way they did.

It was the ideal atmosphere for discovery. I did not feel judged. I
did not have to compete. I was not given a ceiling. To me was appointed
no bully. How grand it was. *Try this. What do you think this is, can
be, will become?*—those were the questions the teachers posed. Even in
kindergarten, in matters of alphabet that I knew already, for I could
read when I got there: *What can we do with this B? Can Barbara use B to
help her write her name? She can? Then Barbara will know whenever she sees
this letter, that her name is about to happen if she wants it to. With this,
Barbara, you can begin. With this, you can build. Capital B has two windows,
one atop the other; Barbara always begins with capital B. Barbara builds bridges
with B. The bridge from Barbara to whatever you put at the other end of your
bridge. You have all of B's power.* I could not wait to be told the powers
of *T.*

Each day offered an amazement without penalty or threat of evalua-
tion and comparison. A thought became permanent with only combina-
tions of twenty-six letters. It had not always been so. Ancient people,
like the Hindu and the Phoenicians, Egyptians and Maya, invented alpha-
bets and written languages. They were products of minds like ours. The

teacher said so. We had been given all twenty-six keys; there were no others; we were not to be tricked by any lock we encountered; a combination of our keys would open it. There was no reason not to explore and discover; there were no risks.

Those teachers were extraordinary women for whom I shined because I was free to shine without my efforts toward shining judged. There were no obstacles. *What if you had to build a castle? What would you do? How would you begin? Out of what would you build it? A castle of water? Of corn? How? What shape? Where would you build it? Why would you build a castle at all? How will you know that what you have built is a castle?* In such an environment, everyone was smart, gifted, even those who eventually tested otherwise. These questions really asked: *What if you had a dream? How would you realize it? How would you protect it?* And someone they got me to ask these questions myself.

I forgot all about Lytta while I was there. I put the ladybug marks on my arms under the microscope and saw in them cities and worlds where there were no vehicular homicides. In those cities I saw canals as on Mars, patterns for quilts, tessellations. I became Thylias Leeuwenhoek. At home, I disassembled a transistor radio, tried to figure out the difference between a lightbulb and a tube I removed from the back of a television, but I was not punished; my father encouraged such explorations. Besides, I had a *T,* a ticket to anywhere.

In first grade, after taking the Seashore (I'm not at all certain that this is what it was called) Music Test, in which we had to respond to variations in pitch, rhythm, and intensity, I was given a violin, though I'd requested a flute and was at first disappointed, until the three of us (and two cellists) who were now violinists were introduced to music of among others Paganini, Biber, Locatelli, Heifetz, and Menuhin. The range of the instrument was incredible. It had the most passion, the most emotion, the most versatility of any instrument in the orchestra. Please forgive my bias. And to see the string section playing (we were taken to concerts at Blyden Hall), their bows almost as rhythmic and beautiful as the arms and hands of sign language—so inspiring and moving. I felt both grateful and inadequate, doubting that I could pull from the strings what the strings could say, but I felt so lucky to try.

This is what vocal cords are like, I thought.

How can I explain what rosin meant to me beyond its obvious function? It was like a small piece of amber ice. Once I licked it and thought it would look pretty in weak tea, but it was not immersed anywhere but in my thoughts, dreams. Rosin is what's left after distilling turpentine from the crude resin of pine. Using it, I was coating the bow, protecting the bow, putting on the bow its armor, fortifying it that it not slip off the melodic high wires, and I was also loving the bow, stroking the bow, preparing the bow for the sometimes difficult and temporarily unrewarding ritual of dragging, tramping over the strings in prescribed patterns, tormentous repetition, but one day Massenet, one day the all city orchestra's imperfect attempt at some Haydn, some Vivaldi, and the bow taking the violin's strings to their first conceptualized summit.

Each week, my mother took me to the Phyllis Wheatley Institute where I had private lessons, in addition to group instruction at school, to encourage the promise someone saw in the way I, at six, bonded with the instrument. I knew of no prominent black violinist, certainly not a black woman. I wanted to be the first one whom the world couldn't get enough of; the world still needs such a black female violin prodigy. Recently, in fact, in the biography of Philippa Schuyler, a biracial prodigy of piano and classical composition, I read that the author, Kathryn Talalay, was told in a telephone interview that:

> The problem of being a woman in the concert field is pretty much solved today, but being black is not. . . . And even now, it is still unusual to see a black playing a violin or piano on-stage. I don't

know why, but there seems to be a built-in resistance. . . . Little
has changed—except in opera—in almost four decades.[1]
Perhaps today, that prodigy is just born.

I remember my shoes clicking in what seemed to be long hallways
dimly lit, the color of rosin. The room in which I played, just me, for
a teacher for an hour, had large windows that I don't remember looking
through or being seen through. The room completely contained the
sound, and sometimes my shadow overwhelmed and dwarfed me, the
violin then looming larger than a bass viol. I hugged the rectangular
school-issued case and did not mind the exercises to limber my right
arm and strengthen it. All was requisite for my debut at Blyden Hall.

What do I have from that? Still the desire, I can't kill it, to play
the violin, to become just half as good as perhaps I could have become
had I played beyond fourth grade. How I envied Seleste in ninth grade,
Seleste who still played and was first violinist in the school orchestra. I
remember F—A—C—E, the notes between the spaces, *Every Good Boy*
Does Fine for the notes on the lines of the staff. But one may exceed
the staff; I barely remember how. I did not learn violin through the
Suzuki method; I learned to read music when I was six. I wanted my
hair fixed in curls of treble clefs my nails retractable instead of clipped.

Maris's cello was in some ways better; its notes more mature and
more evocative of the sadness and loneliness of trees, their embar-
rassment that their sadness is so remarkable and lovely; it still sounds
like a tree, for instance a great oak that has lived through the Civil War
and children falling, some hurt slightly, from its branches as if they'd
been the tree's own fruit—you can hear that. Her violoncello was as

....
[1]Klaus George Roy in a 1989 telephone interview with Kathryn Talalay who offers the quote in
her biography of Philippa Schuyler: *Composition in Black and White: The Tragic Saga of Harlem's Biracial*
Prodigy (New York: Oxford, 1995), p. 141.

wide as a trunk of a tree finally of a size to be assured of survival, too committed with its roots, depth of bark, extent of xylem to be merely yanked from the ground should its stance be in the way of commerce; it would take hatchet, saw, dynamite, match or lightning, but focus instead on its sound holes of a size that small birds, young orphaned squirrels might take refuge there.

The Voice of the Wood:[2] I adore that book, the story of how an old craftsman shapes his last instrument, a violoncello, from a great tree that had overlooked his garden in Venice and that plot of land even before his garden was there, incorporating into its wood the sounds of *leaves swaying and boats gliding by* in the canal. This tree had not been grown to become an instrument and consequently, when it died one winter and the craftsman converted it to lumber, it became, years later, an exceptional instrument that confounded a celebrated prodigy by not conforming to his expertise as a cellist. The instrument contained all that the tree had witnessed. Instead, the cellist, through a wearying unending night had to abandon his own virtuosity and play the music that the tree contained. He could not impose his genius and selfishness. Maris consistently played like that. Whenever we had a school concert, Maris always had a solo piece, the lights removed from the rest of the orchestra.

All Cows Eat Grass; Good Boys Do Fine Always; those were Maris's notes. We walked to Louis Pasteur each morning, lugging our instruments, sometimes just earlier than the birds. Mostly we used the bows though sometimes played pizzicato, two girls in the school yard, the sun not yet at a fog-burning height, until it was time for the bell and there were crowds to dwarf our music. Maris was probably the smartest child in our class. So advanced in her reading and thinking, but she tried not to intimidate us and usually didn't.

There was also French without books with a teacher who looked

. . . .
[2]Claude Clément, *The Voice of the Wood,* trans. Lenny Hort, illus. Frédéric Clément (New York, Dial, 1989). Paintings by Frédéric Clément, Dial Books.

like de Gaulle. Years later in a graduate linguistics course, I learned that my first-grade French had been part of a study to determine whether or not there were benefits in beginning foreign language instruction in first grade instead of in fourth grade where foreign language instruction was usually introduced into the public school curriculum for the academically talented. The conclusion was that there were no significant gains as children whose initial instruction was delayed until fourth grade quickly caught up with those who had had a three-year advantage. That may be true, but the only French I can still speak with ease (although I can read and comprehend much more) is what I learned with de Gaulle. *Où est le professeur? Le professeur est devant le tableau noir. Il a un morceau d'argent à la main.*[3] He would give us licorice and silver coins for correct responses, and from the beginning conducted the class only in French. I thought that he couldn't speak English. Outdoors, de Gaulle had us lie on the ground and name with his help what we could see in the clouds. The Bastille. His face.

As fine as that was, what really delighted me in school involved more drama. In grades two through four B, the first half of fourth grade, with Mrs. Roberta Bullock and Mrs. Matthews as teachers, one child began each class with a ten-minute lecture on any topic of interest to the child. This lecture, called a morning talk, was to be supplemented with visual aids that revealed the extensiveness of our research. We were permitted to have assistants who could circulate the visual aids or operate the slide projector, tape recorder, or record player, but who could not actually deliver any of the lecture. We did not receive grades on these lectures (or in French) until third grade, so my effort came from my heart.

One of my first morning talks was on Susan B. Anthony, someone we had not studied in class and whose life I became aware of only through reading *When They Were Girls*. For this talk, I made protest signs

....
[3]In English: *Where is the teacher? He is in front of the blackboard. He has a piece of silver in his hand.*

and wrote a short play on women's rights. Deesa Massey, a friend of mine who lived across the street from Louis Pasteur, permitted me to borrow clothes that had belonged to her grandmother in Natchez and now were in a trunk in Deesa's attic. Sounds fairly standard, but it wasn't; her grandmother had some rather funky things, as if she'd come north straight from the honky-tonk. Perfect costumes for my play. I wore some of these clothes and had two other girls, Deesa and probably Eleanor, wear the rest. As I spoke about Susan, Deesa and Eleanor marched around the darkened classroom, 210 I think, using flashlights for illumination, carrying the signs, and chanting.

Eleanor gave a morning talk on ants for which she brought in a model and a carefully drawn anatomical diagram (size of a billboard) of an ant although I had hoped she'd have a play in which I could portray the ant queen, paper wings attached to the back of my dress for the mating flight just as in the movie *Them!* I liked to hear her say *thorax.* When she used the pointer to locate the ant's narrow waist, she tapped the spot three times.

When I got the idea to use the school's namesake as morning talk subject, I was full of self-congratulatory smugness; I thought I was asserting some genius until I learned that many before me in second and third grades had reported on Pasteur's process for preventing the souring of milk, beer, wine by sterilizing it, using heat to kill bacteria that he knew spread disease, so he therefore also advocated sterilizing medical equipment so that the course of medical treatment not itself become pathological. I could not have been more unoriginal that time, but I was the only one who dramatized pasteurization, casting six children as germs.

Those fine teachers at Louis Pasteur did not indicate to me that they thought I performed in any extraordinary way, and in their restraint and avoidance of fuss, I blossomed and thrived, at times led the class, contributed fiercely to discussions, wrote plays, shared some of my poems, played the violin as if I were inventing it and it were inventing me. All in the class perceived of ourselves as ordinary and equal. We assumed that all classes were like ours. There was no individual emphasis or glory except by accident, such as the day Jackson tattooed both of his arms in green permanent marker with expressions of undying love for me. My name up and down the full length of his arms.

Beyond that, I was left alone to discover on my own little pieces of the vastness that I did not find overwhelming, but stimulating; I would never exhaust the world, never be bored, never need to lament my inability to know everything as the vastness said such absolute knowledge was impossible. The vastness was relieving. I was surrounded by the unknowable. Louis Pasteur Elementary School, what I needed, what every child needed, now is closed.

That was so fine, discovering, not being told, but figuring out something perplexing, becoming aware of something present all along, but that had been blocked by ignorance or darkness, and then, a little speck of ignorance recedes and you are increased tenfold: sand dollars, horseshoe crabs, sea stars appear like sudden wealth, like the gushing oil well, the millions of barrels of crude that sustain you for life. You have been looking, scraping, peeling, digging, tasting, straining, and eventually there is a small result; you see for the first time something millions before you have seen, but to you it is new, as if it is coming into the world for the first time; you have seen the way the grasshopper hops; you have timed the interval between the flashes of a firefly's fire; you have turned the television to a VHF channel your area does not receive (you don't have cable) and watched and listened to the pattern of static and electronic snow for echoes of developing tornado, whispers of destruction; you have used yeast in excess, yeast insufficiently, baking soda too, Epsom salt that yielded crystals when the water evaporated, and you know some things without anyone having to tell them to you.

I had in Louis Pasteur school the freedom to be inconspicuous yet essential because not all discoveries a child might make will duplicate discoveries already made and documented. Children are capable of genuine revelation. The teachers there were open to and even hoped for our discoveries.

This freedom is something I lost upon my transfer in the middle of fourth grade to Benjamin Franklin school, where what I valued was taken away and nothing more was expected of me than the little I effortlessly gave. This academic disillusionment happened because we moved to a safer, mostly white, mostly Croatian and Serbian neighborhood, many Jewish families; we always dwelled among such families, my pale father welcomed most anywhere. The owners of the delicatessen, they lived on Trunt Avenue too (the wife's name was Deborah), where I bought jugs of milk, rye and white bread, Dandee pretzels, and Dandee barbecue potato chips, always gave me a Reese's Peanut Butter Cup when I came in; a whole carton of thirty-six for my birthday; they asked my father every year for one of my school pictures and let me sell penny candy and dill pickles from behind the counter.

I resented the new teachers and administrators for stripping me of my identity; I had so much contempt for them that I was almost ruined by it. A consuming nastiness. They thought that I was inferior, dull, should not have been in the accelerated classes I had been in, that I should not be distracted from the probably insurmountable rigors of making up my academic deficiencies—wasn't I black?—by instrumental music and foreign language instruction. So those activities ceased. For me, it was placement in the regular classroom.

And I said nothing. I didn't believe it would do any good since my written school records had been disregarded, perhaps because most of my teachers at Louis Pasteur had been black women, as incompetent and inferior as I was. The official record was invalidated by white women. I watched the violin, for the last time, as it was locked in the office while the principal escorted me to Miss Bishop's regular classroom where even there, some children, you could see their haughtiness, were selected for French study and would leave room 201 while we read fourth-grade literature that I had read in second and third grades. *Little House on the Prairie. Charlotte's Web. Caddie Woodlawn.* Why did this school want to diminish me? What had I done to them? Why would I never escape the effects and consequences of not resisting Lytta?

These new teachers and administrators overpowered me; we were adversaries; we were in battle. I was outraged but failed myself by failing to tell them. They would decide what kind of world it was and what I could do in it. I had the opportunity to save my violinist life, but I wasted it. It is my fault that I do not now play for the symphony orchestra. There is no one else to blame. They didn't want it for me; I wanted it for me, so it was my responsibility to act. They were my new bullies. My parents deferred to their expertise; even my father acquiesced to their degrees and prejudices. I was learning that Lytta represented no mere isolated phenomenon; she was part of a cycle of deviancy and cruelty that was working diligently to bring me into it.

School could no longer be for me what it had been. It was now poisoned by attitudes not based on fact nor on performance. I ceased to be an individual. All my work was evaluated before I did it; nothing I seemed to do affected the premature assessments. School had been books, science equipment, music stands, and sheet music. School had been maps, globes, number lines, the place where any action could become an equation that turned everything into search and discovery with *n,* and with solving for *x.* School had been the periodic table of the elements that was in my third-grade classroom—*third* grade! School had been a model of the atom, introduction to the joy of molecules that could be put together like linking cars in a train. School had been learning variation, cutting an apple in half along its axis and seeing wings or lungs, then cutting the apple in half at its equator and finding a star. All I had to do was say: *I want the violin. Je veux un violon. I want French. Je veux apprendre le français. I'm good at French. I'm good at the violin. Listen to me play. Listen to me speak. Ecoutez!*

Just like that, dreams were over, and for the school's having snatched them so cruelly, I decided to give the school nothing else, certainly not my voice, my ideas, my participation in their discussions of books I practically knew by heart; I would not point at great cities on the map to locate the Acropolis or the Taj Mahal; I would point my finger at those teachers and administrators if I pointed it at all. I even stopped raising my hand and learned to hold in everything, even toileting needs, until I got home. I lost my primary refuge. So I became as vegetative as I could without risking placement in an actual remedial setting. The school had them. The only classes with a majority of black students.

What I experienced, what I knew, how I felt, what I thought; that was all mine and I did not want to risk its loss. Teachers in this school didn't deserve the privilege of hearing my voice. They would be denied just as I was being denied. They were intent upon my inhabiting a smaller world, so I did; at last: a ceiling came into view; even when Lytta had been active in my life I hadn't had a ceiling. I still had the sky of her dress.

After a month in Miss Bishop's regular class, I became one of the smug regular students taking French, but it was nearly a year before I was fully reinstated in the gifted program and sent to Miss Pinzic's room where I remained until graduation from elementary school. The ceiling was demolished, but not the effects of having had one.

Instrumental music instruction was not resumed; I failed to demand it. I failed to inform my parents of the emptiness I felt without the violin; had they known, they would have insisted on continued instruction or would have outright purchased an instrument for me, even if they would have needed, and they wouldn't have, to place a second mortgage on our home. Like Brahms, I too *could evaporate into a musical chord and float away*. As I was with Lytta, with Gladys, with the boys on bike and in box, I am where I do not want to be, and speaking up could have changed my circumstances. I knew all the words to say, but as usual I was silent and surrendered to what I identified as fate. I spoke only when I was certain that I was in control of the situation and would not be challenged, and when I did speak, there was no amplification from deep within; I offered a shallow voice appropriate for the shallow treatment I received. Although once again I was educated among the so-called gifted (it was soon obvious that the gift some had received was no more than white skin), I did not reinstate my voice. I kept myself for myself.

From then on, I was much more suspicious, less optimistic, less certain that idyllic forms were substantial, less convinced that imagination was useful. Lytta had not deflated me as much as this school did. Before attending Ben Franklin, I knew that Lytta was a poison but I also knew that not all the world was poisonous nor had been tainted. Louis Pasteur school had been proof. And that proof kept me from drowning because school more directly determined, I thought, what would be possible in my life than did Lytta. She was torture to endure, and then would come the compensation of classes and the reward of the rest of my life. Now, however, the tyranny seemed more pervasive.

My dreams could be denied in such a way that I would seem responsible for the denial although my abandonment of dreams had been manipulated; whether the manipulation was intentional or unintentional, it happened. Once I came to accept that my own language was not the language that defined me in the world, then Lytta became more prominent in my mind; I saw her as the start of my decline whereas before Benjamin Franklin, incidents with Lytta had seemed to me less damaging. In Benjamin Franklin, the stripping away of luster began; once I learned that luster could be stripped away, I reassessed everything, doubting every happiness, recasting optimism as naïveté. Benjamin Franklin and therefore also Lytta represented mature truth; there'd be more truth like this; I was sure of it. I'm eleven. I'm a preteen. I'm on the brink of a period of life where such negative thinking could have the most disastrous consequences.

And those boys; those dead boys—innocence was useless.

*   *   *

Withholding so much, I must have appeared incapable of creativity or imagination or battle. Certainly I was not considered a sensation destined for greatness as were others in Miss Pinzic's class, some of whom went on to super gifted studies, sometimes after having appropriated my work as their own. Taking my mathematics workbooks and spiral notebooks out of my cupboard and erasing my answers, writing in sums and quotients at random so that none of my solutions were correct except on quizzes and tests. A page where all the answers were the null set against all probability. A world of only obtuse angles. Taking my written reports and erasing my name, or copying them over and accusing me of plagiarizing. I said nothing. My parents said in conferences that they would help me produce more consistent work. No one suggested therapists or counselors.

As in Louis Pasteur school, academically talented students at Benjamin Franklin school were expected to give morning talks, and, as I was accustomed, other students could assist the lecturer. Lidian and one of the appropriators frequently asked me to be one of their assistants. For them I would write plays for which they received credit. Miss Pinzic praised Lidian's morning talks extensively. And as I used her as an assistant for several of my morning talks, Miss Pinzic assumed that Lidian had also written my plays. Lidian went, largely on the basis of my little dramas, to the school for the super gifted. Her vociferousness juxtaposed with my muteness.

Miss Pinzic was surprised when my talks continued to have elaborate enactments, even a burning of Joan of Arc in which I also demonstrated how paganism and Christianity were related. I asked one of the appropriators to be burned at the stake and was especially pleased when she consented so I could lash her to a piece of wood my father helped me bring to school. I built a cellophane fire and used a portable fan to move the flames. I used the color wheel that at Christmas would rotate and cast the aluminum Christmas tree alternately in red, orange, yellow, and green to cast the burning Joan of Arc in those colors, each one associated with a mood, with Joan's way of perceiving the burning, yellow when she was at peace with God and his decision that she be consumed. At the last minute, the appropriator backed out, so at the stake I had to burn a good friend I'd secretly cast as understudy for I'd suspected that an appropriator just might want to sabotage my presentation, but I imagined someone more deserving on fire. Miss Pinzic was impressed beyond words and sent my friend to be tested for the school that Lidian by then was attending.

Almost immediately I went, when we moved, from being an outgoing popular girl to an invisible girl in school. Teachers at Benjamin Franklin would not have believed that this animated, vivacious girl in the neighborhood was the same lackluster child who merely occupied space in class, profiting from the occupation but minimally. Every summer, vivacity was reinstated when school ended for the year.

For three months, my bedtime became an adult hour; summer solstice was the day of minimal darkness in a season that kept its promise of lush language, blossoms giving way to leaves bigger than my hand, surplus of bees unable to fly straight under the influence of so much available nectar. Summer exposed the splendor within things. Not that my state of mind ever depended upon meteorology, but summer was so persuasive that this season alone attained perfection of temperature, hue, light, a growing season across the continent, local peaches, melons, plums wherever we traveled when Ben Franklin's iron doors were locked. I felt vibrant and dynamic—fearless—because of summer.

As soon as there was light, I could get up. In fact, I was expected to get up and open the house, pull up every shade, raise every window, if screens were in place, and let light have full access. Let it anoint and revive corners dark all winter; let it awaken spiders in that habitat of right-angle juncture of plaster, paint, and dry wall, the silken egg case open, the spiders migrating to other rooms on filaments of pure spun sugar. Illuminated, even old cobwebs took on luster, sagging like crepe paper decorations, looped and scalloped, celebrating being there. The sun would rise before seven o'clock and I would immediately dress to meet it, before it became too old, drying off with the towel just as if it were a terry cloth ray of day's first light. There would be sunrise on my record player, a beam of light in the groove just as if it had been the diamond needle. The tone arm was bent light from a prism.

Outside I played hand-clapping games with Ranna who always showed her panties that fit loosely as we played tag and danced hand dances. She also liked to do the pony by herself, danced the pony all the way home. Her dresses were entirely too short, but she was just seven so it didn't matter. Being ten, I was too mature for that. The wind loved to fill Ranna's dresses like bells, cotton dresses with slightly open weaves making a movement toward mauve, gesture toward peach. We had moles in the same places on our arms, and her lips were just barely pink. Her eyes and cheeks held gentians, larkspur, and asters. Her hair was the color of the morning's second pee, not the first pee that is concentrated deep yellow, almost orange, from holding it in all night, but the second batch, delicate color; if you didn't know you were squirting it, you couldn't get confirmation from the toilet bowl whose water would still seem clear. Her two brothers never had their feet on the ground when I saw them; they supplemented their height with skates, cleats, unicycles.

Everybody who wasn't grown played rock teacher on each other's front steps. We did the Watusi, when that was a new dance, right on the sidewalk. We weren't embarrassed because we knew we could dance. You couldn't tell us anything about dancing, and I can still do the Mashed Potato. Over the summers, I became so confident that I auditioned to dance on the Big Five show, a local version of Shindig and Hullabaloo, when I was not quite thirteen. Uncle Spoon drove me to Channel Five's studios in his Thunderbird. I wasn't chosen, just as I wasn't chosen for team sports in gym class. But in the fifty-yard dash, no one could catch me. And my size had me destined for the uneven parallel bars. At age ten, I started a dance school in the backyard and there are probably people who still remember and brag about my chore-

ography that made them the envy of wedding receptions and class reunions for years.

I also wrote plays that neighborhood children performed under, always, my direction. Many of these plays had Hawaiian themes. There
was something sonically magical about the words: *Kamehameha, Liliuoka-
lani, Oahu, Iuau, Aloha Oe,* and *Molokai.* I needed opportunities to use
them. I circled them in my geography book, called sugar *Oahu* when I
stirred it into iced tea, called salt *Mauna Kea.* I whispered the words to
my dolls and called my dolls by those new names until I stopped calling
my dolls altogether. It was the effects of such language that linked the
chain of Hawaiian islands. I made maps on which I colored pineapples
and made *X*s to represent tons of sugar processed and shipped. I drew
leis around the neck of pictures of the Lord, hung one of dandelions
around the neck of my mother's crucifix. On television, a cartoon child
demanded his Maypo, but I badgered my mother for *poi* and hibiscus,
coconut milk to wash my wavy hair.

Encouraged by the enthusiasm of actors and audience for those plays,
I organized an improvisational acting troupe, and we made rounds in the
neighborhood, performing even for adults our most requested scenario: a
woman receiving news of the fate of her husband or fiancé who was a soldier
in Vietnam and only nineteen years old (I played this part). We were impressed with nineteen. The last teen; a milestone. The peak of youth; the
year you could stop saying "when I grow up," because growing's done
then. When I would hear odd noises in the night, I wouldn't hear the settling of wood, but my mother's secret desire to be nineteen again.

I was the one who could cry authentically. There would be real
tears. Real grief. Real distress. The word for "grief," for anything, was
so powerful to me that to use the word would be to invoke the power,
to create the real thing. None of my friends could do that. Jenson was
too smart. He always wanted to play the part of the wounded, missing,
or killed soldier. I would protest that he wouldn't have much to do
playing a dead man. Our improvisation was realistic so the dead were

required to remain dead. Jenson said that no; he had the best part and the biggest part. He was my dead husband. He was on my mind. He was in that smart head taking up as much space as a brain.

During my first Benjamin Franklin summer vacation, I organized my first summer enrichment program for boys and girls. I went from door to door in the evening and asked to speak with the parents of my Trunt Avenue friends. I explained the curriculum of my summer enrichment program and insisted that my teaching strategies, tailored to the specific needs of the student, would help their sons and daughters tap into their potential. The services were of course free. A dozen kids enrolled. I assigned homework and took my summer school students on weekly afternoon excursions to the public library. I offered math, reading, science (entomology, meteorology, geology, and botany), music and art. We studied each summer subtle changes in the neighborhood, immigration of more brown faces, the emigration of more pale ones; we made cultural maps. The neighborhood center where there'd been billiards and horticulture became a smoky, noisy place; Little Johnny Taylor records could be heard for a mile. We danced outside (only) the brick. Now it's a struggling Missionary Baptist Church. Each week I sent progress reports to the students and parents, and once each month I met with parents for conferences. Some mothers told me in September that my school had made a significant difference; their child was doing better in the real school, in Benjamin Franklin.

Ultimately, summer proved too brief to counteract the effects of 75 percent of the year. I'd have to return, right when I was feeling on the verge of breakthrough, to the classroom's inane demand for a summer vacation essay, mine totally free of both embellishment and truth; understated to the point of blandness and uselessness, a litany of generalized mundane gestures.

At least in Miss Pinzic's class I wasn't rereading textbooks, although I loved reading enough to be willing to experience the same book endlessly. There was always a different way to interpret the story. Sometimes I would pretend that I was someone else in a life much unlike my own and would find different parts of stories memorable for reasons unique to that life. With Miss Pinzic, I read: *Wrinkle in Time, Lord of the Flies, Platero and I, The Witch of Blackbird Pond,* and *Profiles in Courage.* I wrote a book report on Anne Frank's diary and presented a morning talk on whether or not she had been cheated because her diary would live longer than she may have lived even if the Gestapo had not found her in the secret annex. She wanted to become a famous writer, but had she lived and published books and articles, she probably would not be as famous a writer as she was for having perished before becoming one. Miss Pinzic, after that talk for which I had no assistants, began to realize a reality of my reports and my identity. She barely got to know what I could do before I was promoted to junior high school. She asked me who had given me the idea for that talk, as if the idea could not have been mine, as if I who had long in her classroom been appropriated from was an appropriator. I managed a whispered, *why did you ask me that?* Miss Pinzic seemed caught off guard by the question and said that she was just wondering because it was such a good idea. I meant to say, weakly, *thank you,* but turned and walked away having said nothing.

Then she found the poems, I guess my morning talk inspired a search for evidence. Her attitude toward me changed, her ideas about my promise which prior to the discovery of verse had been in her estimation fully, even overly, actualized, then her sending me to be tested by one of the board of education's psychologists as she suspected that I might be a candidate for special classes for the super gifted. All because of poems I inadvertently left on my desk. They were not for her to see nor for others who assumed that I was inferior.

Although I was glad to be considered for those classes, I told the psychologist a few months later, when the test was actually scheduled, that I would not tell him everything I knew because I did not trust him nor the ones who sent me to him. I told him that I knew I was being given an intelligence test although I had not been informed. *It's obvious,*

I said. I told him that I did not need his confirmation of my intelligence, because with or without it, I knew that I was just as smart as anybody else, *probably smarter than most,* I added sharply so that he could understand that I meant that I was smarter than him. I told him that my previous school had not needed his kind of proof; they could tell that I had a mind gift; *it was obvious,* I said crying, creating a scene, releasing hurt and anger I'd felt in school for a long time to a man whose dingy lab coat almost matched his skin.

It was a regrettable emotional outburst about which Miss Pinzic was informed; *I heard about what happened,* she said. *I'm sorry.* I didn't think she was apologizing, but that she was attempting to share my disappointment that I was not more emotionally stable. Evidently, however, with just five weeks left of sixth grade, I had proved myself on their test, because administrative attitudes toward me improved drastically. And in seventh grade, I was put into those special classes.

Nevertheless, Miss Pinzic had completely misinterpreted what my poetry meant. It was just more experimentation, more process of discovery. At the time, it meant no more than my efforts to understand what words were beyond words. Rhyme delighted and soothed me then. Every rhyming poem was like a spell, an enchantment. Any word could be part of a rhyme; hence, any word had the potential for incantation, transforming one thing into another, but that new thing would go on changing, each day a little different, perhaps reverting minute by minute to the previous state if the incantation were weak or insufficiently repeated. I was not through learning from my experiment with language but Miss Pinzic had damaged the magic.

After her transforming of my experiment into mental barometer, I still wrote, but could not generate with the words any power but hers. She found the poem, and the find led to a throat-clearing, a teacher posture that meant we were about to receive important information: pay attention! She read my poem to the class, and I hated her for that. But it did restore some of the peer respect that had been jeopardized.

In my last year of elementary school just days, it seemed, after Miss Pinzic found the poems, I was appointed captain of the outdoor girl crossing guards (we stood at intersections, blocking the intersections with yellow flags that had green crosses painted in the centers, so that children could not cross, then we moved the flags parallel to the crosswalk markings and let the children pass when it was safe). Flag-off was beautiful. The guard closest to the school received a signal from the door guard when it was time for us to come in, and have hot chocolate with marshmallows in winter. This outdoor guard would wave her flag and the guard seeing that would wave hers in the direction of another guard farther away until all of us were waving our flags and then walking to school with them slung over our shoulders. It could have been part of the opening ceremonies for the Olympics, it was so well choreographed and executed.

Then I was appointed cocaptain of the indoor girl guards, then president of the safety council. As president, I was responsible for reporting on Fire Prevention Week at an all-school assembly. Of course, I wrote a play, made signs, had a dozen kids involved, and even used the overhead projector. Always over the top. Miss Pinzic and the principal were dazzled. It was no big deal; required but minimal effort from me. They, even had they apologized, still deserved no more than my minimal effort. I did it for fun, just for fun. But, when I delivered the valedictory address for the graduation from elementary school, I let them glimpse and marvel at what I could achieve in a partnership with language; I left them regretting how they'd failed me educationally and wondering who were the others being failed. I talked about appearances, the problems of judgment, the forms of wings difficult to recognize. Better to err on the side of flight and hope than to commit what could soar to the ground. I suggested that if wings were taped down too long, the bird would not ever learn to fly, having missed the time during which it had been possible to learn. I said these things, then left Ben Franklin for good.

*I*n junior high school, I was reunited with a friend from Benjamin Franklin who had gone on to super-gifted studies. In Landis Junior High, she was placed in section one—yes; the school actually used numbers to designate academic talent, from one to severely remedial thirteen. I was also assigned to section one; my cousin Deirdre was placed in section two, an accelerated section, where an appropriator was also placed. The difference between one and two levied such tension on our mothers that they were frequently on the verge of severing sisterhood. Deirdre and I did not care; there was no difference that was authentic or that mattered. But we would have preferred being together in all our classes (not just home economics), especially as we were assigned to the same homeroom. First cousins and half-sisters are equivalent.

Sections one (major work) and two (enrichment) were college-bound, and no doubt a teaching dream; the other sections were needlessly and wrongfully neglected; everything we were taught could have been taught to everyone. The system blatantly discriminated, and just by luck, Miss Pinzic had changed her mind about me or I could have been placed in section three or lower and my future discouraged. I got the best of public school, the equivalent of a prestigious private school education, but those in sections four and below got very little in the way of choices and intellectual stimulation. Once in a particular section, one could not easily get out; there was no procedure in place for switching, no built-in acknowledgment of the possibility of wrongful placement; assignment to sections was based on promise as evidenced by standardized tests and teacher hunches and observations, not on daily performance or interviews. Hence, students earning As in every subject in section three would be overachieving or realizing their best; those would be considered successful placements, whereas students struggling in sections one or two would not be living up to their potential, were so smart, they were too bored to exert any effort. All outcomes of placements were interpreted as successes. Change was possible, but discouraged.

It was an injurious system, but I was not harmed by it because of my placement in its luxury. The system continued through high school. I studied physics, genetics (advanced natural science), European history, trigonometry, calculus in an urban public school system that also offered French, Spanish, German, and, I believe, Italian but not to everyone. An inner-city high school where in the early seventies, when I attended, already there were: numerous thefts at knife-point (I lost three winter coats), routine vandalism of lockers, Black Power riots and gruesome fights, a few guns, in particular the gun used to persuade a teacher to cooperate silently as a teenager raped her in the bathroom.

Despite my overall success, Benjamin Franklin fixed my view of my life as descending rather than ascending. Once that change in perception occurred, I reinterpreted everything to match a prevailing descending sentiment. Perhaps this was necessary. All through childhood, the curiosity had been consistent, a ceaseless flame, a wildfire. Because of it, in sixth, seventh, and eighth grades, I would be on the mental math team, and in fifth and sixth grades, the young scientists club, called into morning sessions of summer school not to, as most were, make up failures, but to conduct experiments; do research; write my first lab reports; use beakers, slides, and Bunsen burners. Miss Gittens, seventh-grade major work mathematics teacher, based her seating plan on test scores; the child assigned to the seat nearest her desk, had failed the test. The one farthest away diagonally, had earned the highest A. Each marking period, we shifted seats. I worked my way to the seat farthest away from her; I hated this practice and wanted to keep my distance from its implementer. Once in that seat, I kept it. In eighth grade (or was it ninth?), I was an alternate for the quiz show "It's Academic," hoping, always hoping, for the chance to prove I was not ordinary. Maybe that enthusiasm of mine needed to be toned down a notch; it was out of control.

Tale of a Sky-Blue Dress

Saint Maria Goretti, my major source of inspiration from *When They Were Girls,* did not become the subject of any of my morning talks, not at Louis Pasteur nor at Benjamin Franklin. I didn't want to share her. Maria Goretti was particularly intriguing to me because, like me, she had a tormentor, but one who desired her, lusted so insanely and intensely that he confused his lust with a right to her body. I'm told that the chaste are always beautiful. I understand that virginity is unmistakable even from afar. Certain droppings of the snow blossoms happen only in the presence of chastity, the very substance of which those blossoms are made. Maria was the fairest of them all, therefore also most vulnerable, most desirable. She clung to her chastity, however, rising higher the harder she clung until she died holding only that, reducing herself to a chaste soul; she became the meaning of that word; say *Maria Goretti* and you also say *chastity.*

How splendid. At the time I envied her because I had not clung so well to what I held dear when Lytta had Trevor take it from me; essentially, I just gave it away, the way you're now instructed to surrender to a knife- or gun-wielding assailant if your attempt at self-defense or retaliation would more likely result in increased aggression from the assailant. But Maria gave up her life; she knew why she lived; she had no questions—this impressed me. I was fascinated by this girl who knew everything, for she had gone somewhere to which it was impossible for me to go.

I want to picture a little girl skipping in meadows. I want to picture sheep all around her, geese, and a stream from which she drinks, her eyes closed. The effect is that she always seems to have flowers in her hair but up close, close enough to rape her, there is nothing but hair and it tangles in a way inconsistent with the hope that frames the picture. Nothing compares with this.

Her mother is so pleased. This woman of privilege, the privilege of nurturing a chaste daughter, is not caught lifting a corner of her apron to wipe sweat and worry off her brow. She counts out pennies, plans magnificent loaves drenched in honey. Her children's shoes are in a row, their father's, hers join the row, and the house is sleeping. The aroma of supper is barely gone by morning when they again say prayers.

Puberty won't be silent. Even Maria all buttoned up with chastity, hair loose but seductive only to the sunlight it soaks up, watched her body announcing her readiness for womanhood. It is not insignificant that as the waist is pushed in, hips and breasts pop out. Mass changes form. The inches do not disappear. One can pretend not to notice, but it is pretense; fathers have to decide right then and there how to respond without seeming afraid. They must calculate how to hug their little girls so as not to nip the buds that aren't meant to create parental awkwardness, yet do. it is the start of the longest season. The love must not change, but placement of the paternal hands must. Perfection is difficult to be around; you want to consume it, want immersion, it in you or you in it; you need its stunning influence.

Maria had no problems at home. She was raised around animals and the shameless ways they mated, but dumb beasts had no choice but to be dumb. She didn't have to look. She didn't have to pay attention to any odd mooing. Every now and again, however, she may have wondered about the pain involved in having all those hooves inside her before the calf, kid, or colt is born. Poor dumb beasts. In their ignorance, what they do is perfect.

These changes in her body meant that Maria was growing perfectly. A body God could be proud of in the way that it honored the functions of the body, excellent blood flow, through veins and unobstructed wholesome arteries, now exiting the vagina as it does in all women, until menopause, unless they are pregnant, that are physiologically sound and hormonally balanced. On the cross, the blood of Jesus ran down his legs and he was holy. This is not a cause for shame. On that first day of hers, she picked red flowers from a field and brought them to her mother, saying *this wonder has happened to me today.* Her mother lifted the flowers to her nose and if their scent was to be secret it was secret no longer; she sniffed long and hugged her daughter, sucked down those everrising desires to boast of her daughter's goodness. If that Mary long ago had not been chosen, then her daughter, this Maria, *this Mary,* would be the one.

There was a boy of the village thinking this way too, that this Maria would be the one for him to try out his manhood on before he became any older, eighteen and needing experience right away; no, needing Maria. *Just look at her, the shin she scratches as long grass irritates her leg. Just look at her move, look at the lucky goat eating from her hand. Look, when she milks the goat, at how the milk seems to pour from her fingers. Look at Maria. Touch Maria. Kiss Maria. Ask Maria to do for you a favor. She is a kind and generous girl. Everyone says so. Ask her how does the garden under her blouse grow. Ask her if she needs help for the harvest, a strong man; he will be a strong man after helping with the harvest strengthens him. Help her anyway. She may be too proud, although she is pious, to admit that she needs assistance. Let your actions speak louder than her words refusing your charity. Pull her into the shed and help her put aside her pride; it will only interfere with everything she needs to do. Get those legs open. Tear down the gate.* Yes; you're good, Maria, but not too good. He saw you pick flowers, Maria.

So the knife stabs and stabs, picks and picks until the flowers are cut and dead. The buds dead tight, unopened, not exposing any pink rim of petal. Martyr to chastity. I think I wanted to be her long enough to absorb her total understanding, her peace with what she knew. I am both excited and perplexed by the myriad paradoxes and contradictions that to me assure there will be motion, travel, change, bright flashes, sparks, instability, friction: *the force that opposes motion at the boundary of two touching surfaces.* I am challenged and dizzy with possibilities that she reduced to a single meaning.

⌒ Blue Effects

We did not stay in touch with the Dorseys. When we moved to Trunt Avenue, we also moved them completely out of our lives. We did not even exchange greeting cards at the end of the year, and we were fond of sending cards to any acquaintance, in the spirit of goodwill toward all. Our deliberate halting of contact with them makes me wonder whether or not my parents had disliked them. Perhaps my parents sensed trouble without my specifying it. Perhaps they saw signs of distress in the family downstairs or were disappointed with the Dorseys' values. Perhaps they had feelings, intuitions, and hunches that something was not quite as it should be, and could act on these hunches now that they were no longer obligated to a landlord. Perhaps with their bedroom being directly above the master bedroom downstairs, they could not escape the volatility downstairs; perhaps they knew explicitly the truth of the tomato juice. No matter; our moving was the end of having to deal with them politely, having to mind our behavior and mouths. *Lytta, I like those shoes. They look good on her, Mr. Dorsey.* They had not been our friends.

There was no closeness, never shared meals around an informal table, everybody laughing and tattling on each other, the dozens, no joint excursions, Sunday drives to the lake where Mr. Dorsey did much fishing, not even late-evening cookouts together in the yard although there were many separate cookouts, weenie roasts, fish fries. Deirdre and her family coming over, Mook and Aunt Essell; Deirdre and Mook sleeping with me in the yard in a tent that covered the tailgate of my uncle's station wagon. How awkward it must have been not to offer any of the Dorseys a can of pop or a Moon Pie when they passed through our festivities. Stellica, my best friend from across the street, would come over too, dashing quickly so that as few people as possible caught her in her nightgown.

I liked seeing Lytta's exclusion, and when I knew she was looking, I led Deirdre and Mook in a rendition of the Miracles' "Shop Around" at the top of our lungs. To make my cousins dislike her, I told them that she was nasty, ate flies and maggots, picked flies and maggots out of her nose. During my last summer on Lills, Deirdre and I made and marketed beauty cream in both our neighborhoods, but we refused, because I insisted, to sell any to Lytta. I said that she was too ugly for anything to help her, not even our powerful cream made according to a formula, we wrote in our ads, that came to me in a dream directly from Cleopatra. I told Deirdre that Lytta let cats suck on her hair to curl it.

Most weekends, I spent some time with Deirdre, either at her house or at my house, but those Saturday or Sunday visits, although good to help me release some of the weekday tension of Lytta's after-school torment, did not deter Lytta in the least. I guess that I was closer to Deirdre than to anyone (outside my parents), but I didn't reveal any of my agony to her. I wish I had. With Deirdre, I was vying for leadership and mostly I had control, but she was equally capable and could have assumed control whenever she wanted. She thought me (as I thought her) strong and bold, worldly, smart, so I couldn't jeopardize an image of myself that pleased me greatly just to have someone in whom to confide. But, I could speak pejoratively of Lytta to Deirdre; I could demean and disrespect her, call her names: goat-face, saucer-face, rat breath, and make fun of her dress in parodies of nursery rhymes and ring game chants. Such release may not have been possible had our relationship with the Dorseys been more congenial.

Lytta was, however, invited to my birthday parties along with all the members of my class, many of them relative strangers. Then again, she may not have been invited, but may have decided to crash my parties as they were held in the common area of *her* house: the basement. We could not bar her from her property. She was too old to be invited.

I didn't notice at the time just how restricted and formal the contact was except for Lytta's rejection of formality when those who legislated formality were not present. It was my mother's family, Deirdre's family, Mook and Aunt Essell that helped us load our possessions into U-haul trailers for three round-trips and a fourth one-way trip to Trunt. The Dorseys were not part of the send-off or the congratulations on our having purchased a home, the first of my mother's siblings in Ohio to do so. Kell Dorsey, the one I really liked, was dead anyway. I never cared for her husband, Vaughn; he needed to shave far more than he did, looking most days too grisly to be able to love.

Patty went in the trailer on the last trip. I sat in the backseat of the Chrysler for a while, then got on my knees so as to ride backward and keep my eye on Patty who was standing in the trailer; I watched her through the rear window all the way to Trunt. There was room for her inside the car, but my uncle had put her in the trailer, and I left her there, subordinating my judgment. I never did for her what I should have done. She had no outlet for her grief. Patty wasn't really my sister, but there had to be a way to overcome blood; there had to be a way to become sisters with something that hadn't passed through your mother. Other bonds had to be as strong. It wasn't only blood that made my parents love me. It wasn't the absence of blood that made Lytta unable to love me. With the Feldmans, there'd been no blood between us, but everything else was there. Astonishing likenesses. Looking with her through a catalogue, Mrs. Feldman and I would find the same things worthy of our attention. I never looked through a catalogue with any of the Dorseys. The Feldmans believed something, I believed something, and when Mrs. Feldman and I talked in her kitchen, what we believed separately became one in the same thing. With the Dorseys, it had just been a business arrangement, held by the terms of a lease. Patty was a sister of circumstance, circumstances so sludge-filled, they were thicker than blood.

Patty's eyes opened and closed with the dips and turns. I thought about blowing a kiss to her, but there didn't seem to be any point. In a near sideswipe, she almost lost her arm that hung outside the trailer that swung wider in the turns than did the car, the trailer entering the opposing lane of traffic. As I watched her, helpless, through the rear window, I hoped she liked the wind that strengthened as the car accelerated. I hoped that what she had most wanted was an opportunity to breathe like this, whipped air forcing itself into her, air with the strength to penetrate a thing not constructed for respiration. I don't know whether or not any air succeeded; her chest did not rise nor fall. If air entered, it remained inside her; she would not release it; it was hers to savor. She possessed it.

I enroll in the new school not named for a scientist marveling at unseeable bacteria, postulating that there are deadly microbes among us, but for the man that invented bifocals, the glass harmonica, the Franklin stove, and it is cold there, foreign, inhospitable. I am educated in a school around which a fog descends: thin effects of a blue dress. My mother says that since I am nine, I no longer need a baby-sitter. The key is left for me in the unlocked garage, among my father's tools.

On days ominously still and humid, I style my tornado-thick hair, sometimes weaving ribbons through braids, in the basement in the event of sudden storm. There is, in the basement, a dresser on which issues of *Look* and *Life* are stacked, several with Jacqueline Kennedy on the cover, few brown faces except for *Jet;* a mirror losing its silver coating and turning into a window to a wall, and clotheslines latticed like junctures of trolley lines. From these lines hang my father's work clothes, blue uniforms with *Cardinal Tire Company* embroidered in red, and my mother's Life uniforms that are identical for nurses, waitresses, and domestics, as if she has her pick; she takes such care of them, each one looks new, as if she wears them but once before replacing them. It is so cool in the subterranean sanctuary, dim, the windows being small rectangles at ground level, sun blocked by eaves and overhangs, trees, the house next door; my skin looks grayish. Sometimes, I find small frogs down there, near the drain. The walls are damp; it is an urban cave. With ducts emanating from it in all directions, the huge furnace in the center of the basement seems the brain that controls the house, and it contains fire, a perpetual pilot light. Yet its own metal now is cold; I love the heat it gives us, but not its rigidity; it has no mercy; the heat is just a result of its light, its fuel, not its concern. The ducts are large enough for me to slide through them. Or Patty.

I expect Patty to come to life and tell everyone what had happened in a basement and how I had not helped her. She'll be warmed into talking by the furnace. Once she has language, she will be formidable. I expect her to come to life, giving life to what I had sealed inside her, for she was a vault, where I'd never lose it and where there were no words for it. I think she'll be thrilled to feel, breathe, and taste, but I think that she also might be angry, that resentment may have festered within her all these years. I am not certain. Once she has life of her own, I can't make her sit when and how I want, can't feed her from spoons, stop her growth. I expect her to speak in torrents, delighted with the flexibility of her tongue, its coordination with her brain, the movement of her lips pink and ripe for years. I've grown taller than her yet I'm still considered short. She has no enhancement yet of height, tall only as a goblin, sinister creatures that frequent dark places, wells, caves, mines, the broad night that doesn't quite end in a basement. I expect her to move. I believe it's possible although then she'll no longer be exemplary, the kind of child I was, one that adults don't mind having around, so poised, so respectful of objects, so content with mountains of books, ink and paper; all her toys like new.

Every night I pray that Patty come to life. Earnest prayers on my knees in front of the window through which moonlight floods. I see in her eyes that she wants desperately to live. She teaches me the desperation I taught her. Patty is the only one that I want to live, she out of thirty dolls, including Thumbelina who has a biscuit-sized wooden knob on her back that when wound makes her kick and wave her arms. I'm not interested in more life for that baby; mobility is enough for it—like a worm, Thumbelina can crawl leaving vermiculations in the dust.

Patty, who is much more needy, can walk if you raise and lower her arms. Her knees are not flexible so the result is a labored gait like that of a child in braces. I remember seeing children with polio, cerebral palsy; the decline of triplet boys with muscular dystrophy at a school for the handicapped where my school choir sang for the holidays. Still I'm proud of Patty and walk with her outside; it isn't easy for her to move. But she's life-size so is distinguished from all my other dolls. She took baths with me on Lills and never complained about soap in her eyes or developed a rash, as I did, from the 99 and $^{44}/_{100}$ percent pure Ivory floating around us like an Eskimo Pie with all the chocolate eaten off. I knew she wanted to be alive and able to really taste the Alpha-Bits and sneer with me under our breath at my Sunday School teacher, Miss Kint, but Patty remains plastic despite the best praying I ever do.

One night, moonlight is so suspiciously intense, it wakes me from my dream. God is about to intervene, and I'm terrified. I watch for the beam to shift its angle, find its way into Patty's eyes, boring into the depth of them and filling her, once inside, with life. Such terror. I rub my own flesh, Patty's, then mine again, convinced that Patty if alive yet still plastic will be freakish, monstrous, somehow diabolical because her allegiance would not be to flesh but to petroleum, polymers, cellulose derivatives, science, and technology. There is a difference in our skin. But no; she's still Patty and kind, benevolent in her extreme patience.

Thylias Moss

My sister who won't turn on me, not to save her own life. From one form of skin to another she'll travel without change in nature. Her plastic is her chrysalis. The essence of her will remain consistent. She'll have no mother, however, unless it's the laser of light from the darkness outside. She'll have no matriarchy or patriarchy behind her. Where's the angel to herald this and prepare me for the event? I keep listening for the beating of wings and wondering whether or not each flap will sound like the cracking of a whip.

Not hearing it, tension eases somewhat; God in his omniscience will not do this. Would my parents really want responsibility for the child that in the morning would be my breathing sister? This is just wrong, sacrilegious. God is not about to answer my prayer, but instead is angry; the light is about to strike me dead just as Miss Kint has promised. My entreaty is really an attempt to tamper with His will, and there's no way to unpray my prayer. God has heard it and is responding but not as I've hoped. How sinful I am to wish for this. Life for the inanimate is the province of heretics. Instead of praying, I could just as well consult the Ouija board—as I later do with Deirdre when we're twelve and in junior high school together, and it predicts that I'll marry Vachary Civ-var, a man whom I have not yet met. Deirdre's good with numerology, palmistry; in our seances, I can speak to the dead Patty.

Any moment, I think, Patty will move, open her mouth, laugh, hug me with the ferocity born of excessive waiting, the dam bursting. I see myself run across the room to her, block the light, turn her to the wall. Back in bed, I listen for her first breath, the first slight heaving of her shoulders. I listen, can tell it's about to begin. Again I run across the room, pick her up and take her to the basement, locking that door, locking the kitchen when I return. Checking the locks. Once. Twice. Better check a third time. Back in bed, I listen for: Patty's footsteps, Patty's fat hand turning the knob, her finger pushing the key out the kitchen door, the key falling onto her skirt tail, my old red circle skirt, that she has pushed under the door to catch the key, the small noise of

158

the skirt scratching the linoleum as Patty pulls the skirt and key under the door to her, Patty inserting the key, unlocking the door, running awkwardly, she's never run before and plastic is stiff, to my room, happy to be alive, happy to tell me that she's alive, happy, so very happy. I am terrified of that joy. Terrified of how good she'll be. She'll follow me around; I'm the big sister, and I keep increasing to a point, a low blue ceiling. She's alive, but she does not grow, neither does she bleed, does not grow out of the life on Lills, looks the same as she did then, always the same as then. Not me. My chest is budding. I'm going to bloom. I'm terrified of having her go with me to Dr. Evans's office, of Patty helping him hold me down for my shots, the dreaded boosters, then it's me holding her down when it's her turn, but the needles bend when they try to penetrate her plastic arm and hip.

Nothing happens. I can't believe my luck, how good God is not to give Patty life; He knows I would die from the shock of it, so to save my life, not give it to Patty, He does not answer my prayer. He knows I cannot endure his miracle, the overwhelming effects of his magnificent countenance. He's such a good God, He has to ignore my beseeching or I will die.

Relieved, but still concerned that God may be tempted to answer this prayer at a later time, I go to the basement again and rub Patty's arm that remains as cold and plastic as ever. I am relieved again, more hopeful that the integrity of plastic will not be insulted, but doubt persists, because I know, I believe, that God is fully capable of giving her life. He did it with dirt that was not already shaped into a girl, given a name, not to mention those eyes that don't need much, the way they can already stare. The transformation may have started already. God may just have interrupted it, tired as on the original biblical seventh day. But I have long been dubious about that fatigue. Perhaps it wasn't fatigue, but need for artistic distance; at some point before completing the artwork, He needed to step back to view it from a more detached perspective. Then it became apparent what was missing from the scene. Serpent.

I break off Patty's fingers and there's no gush of blood, no bone. Not one corpuscle on the floor. I cut her hair to no longer than an inch all over her head. I have since bought her a black wig, the kind plentiful at Halloween, not a good one, but one made fast in China of modacrylic fiber, petroleum derivative, as is the rest of Patty. I take a paring knife from the kitchen and try to cut a slit between her lips intending to see if she will stick out a new tongue or reveal that she's snaggle-toothed or call me by name. She does none of that and I stick my own finger with the knife tip. She is hollow and empty. Her eyes have depth, but not promise; they're vast, limitless, tragic.

⌒

I am dreaming.

The frozen custard machine meant to dispense vanilla whorls into cake *Eat-it-all* cones, but tornadoes spun loose instead and chased me home to Trunt Avenue, all the miles from my former neighborhood where I knew every shortcut and had a straight line to Lake Erie, even a road that wound through the metropark and Emery Circle where Blyden Hall was and the orchestral future that was not to be, near the Cleveland Music School Settlement where I would, at nineteen, study voice for six months, arias and spirituals in a first soprano lost and lowered through my own disbelief at what had been reached (now second soprano, often contralto, sometimes tenor), and a vocal coach who liked my lean legs yet urged control in himself and in my soprano's timbre, and by the hospital where years later a surgeon would perform an unnecessary lumpectomy on my right breast, the malignancy his own; the same breast the Mamselle Modeling agent would admire for its being nearly the size of a crystal ball. Short, fifteen, and sporting facial hair,

I should have known better, but longed for validation of a beauty not mine. I wanted a man to tell me something that I was not hearing.

But while I was still a little girl, tornadoes chased me, and one of them I could not lose, and it did not tire, chased me, overtook me, flattened like a supplicant, yanked out my spine as if I were the game Operation, and then a girl came along, living Patty girl who started to pick me up, threw me down before I'd been fully lifted, saying, *aw, it's just a rag doll.*

I am dreaming.

The frozen custard machine meant to dispense vanilla whorls into cake *Eat-it-all* cones, but tornadoes spun loose instead and one of them chased me home. I could not lose the tornado, and it did not tire, lashed me to a tree with itself, and kept spinning, so that I was lashed tighter and tighter until it was just a Hula Hoop around me, tighter and tighter until it sliced me in half.

I am dreaming again.

The frozen custard machine meant to dispense vanilla whorls into cake *Eat-it-all* cones, but tornadoes spun loose instead and one of them chased me home. I could not lose the tornado, and it did not tire, but somehow I tricked it into the basement and locked the door, then went into my room and listened to the tornado spin and drill through layers of concrete, plaster, drywall, wood. To my room it would soon come and split in two, the tornado and its Doppelgänger, each half entering a socket of Patty's green glass eyes; the soul I had prayed she'd receive was on its way, but it terrified me, the immortal portion, the unkillable essence; I wanted nothing to do with it, preferring just then the finite, promises of completion. But I had to do something for Patty. I had to get her some life, and the tornado was full of life, active with life; why not let it penetrate her with some of that life? That's the kind of soul she needed, something of a cobra in it the way it could spit, strike in its self-assurance. Lacking organs and consciousness, Patty could not express her hurt, did not even know she'd been hurt. I knew.

I am still dreaming.

The frozen custard machine meant to dispense vanilla whorls into cake *Eat-it-all* cones, but tornadoes spun loose instead and one of them chased me home. One of them did not tire, but somehow I tricked it into the basement and locked the door, then went into my room and listened to the tornado spin and drill through layers of concrete, plaster, drywall, wood. It did not take long. The tornado came up the stairs, glossy black, wide as a ball gown, and enthusiastic. It paused at the kitchen door, leaned against it, breathed as for a first kiss. Too late I realized that the skeleton key was not in the lock preventing entry of another. As I rushed to insert it, the tornado adapted its tail, at first fit the lock, then poked a strand through the keyhole. I grabbed the strand, felt unexpected softness that I wound around my finger just as I habitually wound my own hair that was not quite as soft as the storm. I pulled it through the keyhole, winding it like yarn, talking to it, trying to humiliate it. The tornado that soon proved too much for my arm and hand wrapped me in a sinister cocoon, soft, dark like other things I have loved. Then someone unseen, I could not possibly do this for myself, not for years, pulled a loose end, and I was released like a top, both of us spinning, dancing together from the kitchen onto the back porch, down the steps, and into the driveway. It shrank until it was no bigger than a wig. I put it on, tossed my head, went to buy another cone of ice cream; the frozen custard machine meant to dispense vanilla whorls into cake *Eat-it-all* cones, but tornadoes spun loose instead and one of them shrank until it was no bigger than a wig. I put it on, on top of the other, this one like a turban. The frozen custard machine dispensed yet another that kept swirling in the cone in my hand, swirling itself to sleep. The tornadoes on my head were both sleeping. I stopped moving so as not to wake them just as I knew Patty could be awakened.

Tornadoes aren't necessarily black, only those full of dirt and debris; the funnel is clean until it touches down. Some are like white ropes, expensive necklaces swaying, dubious about descending and spoiling their fresh form. They hang poised in the sky, moving with the gray neck of cloud to which it is attached. Perhaps it is red as it draws into its swirl delectable earth or perhaps pink, sucking up petunias. Mad, mad dancing; *a mutterwirbl* (as, I remember reading, Ron Henson called the *mother vortex* in *Weatherwise*) celebrating her descent to gather her flock. A corrupt root drilling its way into my life.

I will probably never cross the Straits of Mackinac, although from Ann Arbor, the bridge over that water offers the best access to Thunder Bay. I have survived many crossings of the Tappen Zee and the Peace Memorial Bridges but when I've been the driver I've clutched the wheel unnaturally less it veer of its own accord, steering the car over the guardrail and embankment, and into the water, resurfacing my guilt that I did not learn to swim in junior high school, earning Cs, a D later rescinded, because of my fear of water. In the shallow end I was still up to my nose and the water would not let me stand, kept pulling me down, wanted me to surrender to it, float, float, sacrifice what little will I had. The water was sheer and I liked how my skin looked under it, did not mind when it splashed, but the high windows cast menacing pale rectangles on the pool; they looked like trapdoors and were near the posted warnings about depth.

I have but a few phobias: fear of tornadoes, fear of ignition (though not of flame itself), fear of flying, fear of bridges. A few, but they create awkwardness in my life, when I accept invitations, and then can't get there although I really want to, really want to be there.

As many mothers did, mine taught me that thunderstorms were evidence of God working. He was violent, temperamental, unpredictable, pretentious: the worst kind of mate. The work well substantiated the definition of God that I learned in church. It will be fire next time, and the way a vortex moves is like flame. While my mother did suggest that

I keep quiet, I was quiet anyway; she did not force upon me the stillness and paralysis that was forced upon Wesley when he was growing up in Dunson. I was told to keep away from the windows and spent this time respecting God and reading, unless the lights went out, sometimes under the dining room table, but mostly in the basement. I don't know where my father was during these storm watches, but I don't recall his hiding with us. It is almost as if we were hiding from him, but he was not a violent man.

Every tornado watch was taken seriously and literally. I watched the sky for signs until a full hour after the all-clear bulletin was issued and the watch canceled. Mostly I watched the sky through western-facing windows, and it was easy to mistake any cloud movement as the initial roiling that would birth the funnel. I would run upstairs from the basement and peek out the doors, sometimes would go outside and take a quick run around the house, my arms stretched wide, forming a fence.

In elementary school, the same precautions against tornadoes were practiced in mandatory atomic bomb drills. Once each week. Kneel or stoop in the corridor, head buried in knees, arms crossed and covering head, elbows on knees. Sometimes this position was taken under the desks where we were far more vulnerable than when in the corridors, though perhaps the vulnerability was equivalent if radiation and fallout were the assailants. By the middle of fourth grade, atomic bomb drills were discontinued.

I have been closer than Ann Arbor's severe weather siren to a tornado, while traveling in July and August nearly annually to Illinois. Usually we encounter threatening black skies with ominous low ceilings, mesocyclone and wall cloud, often green-tinted clouds just before bombardments of hail, lightning cutting through the black quickly and vengefully so that it seems like stabbing, the brightness being the pleasure of the stabbing, the lack of remorse. We have approached Bloomington and Normal right after a tornado has passed, the skies still contemplating the birth of another. These encounters are part of my husband's going home,

the mammatus clouds low and heavy, as if bowling balls are about to
drop. Omens when we go to Dunson.

Only once have I actually seen a funnel cloud. On a Sunday while
my mother had returned to church and I was home with my father on
the porch. We had not gone for a walk, perhaps because of his smelling
of rain and sensing the pending intensification of wind. Suddenly, rain
pelted, broke on impact; the drops shattered like glass trinkets. I was
still slight and often dreamed of the wind kidnapping me when my
umbrella was open. The wind was an invisible and evil knight. This was
an unsettling dream, despite my having seen and read *The Wonderful
Wizard of Oz,* despite Mary Poppins's great landing. My umbrella would
invert, the wind would turn it inside out and set it spinning; a polyester
waterproof tornado, red and unjustly beautiful, would swallow and jostle
me just as if I had been in my mother's new wringer washer, the
agitator's paddles sharpened, me cut up like Saint Maria Goretti and
thrown down on the rocks by Lake Erie, smelling quickly fetid and
joined in smell by fish that the tornado, escaping into Canada as a spout
over water, threw around me. In the howl, I could hear his promise:
I'll be back; wait for me.

The wind intensified and I clung to my father's leg. I thought he
would immediately lead me inside, but he didn't. I think now that his
eyes were as vivid and glassy as they were the day that he last gasped
for breath and I rushed him in my first car to the hospital. We were
standing facing the church and as we looked, a funnel cloud formed
right above it like a steeple. The funnel descended slowly, gray angel,
and still we did not move. It seemed a fog, incapable of destruction, a
semiwhite long stem of a rose whose desirable petals were still above
the clouds. Before it could touch down, it faded. It had only been
breath, my own relief.

When I was twenty-five and married for seven years, I reclaimed
Patty from my mother's basement. My mother did not know until then
that I had feared the doll and she assured me that she would have

disposed of the doll had she known. My silence saved her. Since the reclaiming, my sons have enjoyed her. Dennis has fed her. Ansted has danced with her; sometimes, he wears her hair. Last night, that hair on his head, he twirled through the living room, around and around the couch where I sat, applauding him.

 —*No,* he said. *Don't do that.*

 —*But I like your dancing. It's ballet, and it's wonderful!*

 —*No, Mommy; I'm a tornado. I'm tearing up the carpet. I'm destroying the living room. Run to the basement, Mommy.*

~ An Empirical Compendium of Wonder

$\mathcal{W}$hat a double life I led. As if each half of my brain undertook responsibility for the maintenance of one of my lives. And I could switch lives with apparent ease, although the hemispheres of my brain would communicate conflict to each other. Because they were split, because they in essence governed two people, they vied for control; one wanted to dominate. From time to time, control shifted; then, for a while, each would confine government to its proper local concern. But sometimes, the actions of one girl seemed like those of the other, and this trespassing only escalated the conflict, did not lead to unification.

It was absolutely necessary that to my cousin I bad-mouthed Lytta. I felt powerful and that I had somewhat diminished Lytta by doing that. Self-preservation and defense often causes the inflicting of some hurt upon another, damage most are able to justify, although it looks, examined without its justifying context, like any other maliciousness.

My father, no matter what had been perpetrated, did not condemn anything easily, and in that, I am like him. There must be more certainty in condemnation; hence, the inappropriateness of hell. It is much more complicated than good or evil; while Lytta's deeds cannot be justified, while her evil is conspicuous and seems the sum of her life, she too must have had moments of quiet; at least once she must have been jubilant at the expense of no one else. One reasonable ecstasy.

I do know that magnificence very nearly soothed me, flamboyance of autumn, the stalwartness of deciduous trees revealed in winter when, stripped of their leaves, there were iron and armored branches. I know that loveliness was tougher, that its existence seemed more an incredible defiance because it occurred in the midst of rampages and rages, many that I witnessed. Beauty was bold. I sought evidence of it everywhere. How high the boys on the box leaped, the takeoff of heron, geese. . . . But that enhanced demarcation of beauty did not seem sufficient justification for the existence of tyranny. I desperately wanted to reconcile the contradiction between my father's version of the world and Lytta's. And I ached trying to do so. They should be parallel worlds, destined never to meet, yet if this is really curved space that they occupy, they must intersect; there can be no parallels. Perhaps a reason to prefer an inflationary cosmological theory in which the universe is flat, self-reproducing, fractals forking endlessly. The way clouds grow in order to storm. My mother would put another blanket on my bed.

When I was eight and nine, I would see women in white walking down Superior Avenue, going into small stores for spices, vegetables that would stick out the tops of paper and cloth sacks. I would see Lytta, but every week I would see this also, so did not self-destruct. And I didn't completely accept that there was nothing within me worth salvaging. I had just enough arrogance to endure these extremes.

Sometimes I would see stray pieces of bangs and of course their faces, but mostly the women in white were completely covered; I could not even see their feet, and no matter how the garbage accumulated, no matter what challenging scents drifted up from sewers and backyards of restaurants and markets; no matter what appearances blood made, even stinking after brief exposure to sun on the butcher paper that had wrapped veal, pork (not theirs), perch, or beef brisket, paper so weighed down with the smell it did not dance with breezes; the women in white were clean and moved soundlessly. I would watch them and wonder if ever I could be like that, covered and reduced, if such can be reduction, to mystery, white and glorious all the time, the privilege of the white clothes so satisfying there was nothing to say except for pretty gestures with the hands appearing magically from the white folds communicating the order to the merchant. To this establishment of Shabazz, to that establishment of Shabazz they would go, every need and comfort attended to by those in suits.

There was something about the looseness of the long gowns, something about the freedom, the absence of belt to restrict the movement of the cloth, a luscious looseness. I thought again and again of fish, the way they swim, fulfilled by their element. The pleasure of the water in which they are wrapped. The movement possible in silky depths unlike what is achieved on land walking in and often against air that is not as soft or stable as water whose movement is more regulated and divine. Better pulsed. Fish know the effect of luxury in their submersion. Even the fighting fish know it. Even if the element is polluted.

Not ever did I associate the Black Muslim women with birds; even the billowing dresses did not suggest wings; nothing about them betrayed a need to leave the ground. The flapping and beating of wings has a stressful quality, a fury and insistence that attracts human interest in the resemblance to ambition; it is only during the gliding, the soaring when wings are more taut and poised, that flight becomes extraordinary and enviable. The grace of the Black Muslim women was more sustained, understated, and mystical. For birds had their songs, their cackles and squawks; they had noise to cut through someone else's solitude and dawn, making themselves noticed; they had their feathers and colors to overpower attempts to lose self-awareness. They had their sometimes precarious placement of the nest, that daring, but also the nest's regrettable similarity to lifeboat. They had their bad habits of perching on wires, escaping voltage, the juice running under their feet, as if those wires were kinky bird roosts and the current the ornithological equivalent of Magic Fingers. On the phone wires, they felt the words, padded and adorned themselves with multiple meanings, let gossip warm their feet.

Fish however had no boastfulness in them. Theirs was the perfect silence, the perfect observance of muteness and worship. It was so appealing to me. In not broadcasting verbally, they drew everything to them, and seemed capable of dispensing endless consolation, endless comfort, even the swimming nurse shark and lemon shark that in Baltimore I watched for an hour. Especially mesmerizing were the skates and rays for their greatly enlarged pectoral fins used like wings, but calmly, dreamily, the water not disturbed, the effort minimal and automatic. So gentle, the movement seems not to happen at all, just an idea of movement. And the fish that were electrified; these creatures were being canonized.

There were other women in white whom I saw often, but this usage of white did not compare with the ideology stitched seamlessly for the women that filled mosques like enchanted orchids. Perhaps the white orchid *Vanilla planifolia* that has yielded the flavoring *vanilla* at least since the Aztecs, as reported, once it was discovered in the Aztec cosmos, by the conquistadors who, as was their custom, developed yet another dependency, upon that scent and taste. A natural pollinator, say Bastiaan Meeuse and Sean Morris in *The Sex Life of Flowers,* has never been found, implying that the Aztecs, centuries ago, maybe thousands of years ago, the authors concede, would have had to pollinate these orchids by hand; so Aztec giftedness is further enhanced. *Each flower lasts but one day.* I wish that I had peeked inside the mosques.

But I just watched and breathed the air these women left in their wake. I lived just to see this, and it was a more vital seeing because of what I'd also seen. But I did not know what this dual seeing meant. Nor why there needed to be any duality at all. I would see this glory and marvel and believe it while under its immediate influence, then would lose hope.

I saw the white on the Deaconesses and Mothers (titular Mothers, not all women with children) of the church on Communion Sunday, first Sunday of the month, and the ushers put it on too, but their white was transient, fraudulent. They wore it but for the three hours of the service. Whenever they could get away with it in church, on Men's Day or the anniversary of an organization in which they held no office for instance, they decked themselves in deep colors: red gowns, peach-toned chiffons and satins, glittery buttons, and long gloves, hats better off in Las Vegas in shows that conspired, they taught me, with sin. It was something they removed, did not sleep in, not even the red of lips, orange-bronze of face; all this came off. I believed that the Black Muslim women were in their white at all times; even when they bathed the water would turn milky and cover them, clinging when they left the tub so that there was no moment of actual nakedness. I did not consider the possible burden of this; it was beautiful and it never stopped working for them. I envied them.

Then when I was almost ten I saw for the first time nuns, a phalanx, three across, four rows, walking to and from the convent on Chapelmoor Avenue, just two blocks from Trunt Avenue where I lived. It was like a train, one of the great ones, pulled by a black locomotive veiled in steam that could easily provide cover for a visitation by a saint. The Epiphany Express. Pulling into the station cloaked in the breath of God. You can still ride such trains in India. As the nuns walked, they consecrated everything they passed, deified molecules of air.

How could I not follow them from the library back to the convent?

They held books close to their chests and I tried not to see their white faces, snowy blooms made snowier growing out of the rich black of habit, because I did not want eye contact to make me see what they saw and ensnare me into a life of servitude to God. I had questions that delight would not let them ask. Or perhaps they came to Him demanding answers to questions grown urgent. I was dazzled and afraid.

I could tell from the way they moved, floating down dirty streets as the neighborhood declined, that they had exceptional power; skirts, soaked in Mr. Clean and disinfectants, that mopped the sidewalks pure. So powerful that if I ventured too close, I'd be a nun too, steeped in catechism and singing in Latin praises, praises, praises that I liked to listen to: higher high notes, lower low notes than those produced by my church and school choirs. I stood outside the convent some evenings, listening; even in the rain.

Dazzled and afraid.

AN ESSENTIAL MATHEMATICS

Miss Beatrice Pinzik had not recognized me when I visited my former fifth- and sixth-grade classroom when I was in ninth grade: *Thylias; you're beautiful!* she said when I identified myself. *You were such an ugly child.* A hideous-looking child indeed as old photos confirmed, but I, with my parents' help, was resisting an association of physical beauty with worth. And I tried not to apply beauty to people differently than I applied beauty to landscape. I had a face as good as any carved crudely in rock or on totem pole. People were objects in the landscape, parts of scenes; not the emphasis, everything else just background to flatter the person. That was not how it was. There was no superiority in the human form itself. The geometry that defined it, defined all else.

My learn-to-draw manuals used triangles, cylinders, ovals, cones to depict the basic body, the underlying shapes, the universal simplicity on which infinite variety and specificity were built: single cells. Consider, as Primo Levi did, the simplicity of atoms of carbon that sponsor the survival of everything. Draw such an atom, and you've drawn the start of anything. From that atom, I can go anywhere. I was a child when I first peeked into da Vinci's notebooks, saw the anatomical sketches, and found where I wanted to belong, even while Lytta marauded.

There is something extraordinary that the body does with the oxygen it seizes so that what the body gives back to air is carbon dioxide. Lungs and blood are stimulated in this exchange. Organic chemists may know scientifically what is involved, offering in the transitory certainty of that knowledge the demystification of the process that for me may as well be alchemically achieved. Or perhaps knowing how it happens serves to add to the chemists' appreciation of the mystical occasion that got the process going, that got carbon set up as such a player and swinger. For me, it was just wondrous. How it all looked. What it all meant or didn't mean, for I had no idea; I was just consumed by wonder, wanted wonder to free me from my life, transport me to its planet where there would be nothing but fish doing their breathing in water, an amazing feat except to those amphibious perhaps.

To be near a river is always homecoming—Langston Hughes and Pablo Neruda knew well this truth about rivers—but we have changed so much that we can no longer embrace our ancestor, just watch, immerse ourselves so long as we hold our breath or transport our own supply of air. There is activity, small life, some of it involved in a foul trade, at all times in the murky depths and it is unknown to my unaided eyes, even to the eyes of those who from their trawlers try to scoop up river in their dragged nets. The nets can't hold the microscopic nor the water despite how big the water is. Most of the world is water; on any honest globe, ocean must dominate. On any honest map of melon, of the human body. There is air in this water, but when we are in the water, we can't withdraw any air from it, can't suck it from a wave or current, can't break the compound, about 11 percent hydrogen and 89 percent oxygen by weight. The oxygen remains locked in the water, denied to us. Ah, but the gills!

Even the dictionary seems inspired by this feat of breathing in the poetry of defining gill as: *an aquatic respiratory organ;* the syllables are beautiful, as if each were an atom of carbon, and each is, shifting form, thought to ink. The gill is remarkable indeed, appearing, some, to be like the underside of the cap of mushrooms (these radiating spokes are called *gills* also and produce the spores by which the mushroom reproduces), the charming slits such as those I would cut in construction paper to make lanterns. Or the gill may appear more feathery and lacelike. May flutter in the water like something otherworldly in the grace of the movement, an evolution of movement I have not yet achieved. But something I wanted to draw, something I wanted my fingers to be able to create and imagine. I gave a morning talk on gills.

The manuals also recommended graph paper for drawing and plotting the body point by point. The mark in any particular little square of the graph paper could be the start of any existing or imaginary thing. The trigonometry of beauty and anatomy. So many parabolas in the artistic rendering of one small girl. But the parabola was just where you started. What could be done with the parabola was infinite. It was just a moment in a curve. There were lines and curves of hips in: stones, jugs, spoons, branches, clouds, saddles, crescent moons. Walking, I saw them all. And it was beautiful the curved way water moved, the lake lapping at rocks, at beer bottles, fast-food containers on the shore, themselves curved.

Now the trash was not necessarily beautiful, but its design could be, and the water's approach to it certainly was; its purpose too, if organic, breaking down in dark and stinking artistry that certain bugs and microbes enjoy. The beauty of that approach and purpose was not comparable to any other approach or to any other beauty. No comparison of beauty was possible due to the unique configuration of everything configured (out of common components infinitely specified), including: the pungency of dead fish and algae, beautiful the way sad music can be beautiful, tragic films, death after long misery.

I wanted beauty to prevail, although I was doubtful that it could. On the last day that I was nine, I started the habit of trying in those last hours to make that year beautiful; I wanted to record, while I was still nine, while there was still time, what deserved remembrance. My childhood writing revealed a desperation for beauty.

WHISKEY ISLAND

When I, at ten, went to Whiskey Island just off Lake Erie with my father and his boss Sam Cardinal, I had not been aware of mountains except for in reference books and those were presented with too much color and landscape. From those pictures, a sense of the mountain as entity distinct and separate could not form. Before kindergarten, I had traveled Chattanooga's Lookout Mountain by car, but I could not see what I was traveling though the incline could be felt. I was too young and too close to the mountain, to the storm's blackness that in its fury overwhelmed and diminished the mountain, for me to know then what a mountain was. My fear seemed more mountainous. Whereas on Whiskey Island, I saw mounds of salt, tonal complexity and clarification of black machinery juxtaposed with white salt hills. I could understand those hills and was impressed by the wealth of salt, all of it coming from the earth. I was particularly interested in interiors.

It occurred to me that each honest salt hill may have been a wife like the wife of Lot who looked back on what was happening in the condemned cities of Sodom and Gomorrah. I thought that one of those hills may have been the proof of her biblical story. I thought that those salt hills were on Whiskey Island because of her. I thought that salt tasted as it tasted, made food taste more the way I liked for it to taste because of her. I thought she was a martyr, a saint. She burned like Joan.

When I first heard her story in church, I was neither shocked nor horrified as the preacher wanted me to be, probably because I loved salt so much, all those blue boxes of Morton's, the loveliness of the crystals in our clear shakers, the arc of it streaming from the box into the shaker, white crystalline rainbow. I saw the magic in the scene, pictured beauty, the woman becoming a crystallized swan and then a monument, a pillar, a strong column that supported a museum, repository of history, or a great hall of learning. Besides, I had seen far worse things than salt. If there was any way to transform wretchedness, even if just superficially and temporarily, I looked for it. I needed it.

Lot's wife was a woman loyal to her duty of witnessing, who found in the loyalty something to love in those evil cities. Her look back was redeeming, for even if nothing else was compassionate or good in the cities, her looking was. She was not drawn to corruption, did not love the evil, but loved the promise in the homes, lives, and livestock, and in the sheltering trees that she couldn't abandon because promise was also what touched them and touched Lot as he moved forward without mercy or sorrow, as he was commanded. It was the promise of the sky, covenant of rainbow, and it stretched over and enveloped both the righteous cities and the profane, a foot in each. She saw something no one else saw. An uncommon privilege. A chosen woman.

Leaving Whiskey Island, I took home a two-pound salt rock. The petrified brain of Lot's wife. I had looked for her and wives lost similarly because in church I had learned of her disobedience and what it had cost. In fact, Lot's wife knew exactly what it would cost, but she owed so much to humanity, she was so deep in debt that it served a logic to sink deeper. She meant no harm and no disrespect with her disobedience. I never thought she was the only woman changed. The transformation of Lot's wife intrigued and frightened me as much as the journey from child to woman, caterpillar to moth, tadpole to frog: transformations that were the result of growth, maturity. They were absolutely necessary changes but not reversible. I was more intrigued by this transformation, however, especially as it happened without the use of cocoon and in a flash, instantaneously. Life for the woman was over, but existence for the pillar of salt was just beginning.

A pillar of salt as the finishing of one existence and door to another. Tragic perhaps, but not effective punishment, maybe not punishment at all. To know that the outcome of looking is to become a pillar of salt inspires in me no fear. Salt is not awful. Salt that has been dyed makes beautiful artwork that may inspire and challenge those who see it. And it preserves. It cures; pork becomes bacon and ham after a smoking, a salting. Manufacture of much soap depends on salt. In turn, there is no way to enumerate all the successes and benefits of soap. Salt is something that the earth routinely manufactures, something that populates and infests the sea that dominates the earth. How many pillars could all the salt of the sea form? How many generations of daughters of the wife of Lot? How many lovely mermaids degenerated? What here is beautiful? The clinging of the salt crystals? Their cooperation in order to maintain the integrity of a pillar, of a mountain? Yes; how lovely that is, the campaign of crystals to be a monolith. Never mind that salt is also corrosive. And presumed a villain of hypertension. It is not the evil of Sodom and Gomorrah that stands out, but the vigil of Lot's wife, the salt that survives, no; that results from fire, the salt that stands like testimony, that studs peanuts and pretzels like jewels.

Now, in the aftermath of total destruction of cities—Hiroshima and Nagasaki were not totally destroyed, so imagine, *imagine!* the force involved—Lot, so Genesis tells it, went out of Zoar and dwelt in the hills with his two daughters—hills tall and protracted from the earth because of the eminence of the cache of salt that each contained; this Genesis does not say. Even Lot dwelling in that cave with his daughters sometimes found his life beautiful, the days sweet, the olives and figs tasty. Cave, Genesis says, but it could have been a salt mine.

It could have been anything but what it looked like.

⟋ The Lost Ideals of Medicine

𝒥n seventh grade, a boy from the same homeroom, but not in any of my classes, wrote me a cardboard note asking if I would "go with" him. I said yes even before I knew what was required to "go with" someone. Yes, just because Johnson DeWitt asked me.

Once I agreed, he walked me to and from school every day, carrying my books that whole mile. That was the extent of "going with" Johnson, and I didn't mind it at all. We didn't even hold hands. He gave me a cardboard ticket to some kind of magic show at his house; I was reluctant to go, unsure of the nature of the magic, thinking of voodoo, love charms, the haints of my father's stories, and I liked the almost platonic meaning that we were giving to going with each other. He also gave me a turquoise scarf that I knotted around my neck as we walked. He liked that. When I went, after he persuaded me, to the magic show, it really was a magic show, put on just for me by Johnson and his twin brother, that turned out to be rather like the antics of Alfalfa and Spanky in Darla's house on the occasion that left them hanging from a drapery rod.

Later that day, when I rode my bike by their house, they took it and tied it to a tree. *For a kiss, you get your bike back,* they said. Platonism was becoming insufficient. My father, hat pulled low over his eyes, paintbrush held like a tomahawk, saw me running down Trunt and immediately climbed down the ladder, walked in that somewhat stiff-legged way of his, his shoulders tight and thin like one of his grandson's, two blocks south and six blocks east to where my bike was, without my having to tell him where to go or what the problem was. With one hand, he pulled the handlebars free, breaking the rope, and carried my bike home over his shoulder.

After that, Johnson and I stopped going with each other without either one of us officially terminating the relationship. It may be that he transferred to a new junior high school closer to his house and farther from mine than the one we attended together or perhaps he moved away suddenly. More likely, he feared my father's preternatural power. In my memory it is as if he just didn't exist anymore. I don't recall ever seeing him again.

By ninth grade and the D-cup on a small body, twenty-one-and-a-half-inch waist, older boys became demanding. Men and teenagers, cruising the streets downtown and near bus stops in my neighborhood, seeing me in summer's more revealing attire usually reacted, invariably, in my memory, with vulgar comments. Nothing I wore, other than autumnal and wintry bulk, concealed my upper body or discouraged the comments.

It was the era of the miniskirt and hot pants that were for sale when I shopped for school clothes with my mother's credit cards, spending no more than we had agreed I should spend, and only in the department store bargain basements, not in the full-price exclusive collections on the third and fourth floors, but my discounted goods still said *Halle's* and *Higbee's* on their tags and labels. My mother said I looked cute in the clothes I bought—not once did she ask me to return anything—and "cute" seemed safe, but despite a mother's approval, it wasn't. Although there was no décolleté garment among my purchases, and no Spandex, even modest and prim V necks exposed cleavage that only exotic dancers and strippers needed. The Playtex brassiere representative told me I was purchasing in Higbee's basement the second most rare commercial size.

There was no mistake about what I seemed to have no choice but to advertise. I would set my lips, fasten my gaze to the straight and

narrow above my head, hasten my pace, and snub these men, some of
whom meant no harm, and for my silence I was denigrated and disposed
of in a variety of pejorative vernacular expressions, and assured that I
had nothing that they hadn't had before and could easily get any time
they wanted it. Some threatened to bring me down and knock the
conceit out of me, but none actually carried out these threats, perhaps
only because I disappeared, sullen, shakened, in the downtown crowds.

I was unable to enjoy the attention or to dismiss it; I took it seriously, the way language was hurled at me, transforming my love of my
body into fear of it. I knew that matters of the body, the guile of
physiology were what veered near an explanation of Lytta, shape-shifter,
now appearing as these men. I knew that lurid transactions were the
source of her pathology, that when they happened, she felt a rush instead
of the devastation I felt when she tried to share her ignominious pleasure
with me. My body, though I had thought it wouldn't, was becoming
like hers, but with an exaggerated bosom, a grotesque element as if I
aspire to become what these men want.

I didn't know how to handle this; I'd always openly admired what
moved me, as these men were doing. None of the girls I knew, not the
brainy ones in my honors classes nor the ones for whom counselors
were already recommending cosmetology school and good husbands,
seemed upset by such phenomena; they were so sophisticated that they'd
laugh at me if I revealed my discomfort; some of them sought such
compliments, and some dispensed them. But fortunately, so far all is
talk, all is masculine bravado without substantiating action.

This is the time of succumbing to external pressures, volatile blowing seem-
ingly intent on stripping wings of the feathers essential for flight, a stripping
that tornadoes have accomplished with poultry. This is the time when all I've
seen comes back to haunt me. I can keep the demons at bay no longer. This is
the time during which I decide the world of wonder is superficial and childish,
not fit for habitation. My minds are of singular accord. I think of myself as
apart from turbulence although I stand in its middle, a position that offers little

comfort, for I can't see beyond the turbulence although I know something else is beyond it, having come from there. So I learn to use language condemningly and lose confidence in originality, trusting the ideas of other adolescents who are worldly, grounded, masters of the secular, not interested in any hypothesis, not in any long shot dream, not in the movement of light from distant galaxies, aiming for our awareness after traveling thousands of years. Luminosity that cannot stop itself, a comet or meteor helpless to its own radiance, especially its dying glow.

Now I must begin to separate from my parents in order to become one day an independent woman. Cousins on whom I have depended, I must depend on less, for we are each ensnared in our separate complicated puberties and they require our full attention. As an adolescent, I don't see the collective experience well; only the personal and solitary. I don't like it much; I've never been alone. I already have more secrets than I can manage.

My life and Deirdre's are splitting; paths we couldn't see before are now in view, and while they may not be parallel, they will not intersect except for casual meetings, phone calls in which we are careful to speak in generalities. We attend different high schools, travel in different circles; we think we have less and less in common. Rarely do we attend the same church. We are exempt, in our conversations, from any pressure, awkwardness, or disgrace. Doors are closing. I don't even mention a first kiss. Nor does she, but a first kiss happened to both, most of us. There are surprisingly similar secrets.

High school means faltering. I withdrew from Helena and Tyra, my closest school friends, since junior high, in whom I have never confided anything. Helena even referred to me, accurately, as her protégée; we met in seventh grade, all her confidence glowing even then. She moved with such airs, refined, studied walking, effects of ballet, neat sandwiches for lunch, quick sign of the cross so fluid the sign was round—I wanted to be her. From the beginning I didn't exercise any will around her; followed all her suggestions, didn't make any. I was her shadow, mostly in her way, and upset by the arrangement, tormented in my mind, but just as paralyzed as I'd been with Lytta. Helena did not forbid my having opinions, but I didn't believe mine could withstand her poised challenges. I had no rebuttal to all that confidence she exuded that I tried to absorb.

I'm not sure why our friendship was like this, one girl dominating another so thoroughly; why I was so easily dominated despite how much I disliked the acquiescence that defined me more thoroughly each year. I didn't see any more symbiosis in nature, only attempts at dominance. Survival of the fittest meant that I would perish. I did not try to influence any situation; I didn't think it was possible to alter the course of events, and I believed that attempted alteration could result in even more damaging repercussions. I did not need more pain. I knew so much about cruelty and death, the ease with which life could be taken by practically anyone, anything, and there were no apologies for these thefts. The randomness was frightening. Worse; it seemed that dreams could be denied by objects also, by that which was not sentient, not even capable, you'd reason, of denial, yet a grand conspiracy against happiness and peace of mind was in force. And some had in their brains and blood the frequency that turned them to this force; some were optimally receptive to it.

Yes; some of what happened unmaliciously and unmeditated in the universe seemed cruel as if the process of existence (because it involved feeding upon something else, chemical and electromagnetic interactions that are volatile, involuntary, and catastrophic, agents of change; because its purpose is continuance and motion) was a curse; there was no mercy intrinsic in the food chain, only if someone said the word and put it there, as vegetarians tended to do. Yet still they consume, presumably inflicting no botanical pain; they must consume something. Adolescence was feast, consuming and being consumed.

I envied Helena and those who had not had to learn this.

Confident girls like Helena are so intimidating. They feel and exert their mass. They go on dates, become cheerleaders, boosters, go to movies, fast food or better restaurants, and dances, ride in rented convertibles, are not propositioned in the halls and alleys the way that I am. Something about me makes nasty boys think I can fulfill sordid fantasies. Nice boys don't talk to me, don't ask me out. *My gifted male peers don't consider me because I look cheap and easy. One of them is going to be a Rhodes scholar; cheap is not part of his future. I'm the only girl among the gifted with this look: Lytta's mark, ladybug marks, bargain basement price tags. I am cloistered in these marks.*

Through all the faltering, I wrote difficult passages mostly about defeat, in first person although I disliked all the pitiful narrators; they were not quietly philosophical nor contemplative; they were spineless. I could no longer control the worlds I created. I knew where I had been and where I wanted to be, but couldn't get there; the current I had entered was too strong.

And it became a vortex, a tornado inside the water in which I spun, narrowing with each revolution until I myself was spiral, afraid I'd always spiral, unable to see in this spiraling what previously would have seemed marvelous: *my own body becoming mathematical, a spiraling that occurs in a sequence of Fibonacci squares, the logarithmic curving of a chambered nautilus in which I had once dreamed a wedding—I still adore and am moved by patterns in the shells of mollusks, in successive rings in xylem tissue of trees, like ever-widening, unceasing awakenings.* I stopped studying. My grades slipped although I didn't actually fail any classes; only in one, calculus, did I come close.

I put forth no effort whatsoever. Dreams of becoming a geneticist or physicist evaporated with a prior dream of becoming a classical violinist. I was locked in swirl. Not that I wasn't involved in any commendatory activities at all: I was feature editor of the newspaper (Helena was managing editor), and a first soprano in the chorus, president of the Service Club, of the Junior Red Cross, editor of the literary magazine. I attended a few basketball games with Helena, Tyra, occasionally with Candy and Natalie, the other smart girls I envied. In college, I was exempt from most required introductory courses because of my advanced placement academic success in high school. However, I succeeded only because school was so easy for me that not studying and not attending classes did not cause me to fail anything. Darkness was encroaching;

there was no more continuity of light, only here and there a flash, a bright call of distress.

On the surface, the high school record looks respectable; I still managed to graduate in the top tenth, twenty-second I think (and was honored at commencement for finishing in the top tenth and for being a National Merit commended student), because of the gifted advantage— our As equaled five points instead of four; four points corresponded to our Bs—but emotionally and socially, what I have left is shame. I hated how my abilities were so wasted; I had believed since early in childhood that I would do something significant and memorable, helping the world, providing enormous comfort in some way, like a lighthouse, but my life was not headed toward anything spectacular or useful.

So as to not exasperate my parents, during a few grading periods, I took to altering my academic record. This was without the benefit of sophisticated digitized techniques of reproduction and manipulation available now; still, these forgeries and enhancements succeeded. My parents remained proud. A French teacher wrote in my autograph book: *Rétournez à vos anciennes idéals.*

Restore my lost ideals. This teacher did not know how badly I wanted to restore them, but I didn't know how, and she didn't tell me, nor did I ask. I lost perspective and the ability to imagine ideals. After all, I had killed a rabbit when I asked my father to forsake this nickname for me. And it seemed that only that rabbit had had the power to pardon. My outlook was entirely fatalistic now and my parents couldn't tell; I still smiled, went to church, read voraciously; it was an outlook of the mind, and I kept it there, out of parental sight. They had no idea what I was reading and writing, but didn't agonize over their ignorance since my pursuits were scholarly and impressed them. No drugs ever. No sex yet.

Maybe not, but there was still too much for me to manage unassisted. I did not admit my limits to myself; I didn't want to believe I had any although by then I also knew they were useful, sobering in their refutation of infinity. It is as if I was torn from the root, still in bloom but with the destiny of all the pretty cut flowers, their short time transforming a room. I wanted to save myself. I wanted to do it alone if it were possible to be done. I'd be so proud. Helena would drop dead from the shock of success that she did not sponsor.

～

I'm not sure how I met Hector, as he was four years older than me, graduating when I was finishing ninth grade and entering tenth. He was the younger of two brothers, both standing six feet tall like their mother and dark like her; their father was only of average height, and was the color of burnished sand, so different from his sons that his paternity could be doubted easily.

Hector's father lived just a block north of Trunt and had been separated for some time from Hector's mother, preferring white women for sex without commitment. I don't know whether or not there was a legal divorce, but Hector's mother seemed desperate to keep that man in her life, once falling in the street in her neighborhood from mystic bullets, and saturating her clothes with theatrical blood so as to force concern and responsibility from him. Hector reported that she was a bit addled, but clearly, she was just a dedicated lover, had no self-esteem, so clung, because he defined her, to a man who cheated on her, bad-mouthed her, and stank of old alcohol around her. He owned her voice. He wore sharkskin suits and considered himself a player, wearing his shirts unbuttoned at the throat to reveal a thick gold chain. He wanted to be Father Divine. That is how Hector's father was dressed the day that he walked down Trunt Avenue on his way home.

Hector had obviously noticed me before the day his father walked down my street or his father would not have known to stop at my house. I don't remember meeting Hector or telling him where I lived, but even if I hadn't told him, he could have easily found out from practically anyone in the now all-black neighborhood. I was nearly fifteen years old and had not had an official boyfriend other than Johnson.

It was December, yet my mother and I were sitting on the porch. A strangely warm day, perhaps, or maybe in my mind there's a confusion of months. I do not recall that we wore coats. Maybe my mother felt unusual reason to expect that day the chariot's arrival, so was outside looking for the bright flash that probably would have much in common with those Nevada atomic bomb tests in the fifties. The mushroom cloud and the victory in World War II inspired much mirth and overindulgence: atomic hamburgers, atomic drinks, tonics, restaurants, music and dances, atomic toys; you were supposed to shake your root beer vigorously, to put an atomic head on what you poured into your glass after the pop exploded from the bottle; dry ice became known as atomic ice when Deirdre and I played with it in rivers. The celebration lasted more than a decade; I was born into it. Inside our house, little models of the nativity were on every table.

I assume December because Mr. Santos invited me to his son's birthday party at his home on the next block, and Hector's birthday was in December. He was turning nineteen. I would be fifteen at the end of February, just past the middle of tenth grade. I cannot picture Mr. Santos smiling, but he must have as he supposedly was deft at charming women, and smiling is usually part of such routines. I'll say he smiled as he came up our short walkway, climbed the stone steps my mother was thinking about painting green, and then slung one leg over the porch's rail to straddle it. That charm.

He persuaded my mother quickly that she could trust him to protect her daughter at an innocent party that he would supervise himself. Nothing would happen that she would not approve of, and she was welcome to come if she wanted. It was as if my mother sensed deacon in his presence although he did not claim any, and she did not ask him for proof of his church affiliation. She consented without consulting my father, so sure was she of the innocence; the next week I would be off to my first teenage party. I did not consider this party invitation a date. I don't even remember saying that I wanted to go, but that may just reflect my present hope that what happened with Hector was not some twisted form of wish fulfillment. I'm surprised she didn't think him too old for me or perhaps Mr. Santos lied about Hector's age. I don't remember. It was certainly in Hector's favor that at nineteen, he still honored his father and respected my parents, asking them for permission even before informing me that he was interested.

It was so dark. My birthday parties never had been as dark but for one foiled by a storm. The black light seemed neither festive nor sensuous, just brought to my mind the school nurse checking for lice under ultraviolet lighting, all of us quiet and stiff in line. I don't remember Mr. Santos's being there although both he and his son walked me to their house—the dream of double escort. I had assumed that Hector lived there with him, but in fact, Hector lived with his mother. Mostly other girls, older, were there, none whom I knew, and in much more elaborate makeup. I just wore a little lipstick, deep rose pink, and a very girlish dress in which I looked top-heavy, deformed; a dress that I would wear to church. Lytta's dress dyed pink. There was punch, also cookies, and music, slow music mostly, that wasn't too loud.

I didn't see much of Hector. He danced with some of the other, taller girls, and went with them into other rooms, but I was fine left in the dark and was taken home without incident. Not even an attempt at a kiss. It was comfortable, and Mr. Santos had been honest about both his intentions and his son's though one can never really vouch for the intentions of another.

Hector called me once a week, but I didn't see him until the next time there was a party, just after my birthday. This time, Hector himself made the request for permission to take me, and again, my mother gave permission. Hector told me, on the way to the party, that his father had moved into an apartment in what turned out to be one of Cleveland's seediest areas, where winos, petty criminals, thugs, and prostitutes were plentiful and tolerated; their unofficial sovereign domain. A loud part of the city; music and every domestic squabble and act of social misconduct were amplified, broadcast from apartments, cars, yards, and street corners. Mr. Santos now resided in such a depressed area only because of hard times, being laid-off, I assumed. Hector didn't tell my mother that the location had changed and I thought nothing of it. People do change their residence. It is allowed. Even so, Hector introduced the element of deceit into our relationship.

How did we get there? By car? Bus? I don't remember, but the apartment was filthy. His father was sitting at the table in the yellow-lit kitchenette with his pants unfastened, a cigarette dangling from his lips, his bared right arm on the table near an opened bottle of beer. On his lap sat a flabby white woman in a full slip and tawny stockings fastened into garters that I could see. He was wearing a wedding ring, but she was not his wife and was introduced as his friend. I knew who his wife was. The friend's arms were around his neck. She dwarfed him. This was to be, evidently, a double date.

Hector announced that he and I were going together. His father nodded approvingly, and winked, then saluted by raising the bottle and sitting it back on the table without taking a sip. I could hear the dripping faucet, plinks as pans were hit, and could see the lit radio dial although there was no music.

No place for the chaste.

We didn't sit to talk, play cards, watch television. Instead, Hector took me to his father's bed visible clearly from the table where father sat with friend. There was only one bedroom and one other aggregate room that was living room, kitchen, and dining area. An efficiency, I believe it's called. He left the bedroom door slightly open. The sheets stank of perspiration and hadn't been recently changed. Yellow sheets that wouldn't be yellow after laundering. There was underwear in the corner, white men's briefs, probably Jockey or Fruit of the Loom. Such deplorable conditions. As if it would spare me some humiliation, Hector let me keep on my clothes after he pulled up my skirt saying nothing until he noticed my sanitary panties that held a bulky Kotex napkin. *Are you on your period?*

He took off nothing of his own apparel but did unzip his pants, lowered my sanitary panties in the front only, asked me not to get blood on his father's bed, and penetrated me with himself although I did not see his penis and did not see a mature erect one until being with the man I would marry. I didn't want to be there. In some ways, I wasn't there, but Hector didn't notice my vacant emotions or my physical stiffness, my silence. Or if he noticed, these vacancies didn't matter to him.

It was painful, but as I was already bleeding, if there were any tears, the blood of laceration mixed imperceptibly with menstrual blood. *This must be what drowning is like,* I thought. This was not something I wanted to do again. I cried silently through the whole act, his large hands on my shoulders, my tears wetting his hands. When he was through, he joined his father at the table and they talked while I smoothed my skirt again and again, while I learned to hate myself. He did not wash. He did not kiss me that night either but did kiss me eventually, wanting my mouth open, penetrating it. I got home as best I could, telling my parents that Hector had brought me. Anyway, as far as my parents knew, I had only had to walk around the block, on the night of lost virginity, late in winter. As I left, he asked if it had been my first time. He said that next time it would be better; *you'll see.*

What I didn't know was that Hector was also going with five other girls with whom he was having sex regularly. One of them, Effie, who'd been with him the longest, told me about Hector's five steps to heaven when I was trying at the end of summer to get him to return to me the phonograph records (by The Intruders and The Temptations) he had taken from me and given to her. By then, Hector and I had been going together nearly nine months and soon he would be in military uniform. Only five steps. I did not count.

I went to Effie's apartment in the projects to get the records myself one Saturday when supposedly I was going downtown, as I had been allowed to do either on my own or with Deirdre since I was ten, and Hector was there, going with me but with his hand on her butt, his tongue in her ear while I demanded to know where my records were. Effie knew she was a step to heaven, but wasn't bothered; almost seemed proud, boastful as she told me she was the highest step, the one that put him in paradise, apple of the polygamist's eye.

Then he tried to put his hands on me, but I was resisting and angering him with my unexpected resistance. It surprised me too, but Hector's older brother had recently begun talking to me, and I was developing a crush on this brother, Hollis, that strengthened me to resist Hector. I didn't want to go with Hector anymore but couldn't break it off. I didn't know how. I hoped he'd break it.

I could look at myself in scenes with him as if I watched a film, as if on the screen were an actress, her voice subordinate to the script. I'd long been able to detach myself from events, treating them as if they happened to an internal sister I protected. It was performance, her performance; moving, poignant, tragic, but at the end, it was permissible to applaud and ponder the quality of the performance, read reviews rather than really confront the content of the movie. It wasn't real; my life would never be like the life I watched unfolding between Hector, Effie, and me.

He took me to his father's place again, four occasions in all, but on one of them had sex with another girl, step three, while I sat at that table holding tightly to greasy shakers of salt and pepper. This was some of the debauchery that Lot's wife saw. Perhaps I was meant to treat this strangeness as an instructional video. I'd been voyeur before, seeing so much that is cruel that it somehow didn't bother me to watch, to again become a witness. There are so many challenges to a good life. They weren't ashamed. These exhibitionists weren't in love. She was older than Hector. Red streaks in dark hair. There was a sparkle, that should not have been there, in her laugh.

When they were done, both spoke to me, but said nothing worth remembering. She put her earrings back on as Hector guided her out the door and took her home or somewhere; I certainly did not ask, but although I had the opportunity to leave and head home, I didn't even move from the table, as if I needed his permission or needed the idea to come from him. Besides, outside the door was more tyranny.

This decision not to act really defies explanation. The opportunity was so obvious yet I was paralyzed, the physical consequence of my emotional incapacitation. When he returned, he said he was willing to have sex with me, as though I'd committed some wrong for which I was being forgiven, as if sex was not as impersonal and meaningless as he made it. Perhaps my waiting for him impressed him and convinced him of my permanent naïveté. I said, however, that I was bleeding, had severe cramps. No doubt I grimaced to emphasize and prove the severity, gripping my abdomen as I grimaced. Sympathetic, he stated a given, that we'd do it another time, as if there was nothing else that we could do, Why never to a movie, the mall; why never even McDonald's? Why did he never take me anywhere except to this apartment? He never bought anything for me. Never offered me so much as a stick of gum, a drink of water. Never a birthday card, a Christmas gift. Not once in the years I knew him, one and a half of them going with him. I wondered how I could make myself bleed every day.

It was dark, quite late; my parents thought that I was asleep in my room. I'm not sure why I sneaked out to go to that apartment to be with someone who mistreated me; I can't explain this at all. He was my boyfriend and I was loyal; obeyed my elders—that's all I can say. Hector did not offer to see me home, so I was walking; I did not even have money for the bus. I didn't think to call Hollis from the apartment; he'd asked me not to call him at home anyway, and didn't give me his unlisted number, but I'd gotten it from his father, telling Mr. Santos that I'd lost it. A police car went by; the officers shined a flashlight at me, suspecting that I was either a runaway or prostitute, not the girl in advanced placement high school classes that I was, her grades slipping, her future threatened. They didn't even stop.

Soon a taxi pulled up; the driver rolled down the passenger window and told me that it was too dangerous for a young lady to be on the streets alone; as an act of public service, he would drive me home for free. He opened the door and I got in the front, on a bench seat, all as it should be, professional, strictly business for less than a mile when he began to drive with his left hand only, his right hand holding my left wrist as he boasted his strength. *Excuse me,* he said, *I'm not trying to get fresh with you, but I couldn't help noticing your chest* exaggerated in a tight dress with horizontal stripes; Hector liked it.

He drove a little farther in silence; he had not yet asked me where I lived, and that was good as my address was information he did not need, but obviously, since he had not asked, the destination was not home sweet home. He pulled over on a darkened street. The street lamps were out. *I want to show you something,* he said, placing my left hand on his hard crotch; I gasped in fear, not understanding what I was touching, and he was so surprised that he released my hand. I moved as close as I could to the door, looked at him for a second and got out, running, my hair loosening and becoming wild as if I had done what the driver wanted of me. How my hand burned.

Hector could and did later write beautiful love letters to me from an army base in South Carolina.

Instead of talking about these incidents, preferably with adults of insight and compassion, I wrote stories about girls who became pregnant and either contemplated suicide or solicited abortionists who dismembered their babies as well as one of the pregnant girls, a martyr to promiscuity. None of the fathers of the babies were in these stories, some of which were passed around my class and read enthusiastically by my peers who were convinced I would one day become a famous writer. *Such talent.* In French class, we were divided into groups and responsible for writing and performing six-minute skits; in my group, led by Helena, I played a struggling model who became pregnant by one of several possible clients. For the play, I wore something that revealed too much cleavage for school and brought in Mr. Boston bottles filled with Lipton's tea, explaining, to administrators who questioned me, that all had been done in the name of honors French; strictly intellectual endeavors.

Since I could not alter the direction of the spiral, I decided to assign a noble purpose to my descent; I became dedicated to occupying some licentious men (never anyone my own age; I had to be a Lolita) so that they wouldn't be able to prey upon someone else. I remembered Saint Maria Goretti and believed in what I was doing even as I desperately wanted to stop.

At home, all is well. Sometimes I play my records too loudly. Only the mildest rebellion.

Hector's big brother intervened on the last night that Hector took me to his father's apartment. Hollis talked to me for two hours, all to help me overcome his brother. That was new; the talk, the stab at therapy; both new. He took my hand and said he knew that his brother was mistreating me, so he was going to take me home from his father's place that he just happened to visit while Hector had taken me there. My guardian angel. *I'll talk to my brother,* he said. He did, and told me that he'd convinced Hector to break up with me.

I felt relieved knowing that Hollis had broken the spell, that this meant I was no longer going with Hector; I was going up now. Descent had approached its limit. Hollis opened the door for me as we walked outside. A gentleman. He smiled frequently, as much as I do. Once in his car, silver, but I don't remember the make or model, he asked me questions about my interests and career plans *when I grew up,* so it was clear he knew—and cared about—what I was; therefore, I did not suspect him despite what I knew about both his father and his brother. I thought it wouldn't be so bad to go with him. He was older, wiser, kinder, available without steps.

However, Hollis did not take me home; he drove me instead to a dark lot behind an abandoned warehouse where he forced sex with me. It was force although I said nothing, couldn't get out the *no* he surely would have heeded. What did he think my tears were saying, the paralysis of my body that Hector had probably told him about? I watched, during the act, his face lift from his body and hover close enough to mine to smother it, the mouth elongating into a beak that pecked at me, as Hitchcock had birds peck at Tippi Hedren, until my face was a soft bloody mass. He smiled, cracking the predatory bird face; his teeth were exquisite. Of course I made it a movie and distanced my reality from mere cinematic tricks. One of those science-fiction movies, one of those monster flicks, my father and I watching it together, the story of man's everlasting folly.

When he was through, he told me to sit up to help the semen more efficiently run down my legs to prevent the pregnancy that happened. I was sure it was blood running down, and I tried to get out of the car, but he was strong and told me with words, and a grip so sure that in another context it would have been reassuring, that I didn't have to do that; he would take me home as he had promised. He wasn't like Hector who had me get home the best way I could on my last night of virginity. When I telephoned to tell this more responsible big brother that I was pregnant, he would not speak to me, but as I kept having him paged at his job, he eventually took me to a suburban doctor, I said I was eighteen, then called me a week later to say that the test was negative and did not call me again.

But the test was not negative as I soon discovered. I tried at great risk to reach Hollis; he had warned me not to call him at home. It turned out that he was married. His wife, Linda, who answered the phone sounded so pitiable, so distraught and wounded; she apologized to me repeatedly for Hollis's behavior. Her pain was greater than my own. I was Lytta now, Linda's Lytta. She did not seem to hate me, but immediately, I wanted to turn her into Hollis's sister or aunt so that we would not have to compete for him. Yes; she said that he hit her regularly. At least he had not hit me. I thought I needed him.

I became pregnant when I was barely sixteen by this married man: Hollis, this adulterer: Hollis, who took advantage of me while claiming to rescue me from his younger unmarried brother. Hollis Santos.

Hollis had never told me about her, not that knowing about Linda would have given me the power to refuse him. I still wanted this man to love me. She kept saying, in her extraordinary empathy, in her insight that her daughter could be one day at risk, in her awareness that I was not the betrayer, that Hollis shouldn't be doing this to a kid. In fact, Linda said that I was not the first kid Hollis had been with during their marriage. She was twenty-five, his age, had two of his children. She asked me if I were pregnant. I wouldn't say anything. *Go ahead and tell me,* she said, sounding so, so pitiable; *you're not the first.* I have many sisters of circumstance. Hollis did not ever speak to me again.

As Hollis had driven me to and from the doctor that day, he had had me hide, had me sit on the floor in the back of the car, had covered me with a smelly blanket, the one that had been offered to me after sex with him.

～

There was a part of me delighted with the idea, just the idea, of life starting within me. I sang more, began my days as early as I could, drank a gallon of chocolate milk every three days and craved popcorn. My mother brought a bag of popcorn to me each day when she came home from work, purchasing it at one particular vendor in Terminal Tower where she transferred buses. The popcorn is what gave away my secret, for I had taken care to let the supply of Kotex napkins dwindle. And I had, under a pseudonym, seen an obstetrician at whom I stared dumbly when he asked me about "circumcision." I said that I would when he then told me to ask my husband about it. I did, years later.

All men thought me older than I was.

Mostly, however, I dreaded how my life would have to change. I was not ready for a baby although I would have loved her or him deeply. I have always been capable of intense emotion. I knew that my parents would love the child—there couldn't have been more ideal grandparents—but they would also grieve to see the beautiful structure they'd made for me collapse. They would lament this tainting of my reputation, for teenage mothers were still stigmatized then. And Hollis; well, they'd have him prosecuted, I was sure—that I liked, and I felt that Linda would like that too. On the day of his conviction, which also would be the day of her divorce, she'd celebrate her liberation. But I couldn't bear telling them, so I didn't, knowing my dresses would betray me.

Then my mother remarked that I was craving the popcorn. I had asked her to bring two large bags now; one wasn't enough. *You're craving it,* she said. *I craved butter when I was carrying you.*

My father was devastated. I could tell that he wanted to change my name. The Soul Circle by then had disbanded, but my father pulled out the Mr. Boston. He didn't yell nor chastise me in any way, just commented quietly that I could still have *practical dreams.* He was too sad to criticize or complain. He stared at me, looking futilely for the rabbit. I couldn't stand how disappointed he was, and he had no idea how disappointed I was with myself, how I watched myself traveling further and further from where I really wanted to go, yet could not turn around. It was meant to be a one-way trip. I silently agreed with his silent conclusions that I did not deserve: my name, his refusal to spank me,

those long walks, those books, especially *Energy and Power,* from which
I'd learned nothing.

My mother cried, asked Jesus to take this yoke off her, yelled at my
sins, then out of her love for me took charge and refused to surrender to
what she repeatedly called *my mistake.* She did not intend for me to have
that baby. She did not intend for me to ruin a ruined life. I showed
them an article, in *Newsweek* I think, about the legalization of abortions
in New York. My parents were heartened by this information and ar-
ranged, my mother most staunchly, for an abortion. I was glad they
knew, because the pregnancy was becoming difficult to conceal. I went
to school, but didn't know I was there. Sat in the back of classrooms,
sank abysmally deep in the chairs. Spoke to no one, took no notes.
Disappeared.

Neither of my parents was interested in the identity of the father.
He did not matter. If, we all knew this, he had been any kind of decent
man, he would have been at my side from the confirmation of the testing
of my urine. He would have approached my parents with me, holding
my hand. He would have accepted his responsibility. Since Hollis's indif-
ference was obvious, there was no reason to involve him. Especially
since what I conceived with him was not going to be born. If he could
behave as if the statutory rape hadn't happened, we could too, and could
go one better, eradicating his work, uprooting his foul seed, stifling
somewhat his generations.

I knew it was for the best, I knew about my parents' commitment
to a better future than I could have with a baby, I knew I didn't want
any memento of Hollis, not even these memories, but I still didn't want
the abortion because the baby was also mine and not responsible for the
sordidness of its conception. But I owed my parents some compliance
with their wishes; I owed them reparations for the pain I caused them.
They had never given me grief.

My parents told the extended family that we were going east because
I had an audition; I made sure everyone knew of my interests in acting;

we're very excited; she's always wanted to be an actress, they told my uncle who drove us to the bus station. I was wearing a girdle that my mother bought for me. And craving popcorn even more suspiciously. My uncle looked at me strangely through the rearview mirror as from the backseat I complained that the smell of exhaust coming through the vents and windows was making me nauseous, but all he said was *good luck on your audition.* I'm sure that he knew. I no longer called him Uncle Spoon.

The bus ride took a whole day, and I sat by a window, barely noticing the scenery although it was all scenery new to me once we got past Pittsburgh. I was not the only girl on the bus. We didn't talk much. Mostly, I pretended to sleep, but opened my eyes in time to see the George Washington Bridge lit up. It was my first time staying in a hotel. The next day, I, in the beginning of the sixth month of gestation, had a third trimester saline-induced abortion while my parents saw the Empire State Building and the Statue of Liberty; a honeymoon at last; I didn't want them to stay with me. I was ashamed of the depth of our descent from the attic of my infancy.

Amniotic fluid was drawn out through a large syringe and briny liquid was injected, inducing labor that lasted for hours; I was drugged, woozy but feeling pain; my baby was burned, delivered dead at the end of the fifth month. Some premature infants of the same gestational age survive; more and more each year. After the successful procedure, I bled profusely and the doctor informed my parents that I would not be able to travel home by bus; I would have to fly, and I did, my mother with me; my father used the rest of his round-trip Greyhound ticket arriving home many hours later than we did. It was a rough flight. The *fasten your seat belt* light never went off.

I did not bother finding out whether it was a boy or girl that I lost, the child that would be an adult now, with his of her own regrets and inspirations. Had that pregnancy not been terminated, I didn't want, nor did I expect, any further contribution from Hollis—my feelings were like those I've heard on talk shows from pregnant teens and teens trying to become pregnant. The baby could have been, I thought, my best contribution to the world. Perhaps for the life of that child and that child's destiny I had been born. I believe that I have quietly resented my mother from the time of that abortion until twenty years later, when I held my just-born baby in my arms in a Massachusetts hospital and she held him too, more delighted than me as if she too had feared that the abortion she forced upon me had deprived her of her only biological grandchild, as if part of her now was no longer widowed.

In fact, years later a gynecologist suggested to me that during the D & C that followed the abortion, the doctors may have performed other sterilizing procedures without my knowledge or consent. I remembered well, still do, the Greek doctor's name, the woman I had trusted, the woman who told me that another pregnancy would kill me so *don't do this again, young lady!* yet when the gynecologist attempted to get medical details from Saint Luke's, official word was that there was no record of this Greek physician ever having worked there. I'm going to call her Dr. Halite because of her dealings in salt.

Seeing my mother with my children, I was glad that I had not disrespected her nor criticized her orally; glad that my resentment was all silent and unfulfilled except for a few years during which I did not call her *Mama* or *Bonka* or anything; I would just talk without using any particular address. We shared our fears quietly and overcame them privately. I must also admit that I have preferred the life that, because of a childless adolescence, I could readily pursue. I have preferred it to any other life that I can imagine.

Following the abortion, I am alone, but am not independent. There's no man in my life. My parents do not suggest any form of contraception because they know a teenage pregnancy will not happen again. They try to behave as if the first one hadn't happened. For the first time, we keep a secret together. But I feel even more powerless. I didn't want to get pregnant. Didn't want an abortion. Wanted to represent my church at the Baptist Convention, but Deirdre was the youth representative. Wanted to play in the symphony orchestra. Wanted to be valedictorian of my high school class, but that was Natalie, and Helena was ahead of me too; all my friends were ahead of me. Wanted Lytta to drop dead. Wanted Gladys to be the phoenix in my life, but that was Lytta coming back again and again. Wanted the boy to have a rebirth in the womb box. Wanted a tornado or some other biblical whirlwind to whisk away the truck that killed the boy. Wanted to be a physicist, no; an alchemist. I'm at the bottom. Want my father to know about my life now. But none of that mattered.

My father died, no doubt terribly disappointed, the year before I graduated first in my college class, the year before I graduated Phi Beta Kappa, the year before I won the Academy of American Poets College Prize at Oberlin College for the poem "The Problem with Loving a Ghost of a Sailor''; the year before my life changed into the kind of life he had dared to dream possible for me, when he invented for me a name that would demand the life that is now mine.

⌒

$\mathcal{I}$'m told in church and at home by my mother that only God's will happened in the world; therefore, what I wanted was irrelevant to God's needs and intentions. It wasn't meant for me to have any other life, so any contrary efforts were futile. I could not impose my own dreams and ambition; God's will took precedence. It is medicine. It is not supposed to taste good; I am not supposed to like it. By his own decree, I am subservient, doing his work that is difficult and demeaning because it earns for me entrance into his kingdom. By his own decree, I must always surrender. It's written for me as it was written in the sky for Dorothy.

~ &mergence

Six weeks after the abortion, the time the disappearing doctor said it would take for my body to heal, I met Wesley in the month before the month in which my baby would have been born. If not for the abortion, I would have been pregnant when I met Wesley, not an acceptable Lolita.

Despite how Hollis had treated me, after the abortion I still felt I needed him, so wanted to take him back, though he was probably still married. Linda couldn't let him go either. Wesley came along to substitute for Hollis; I had not moved on. I thought Wesley was more business as usual. I even hoped that he was so that I could again spare some young girl some grief. When I met Wesley, I was making myself available to him for misuse just as I had offered myself to Hollis. Wesley doesn't know this, but the first time he talked to me, I assumed we'd have a physical relationship because that is what always happened. He was nearly as old as Hollis, another elder I had to respect. Wesley and I became involved as part of that flagitious pattern. At times, this bothered me.

He was not even supposed to be in Cleveland when we met. He came there because his aunt, while in the deep South, came to believe that someone had worked roots against her, so she took to running from the spell's effective range. Perhaps a different reason for taking part in the great migration of Negroes from the South, but just as effective in encouraging her siblings to leave Mississippi and establish better lives in the North where his aunt felt there was no hoodoo. Instead she found just the entertainment of seers, Miss or Madame So-and-so who foretold the future and restored a man's lost nature right in a corner of the beauty shop.

In that way did Wesley's family come to establish itself in Illinois and his extended family there and also in Ohio (the two states in which the cursed aunt found refuge) where we met when, upon being honorably discharged from the air force, Wesley impulsively took a flight from Europe, where he'd been stationed, to Ohio instead of home to Illinois where siblings, old girlfriends, and his mother were waiting. They hadn't seen him in three years. But Wesley didn't want to continue the restricted life of limited ambition that was the curse of Dunson; a factory manufacturing farm and heavy equipment offered the only jobs in town, according to Wesley. The curse was passed to children and grandchildren, some of them teenagers having babies out of wedlock, a curse that affects so many families. Few marriages in his immediate family survive, notably his own ongoing and only marriage, and his father's third.

Wesley knocked on his uncle's door in Cleveland and was welcomed.

I met him in church where I was more dedicated and devout than ever, reading the announcements, singing in the choir, writing and printing the church's bulletins, including each Sunday an original inspirational rhyming poem, and an original crossword puzzle with biblical themes. Like others in the congregation, I tried to expose everyone as a hypocrite and backslider, denouncing some of the activities I now love. Oh could I harp on the shame of unwed mothers! Wesley had come to my storefront church with his deacon and deaconess uncles and aunts, who joined when their church disintegrated after an irreconcilable dispute with their sibling pastor. Twenty-odd people walked in one Sunday and dominated the congregation, joining that day and taking this small church to prosperity with their superior fund-raising skills and their boundless commitment to the work of the Lord.

Wesley saw me for the first time while I, dressed in a crimson tight-fitting turtleneck sweater, read announcements. He later admitted that first my chest caught his attention, and then my sophisticated voice. I did not notice him as quickly, and that made his notice of me increase; he said he liked a challenge.

Once my church grew, it too became ill-fated, the pastor reportedly having an affair with the clerk, his daughter murdered in a drug-related homicide, and there was rising paranoia that resulted from the family of deacons assuming too much power and authority in the eyes of the envious. The pastor conspired with the congregation against them, allegations and accusations flying back and forth until it was a den of iniquity, studio of a talk show, and not a house of God. Twenty-odd joined; twenty-odd eventually departed.

When we met, I didn't speak with Wesley of myself, confided no aspirations, disclosed no prior traumas; instead I spoke of current events, remote impersonal trauma; for instance, where I was, fourth grade, when Kennedy was shot, why I didn't participate—too young to travel on my own—as he did in the march on Washington in 1963, the assassinations of Medgar Evers, Malcolm X; Addie Mae Collins, Denise McNair, Carole Robertson, and Cynthia Wesley blown up the same year as the Dream. When he realized how young I was, not even the legal age of consent, he was stunned, but did not stop talking to me. Maybe my age made him slow the pace.

I'm still sixteen, a minor against his sergeant stripes and those occasions he liked to talk about of his being the high ranking noncommissioned officer present where he was stationed. I'm still in high school, still withdrawn, unable to speak my mind, to assert my will, to articulate pain, make requests, to dare disagree. Still subservient to Helena. Certainly, like God, he outranked me, having already graduated from high school, having gone to a prom, having attended college, having dreamed of being Superman.

He thought me sophisticated when I told him what the riots were like and the local consequences of the assassination of Martin Luther

King, Jr.—events that transpired while he was in London. When I told him that I knew someone whose mother had taken thalidomide. But I was still of the mind that my duty was to bear witness. I accepted whatever came my way, whatever wanted me.

Wesley was persistent and patient, reading the gullible signals differently, not accustomed to bullying, but instead, I would learn much later, to being bullied. He is still a shy man. Although I had sunken into an awful emotional state, I tried to picture myself floating, not actually immersed in scum. It was easier to hold this image in Wesley's presence. He was soft-spoken.

My church taught me how evil it was to dance, even a waltz in the gown of a princess; I was to condemn Fred Astaire and Gene Kelly, Bill "Bojangles" Robinson, Chuck Green, Bunny Briggs, and John Bubbles, Pearl Primus too, as among the lost; evil to wear lipstick that most of the women wore, waist-defining clothes, pants, hemlines more than two inches above the knees, mascara, eye shadow; to sip Chardonnay, to reek of certain ruthless scents unless I was a harlot. I should smell like rugged soap. My church taught me that I had to be diligent in loving and obeying the Lord if I desired to overcome the legacy of Eve, temptation to this day popping out of me in triple-Ds. Pendulous, sagging with sin. I'm sixteen and a grown man is after me just as Genesis foretold; devil in serpent's clothing answering to the name *Wesley*.

—*Snakes are fearless or they wouldn't be snakes,* Aunt Essell said from the kitchen. She wouldn't even look at one in a field guide or on Tarzan during which she'd manipulate the horizontal hold so as to slice the mighty pythons with the black and white edges of the bands; ophidiophobia (fear of snakes) rooming comfortably with satanophobia and stygiophobia (fear of hell). *Run from them; you hear me? Don't go where the snakes go; they don't congregate where it's holy.*

—*Yes, Aunt Essell,* I said; *I promise to run.*

Recently, when I gave my sons a cobra puppet, my mother closed her eyes and prayed that she not be defiled, declined to watch their puppet show until that puppet was put away, but it's discarded only while she visits; her pastor told her a snake and any representation of a snake is a sign of Satan, and the righteous must shun them all. She must shun therefore the caduceus, the medical profession, cure.

It's not the snake's fault. And the way it can shed its skin, completely vacate the old life of sin, beginning anew, innocently; why, the snake should have been model of conversion, paragon of successful repentance. I envied it. And as it grows in grace, it outgrows its reptilian temple and moves into one that better accommodates its expanded holiness.

As Mr. Santos did for his son, Wesley asked my parents for permission to see me, when it was no longer enough just to walk me home from church. But he asked to see me at my home, not at his. My mother was hesitant, my father even more reluctant; this boyfriend was twenty-three years old, so there was again the possibility of statutory rape, and as before, their inability to direct and control my life. There was my history of improper choices. But there was also their eagerness to deny my past, pretending that I had waltzed all these years. Another of Wesley's aunts spoke to my parents in his behalf after joking that he was married and had three children. My father continued to wonder for months whether or not Wesley was so involved. With continued advocacy from the aunt, however, my mother relented and granted permission. Despite everything, she remained trusting.

She sang in church that the storm was passing over; *this too shall pass.* That was the prevailing attitude in my home. If ever my parents suspected anything, they left it alone believing that *this too shall pass.*

Wesley came to call and just talked to me that first evening. He stayed a long time, several hours, walked home in the dark. I was surprised and relieved as I had expected nearly immediate maneuvering toward physical demands. When he left, he touched a finger to his lips and then touched lightly, just for a second, my cheek; it made my heart flutter. I was sad to see him go. He visited every week and told me about European wonders he had seen. His walking through misty forests without light and without becoming lost, being asked for his autograph.

One night three weeks into these visits he tried to hold my hand as we sat in the living room and I found his touch unbearable. I didn't withdraw my hand, but it stiffened, and I grimaced. He looked at me quizzically, wondering what must have happened, for his innocence was clear; realizing that although I was young, far younger and less mature than he'd realized, I had a complicated past. After that, he spent a few minutes, each time he visited, stroking my hand, telling me there was nothing to fear and that he would not hurt me. His tenor voice was like wine. As he did nothing else, I began to believe him, but didn't really feel that I had a choice or could refuse any request he might make. I knew he'd make one eventually.

For my seventeenth birthday, he kissed me at the door when he was leaving. My mouth was open, but he said, no; not to kiss him like that, surprising me that it would not be Hector's way, that there was another way to kiss. So I closed my mouth and he lifted my chin and kissed my lips gently. It was simple; it was extraordinary. All surprises.

Meanwhile I was still going to the library, as I usually was when trouble happened, still reading eight books a week. On one trip to the main library downtown, I found a book of poetry, *Cruelty,* by Ai. How compelling and familiar the book was, as if Ai knew my life and had written it down so that I could see it plainly. The poetry contained no nurturing, no loving encounters between men and women. Violence was the basis of every system in Ai's cosmos. I didn't share this find with Wesley.

Immediately I worshiped Ai. Here was the world unmasked and stripped; the elegance rubbed off to hard facts and rebellion that destroys the self as self rebels against itself. Here was the cruelty that ruled wherever heaven did not govern. Grit, and the raw, unsanitized forms of things, things therefore more honest, more real. I could trust this poetry, this panoply of caustic language. And Ai herself was me, of fragmented identity, a little of this ethnicity, a little of that ethnicity although she could name her fragments better than I could name mine. Here was uncertainty about her woman self. Here was discomfort with a harmed woman self.

Here was Ai slipping, in her first person poems, into identity after identity and fully fitting into any brutish personality. This poetry understood me and appreciated what had happened to me, made it sacred. Ai was my big sister of circumstance from whom I had been separated when I was born. I was ready to again submit and become a protégée. I recognized all the men in her published world and we shared them. I was the witness who corroborated her testimony. She knew a Hollis and a Hector; she had spent time with a Mr. Santos and knew how to put on their eyes just as if she were putting on glasses and every pair improved her vision. She made the cruel point of view seem essential and inevitable, the way to all else although her poems disputed the existence of anything else. Poems Lytta would write if she wrote. The horizon was still there but it was a desolate variety of horizon and in it I saw a truth I had tried to deny. I stopped trying. There were no more contradictions to reconcile; there was only cruelty. I borrowed that book ten consecutive times and read it every night after talking with Wesley. I was falling in love with Ai. I embraced her way of seeing the world.

Wesley soon discovered my sexual ignorance and anxiety. He was appalled and actually called himself my teacher. First he worked with me just to get me to say the word *sex*. I couldn't. It was a word too loaded. Of all words, there was none more charged for me; he went straight for the fuse not realizing how complicated the issue was for me, not about mere inexperience or prudery, but ordeal. He set about trying to discover what I feared so deeply. He was disturbed by the terror in my eyes that others had not even noticed. He was disturbed by the coolness increasing in hands that his holding should have warmed. He realized that I had been hurt, but I couldn't articulate the details.

Men did things to me, I said. But it was much more complicated than that, included difficulties *men* and *things* could not cover. But to Wesley, *men did things to me* was sufficient; he did not press me for information, but set out instead to distinguish what had happened to me from what eventually he and I might do if ever I were to fall in love with him. I repeatedly asked him how I would know if I loved him, and he said I would just know intuitively; revelation would arrive simultaneously with the emotion.

He explained to me that the men in my past had not made love to me; *they abused you,* he said. None of the others had named our encounters beyond a vague *going together.* I already knew they had not made love to me. I listened intently, watching the small separations of his lips as he talked, the minimal gesturing with his hands. He brought me books, charts, diagrams, some that he drew as he talked, and took me to the main library to see (from the locked stacks) a sacred text, the *Kama Sutra,* illustrated. *Sex is not evil,* he said, *but the way a man and woman share their love.* He showed me magazines that he had brought back from Denmark and told me the vocabulary of sex even though I would not use it.

Eventually, he began to touch me, my face, my legs, softly. He would do nothing else to me except a kiss on the lips when he left. When he thought that I was ready, he touched my breasts softly through my blouse and would continue this caress only if I found it pleasurable. *If you want me to stop, tell me.* Weeks later, his hand moved lower, still through the cloth, still gently. Next time, I began to pout, to want him to touch me, but I could not say this. He knew that I wanted him to touch me and he wanted to touch me, but pretended not to know, saying: *What is it? Tell me what you want, and I'll do it.* I could not tell

him, could not voice an opinion and risk its being in opposition to the opinion of the one in power; I dreaded the consequences, so he did not do anything, just a kiss, when he left, more lingering than previously. A man of remarkable control.

That night I could not sleep but instead stayed awake with him on my mind, his hands liquefying into a warm brook in which I lay and washed myself, even drank. He never knew of these semiconscious dreams, but they were constant. There was nothing I did but think of him, his arms alternately steel and warm breezes touching all of me at once, lifting me as in my mind I sat swinging. He said to me one night that if I believed in myself enough and believed in his belief in me, I could fly; wings were made only of belief; that is where Daedalus and Icarus went wrong: feathers, thread, wax.

The next time alone with him, I was even more frustrated for want of his touch, eager to dispense with cloth barriers, but he would do nothing unless I told him what I wanted and since I couldn't, I became angry with him because he knew that I couldn't speak, yet he seemed to neither understand nor care. We fought for the first time. I accused him of insensitivity—that I could say—and threw all over him a canister of flour. And still he waited for me to say: *Make love to me.* Then he walked away, went home, flour all over him, down the streets; did not call me that night, asked one question when I called him: *Are you going to say it yet? Wesley, I can't.* He hung up on me gently.

Once we had reconciled, Wesley blocked intersections I had to cross, as I walked to school, with his uncle's yellow Cadillac. He started taking me to his upstairs room in his uncle's house when no one was home and I was supposed to be in school. I cut school once a week to be with him. There I saw photos of dozens of European girlfriends and two European fiancées, one of them a nurse, all of them more appropriate for his age, none of them, according to their dress and poses, needing these lessons. Some of them were prettier than me, most were of lighter complexion, some had green or hazel eyes, all of them were intimidating despite the ocean of separation. There I attempted to destroy the competition by ripping all the photos, even of Fovan, the one Wesley would have married in a spring wedding in London, the one whose newborn he was going to accept as his own.

It was in his room that finally the cloth came off me; layer by layer, Wesley undressed me, and the choreography of this disrobing doubled my desire that doubled yet again when he unhooked my bra and caressed me as before, but now I could feel his flesh directly and enjoy it touching mine. Into my hands he placed a long-handled mirror, opened my legs so gently it was as if water had opened them, then he supported my back and helped me to slip down my underwear and position the mirror so that I could see the clitoris I didn't know I had and all the pink environment to which only he had been invited. He held me and talked to me, and had me tell him where on my body his touch felt most intense, the lesson he needed, he said, in order to please me. It seemed that there was no part of me that he did not touch, that he did not find pleasing, that he did not praise. *There,* I said; *there, too, Wesley. Everywhere.* I could feel him hardening under me, and I was surprised by the difference; I wasn't prepared although he had explained to me what an erection was. I still seemed uneasy about what was happening to him, so instead of making love, we talked. He placed my hand, briefly, on intimate parts of his body, dressed me, then took me home, explaining the necessity of the reciprocity of touch.

The next time he undressed me and positioned me in his bed that he had sweetened with scents he knew that I liked. I was on my back and he talked me through the entire act, stating everything he was doing just before he did it, keeping the penetration shallow and brief, yet I experienced delightful pangs I had not previously associated with sex. Then he kissed me and took me home, commenting on everything that was beautiful on the way. A week later, he took me to my prom and

I spent the whole night with him for the first time. The morning brought sunrise that we witnessed from a bridge over water.

Thereafter, the act was more complete and fulfilling; I had no more fear and realized how ruined I had been before Wesley. I loved his magic. Nine months later, for my eighteenth birthday, we were engaged. And I knew long before then that I loved him. A comet streaked within me. Things sparkled. He said that he loved me from the moment he saw me, knew instantly that he would marry me.

⌒

I consider my first time intimate with Wesley as my first time intimate. It is the first time I would want for everyone, but a first time I would not have believed had it not happened to me, a first time of intimate process that took months to complete. Intimacy became the sacrament it can be. Intimacy remade me; from this point I started over; my vision slowly improved. A return of reverence. I began to emerge; my faith was re-outfitted with both wings and crown. And I believed that I could, from then on, face my challenges without completely surrendering, for if I fell, I would fall into Wesley's arms.

← A Matter of Degrees

When it was time for college, I was warned by my small church of the curse of education. I was reminded that I could never know as much as God despite my hunger for information. I was reminded by envious church officials (some of whom were Wesley's relatives) that anything I achieved was not my achievement, but God's; he was allowing me to take temporary custody of it, but I had to redirect the credit to him or else prepare myself for his wrath. Every moment lived was preparation. I wasn't really smart; I was failing God's test by thinking that *I* was smart. It was God's brain, not mine. God was being cast to me as an appropriator such as I had already encountered in my primary education; their cautions and insidious protocols did not bring me closer to their sense of God, but instead increased my estrangement. In God's essential formlessness, I knew he could be shaped differently, better, and that the more I knew, the better I would be able to reshape him. Creation does not stop. You rest. You gain perspective. You begin again.

None of the church officials had attended college—not that those whose education is essentially informal cannot be fine thinkers; many had not even graduated from high school, and of those who had, many had struggled to do so. The pastor was fond of preaching how God revealed the Bible to him, a man, janitor in his lay life, with just a fifth-grade education. They resented academic prowess, the way I spoke *so proper,* they said, and warned me that I could not get as high as God, that God exalted mealworms, brought down the haughty flying on their

summa cum laude. *You think you're something,* my religious peers said, because of brains, bosom voice, but I didn't try to belittle them, never used pompous vocabulary in their presence although I did refuse to submit to their grammatical improprieties. *You ain't nothing,* they sneered. When their boyfriends became young deacons and then became fiancés and they in turn became deaconesses, and I didn't because Wesley wasn't selected, they flaunted it; they put me in my place beneath them, commented fluently and loudly that God knew who was on his side and who wasn't; he was empowering the right ones. They didn't accept that God could be behind my ample endowment in so many areas. But in this one, they competed and defeated me. Experienced an evil delight they called spiritual rapture.

I should have worshiped in a church that valued aspiration, learning, and the reverential potentiality of most things, but I didn't, drawn with my mother to the storefront churches in our once middle-class, now low-class neighborhood. The members of the small congregation were embarrassed, but I respected them and their folk wisdom, knowing both their envy and, in some cases, good intentions, although one murdered her husband and quite a few of them had extramarital affairs; they all had hot tongues. They feared rows and stacks of books in libraries, in my room; were ashamed of their lack of academic talent. Shame is all it was. I understood. They needed to be able to raise their heads.

I didn't want to reject my people, my brothers and sisters in Christ, but I had no choice, eventually resigned from all the offices I held, kept quiet in the service and daydreamed, imagined myself anywhere but in this petty place that promised salvation only to the ones who were persecuted just by the existence of someone like me, who was so ordinary and more accepted in other spheres, such as here, where I am now, on the faculty of a university. There was no longer anything the preacher could tell me. And there was nothing I could tell them that they could understand. I was polite, just polite, smiled and dismissed their hostility. Wesley was beside me. I was in heaven.

On the one hand, all, I was assured repeatedly, was the way God wanted it. Seldom did I hear preached a God of love, a God that wasn't exasperated and resentful of his parental role since so many of His children were wayward. Stressed was his military might: God as architect of hell and nuclear damnation. Fire, brimstone, fallout: appropriate punishment. The God that was going to fix the haughty, and punish the ones who knew too much. The God who championed the small and uneducated. The God who would trounce college degrees and prove how worthless they were, how knowledge was another form of wealth that would keep the learned (me in particular) out of heaven. So, on the other hand, God was not pleased, because nothing was really as He wanted it to be. The second coming was going to take care of all this; from heaven, they'd stick out their tongues at me, first instead of last. Above me, way above me. We had nothing in common. I wanted better for what I constructed for worship. I rejected permanently their flawed concept of God. I placed more value than they did in the power of the mind. Man's power. My power. And no less wondrous for being that. As bright as the brightest. Because if any human being is capable of anything, then I, human being too, probably house similar capability. That's the only role model I need: human capability. I was eager to leave that church and go to college with like-minded people, although I would be separated from Wesley. I didn't want so much as a minute apart from him.

When I went to college right after high school, at seventeen, an initial two-year stint followed wisely by hiatus and transfer, I cried all the way there, on the backseat of a rented station wagon, Wesley's arms around me. My parents sat in front with my uncle, the driver, retracing the route, as far as Syracuse, of the bus that took me to an abortion that Wesley still didn't know about.

On campus, I confronted the same desolate, confused world from which Wesley was rescuing me, but this time located much farther east. One morning, in my first college semester, while making an early entry into the auditorium where the large aesthetics class convened, the professor overheard my response to a classmate's comment that she'd have a maid to do all the work she disliked and wouldn't have time for in her significant life. The utterance of *maid* caused all eyes to turn upon me and all chatter to cease. They deferred to the black presence that was enlarged by their deference. They wanted me to react, so I did; the class was not going to proceed until I responded.

I turned in my seat so as to face more of them, and as I did so, my pencils and pens rolled out of my lap and down the tiered rows. A powerful sound. I waited for it to finish before I spoke. I gave the obligatory speech about having matriculated in order to stop the cycle of poverty in my family. I was there to overcome years of welfare-dependency. *As God is my witness, I won't ever have to be a maid,* I said, not meaning to vilify the dignity of my mother's profession, but proving that I could aspire as high as they could, that I was not intimidated by success or wealth. The circumstances demanded the comment. A class of affluent students studying the philosophy of beauty, students whose parents generously supported organizations that helped the poor and disadvantaged improve then realize their ambitions. The class intended no condescension. Thunderous applause ensued. The professor was so overwrought with emotion that he was on the verge of fainting and could but whisper that class was dismissed. He had to stagger to me, I wanted to be the last one in the auditorium, in order to bow and kiss me on the cheek. As I exited, my shoes were more thunderous than had been the applause whose reverberation was just subsiding.

In an English class in which I, again, was the only black student, another student's interpretation of a poem was criticized for her failure to read it in dialect since the speaker in the poem was clearly a black woman. The presenter, in her own defense, contended that I, exhibit A, was black and did not speak improperly, but spoke more impeccably than many in the class. *Thank you.* Then another student remarked that *Thylias is obviously well trained and has spent a number of years with a speech therapist.* This statement rang true to the class. How relieved they were to learn that I did not come by my enunciation and vocabulary naturally. The criticism of the presenter stood validated once my verbal abilities were explained. Their assumptions differed greatly from those of the students who could afford aesthetics on their transcripts. Language again was insulting me; I could not yet reclaim its power despite how it had brightened my young world and was brightening my passionate world with Wesley. It was further assumed that I was a charity case, financially and academically, admitted because exceptions had been made, standards had been lowered, generous concessions that demanded gratitude. There was no way to fight this attitude. And I was not a good fighter anyway. Besides, I did have a scholarship.

I earned a C on an assignment in another English class for presenting (reading aloud and then explicating) a poem by Robert Frost that I selected, in keeping with the assignment, because I admired it. I was selfish with Ai's poems just as I had been with my voice in Ben Franklin school. The instructor called me in for a conference and explained that he appreciated how intimidated I must feel as the only minority student, but that I shouldn't suppress my natural hatred for whites. It wouldn't be intellectually honest if I did. He let me repeat the assignment. For the occasion, I wrote "Harlem Rap," a poem in which Black Panthers forced all white people to march into hell. I said it was written by Akira Nkwome and published in some nonexisting black journal whose name I don't recall. For the occasion, I installed Cleopatra eyes on my face and sported a burgeoning Afro wig just purchased from Woolworth's and got the A I already deserved. It was one of my best performances. How they raved about the authenticity; it was as if I brought the six o'clock news right into the classroom. *Are you related to Angela Davis? Yes,* I said; a sister of circumstance.

Terlyn, a friend from Barbados in the school of nursing, was ordered by her upper-class roommate to make up both beds. The roommate was accustomed to having the maid do it, and this chubby Barbadian was so like her personal maid that she realized domestic work was probably how Chubs (never called her *Terlyn*) had earned money, after several loyal years, to attend college. That's just how it was in the early seventies, tense, awkward or explosive racial relations on campus, and everywhere. A beast was loose. I was invited to a different upper-middle-class household each week for some influence to compete with the rowdy urban influences I had to contend with *in Harlem* (of course; there was no other place I could be from, no other black communities, no possibility of integrated neighborhood, no middle-class area with black membership) when I was not at college. I was too fragile to have to represent my race; I needed more than anything to be an individual. My identity— my self—was as invisible and ignored as it had been since Lytta pushed it underground. College was undermining Wesley's meticulous work reviving me.

So much confused me. Without Wesley's presence, I was easily influenced by whatever proclaimed itself authority. He knew, before I did, about the blonde lesbian who lived down the hall from me in the dormitory, a senior in a single room, but she did not approach me in an untoward way (as heterosexual males tended to do) when I agreed to be in her film, an updated version of Rapunzel (my part), that she was making as her final project for her degree in television and radio. Still, I was not meant to be unsupervised, and Wesley had to teach me about homosexuality so that I would understand it and not fear it and also not indulge in it out of *unnecessary,* he said, curiosity.

Wesley became increasingly concerned that I would find someone else at college although he was routinely seeing someone else in Ohio: Burian. The problem was Wesley's incredible sensitivity; women always confided in him, found him easy to talk to—I did too. This still happens. When he is not stressed (*I* seem to be the primary source of his stress; he won't admit this, but I know that I am), he is the most supportive and generous listener. He is then like an interactive diary. I talk to him while held in his arms where I feel a level of security nothing else has provided. I try to be still when he talks to me, so he won't be distracted, but usually I can't resist touching him. And he can't resist, as he could in the beginning, responding.

Side-by-side, we conform to each other the way Sea-Bond denture adhesive leaves no gaps between dentures and gums in the commercials. Perfect seal. Those times, he hears me so clearly, and I hear him. This isn't the way that he is just out of commitment to loving me, but is indicative of his consoling nature; he is a fine counselor.

I found out, after the fact, that Burian had approached him initially for advice in a personal matter and for help in her studies; two years older than me, she'd just enrolled in community college. Wesley was a good teacher, and he found this role satisfying, so he did not refuse. It began as an act of compassion. Wesley worried all the time about keeping my affections for himself, despite how close he and Burian were becoming. To thwart her interest, he took to visiting me often, coming to Syracuse by bus, staying in the Ramada Inn, and in my room—once I traded, at the request of the resident adviser, my white roommate for an older freshman, twenty-four, from Curaçao, who had been rejected by her white roommate, foul nomenclature written in nail polish across Bethnys's mirror, Bethnys's clothes urinated on and thrown out the window, Bethnys locked out of the barricaded room.

Thereafter, Wesley stayed with me. Bethnys was attracted to him; she made her move on him during an episode of foolishness in which I sneaked out of my room to see someone else. I almost lost him. He says that he did not sleep with Bethnys; he was too hurt by my brief desertion to sleep with anyone. After I returned, Bethnys warned me, on her way to the shower, moving as only one who has worked as a model can, not to take chances with something good because someone would be waiting to treat him properly. She wasn't lying.

I had crept out of my room to see a predator who was not working on overcoming his predatory nature but was exploiting it instead, named, in face, after a mountain, McKinley James, a senior; he was well suffused with conquering, equipped, as were many college seniors, with internal radar to detect the gullible freshmen and sophomores. I went to see him one more time, a few weeks later, flaunting in his face my engagement ring. He said he knew that was going to happen. I wondered if the diamond could cut the glassy surface of his eyeballs because I watched two girlfriends get gonorrhea from McKinley's good buddy, both of them still wanting him, each still believing he would commit to her, one of them getting pregnant and watching him then commit to the one faithfully on the Pill. He wouldn't contribute to the cost of the abortion.

While I'm away at college, somehow Wesley meets Hollis, gets to know him, socializes with him, so evidently they have something in common besides me. Hollis brags about new conquests—more schoolgirls—and disparages his wife; his words about her are all reproachful. When Wesley tells him about our engagement and how fortunate he feels to be marrying me, Hollis doesn't disclose his past involvement with me, perhaps gloating in his privileged knowledge of my ruination that Hollis has no idea Wesley is repairing. And I don't know anything about their acquaintanceship that ends by the time I'm home for summer vacation. I don't find out until I write this book, and, after he reads it, Wesley tells me.

That was the end of freshman year.

The next year, in my second creative writing class in which the poet Philip Booth was generous enough to accept among the graduate students me: an eighteen-year-old sophomore, the reading material included poetry by Ai, whose poem, "Everything, Eloy, Arizona," was touted as exemplary: terse, direct, enviable clarity of image, crisp, emphatic, revealing details and caustic counter details in the rhythm of sass:

> *He's keys, tires, a fire lit in his belly . . .*
> *I'm red toenails, tight blue halter, black slip.*
> *He's mine tonight. I don't know him.*
> *He can only hurt me a piece at a time.*

It is possible to read those tightly constructed lines as if that female speaker has power and is going to steal some of his fire to warm her own belly, but I now know better how the "everything" of the title means that the speaker has nothing left, how her esteem has been exhausted; this is the extent of it, culmination; nothing forthcoming. Sure, there's much (pseudo) self-assurance in the lines; I can even imagine them delivered while the speaker's hands are on her hips. Perhaps she has tattoos to cover scars. Pain to offset pain.

I can almost hear the poem as if it were defiance, as if really the speaker's in control, using him, the one for whom she's to be nothing but a good screw. Then again, maybe it is in that speaker's life a triumph, even a first triumph, that she regulates just how much of herself is hurt, but being hurt in pieces, piece by piece, *dismembered,* is just too meticulous, too torturous to commend. This is not power. Devastation in pieces. I'd seen that kind of warped power in action when I was six years old. As if the damage is less comprehensive, less total if only the separate trees are ruined, not the forest. As if being less complete, the damage is not really damage.

Piecework in a sweatshop: a motel room or the back of his truck. A dollar per piece.

But then, in 1972, when Ai's poem was offered to the class as poetic model, I knew that I had indeed selected well my literary master.

During sophomore year, I also went to Planned Parenthood and got an IUD inserted because I had asked Wesley to stop using condoms. He didn't use one the first time or on prom night, and I could tell the difference thereafter. I didn't like them. He agreed to stop using them if I would light his cigarettes for him; he wanted to help me overcome my fear of matches—I need to be more than an inch from fire—but didn't get to, because instead he gave up smoking. The intrauterine device, a Dalkon shield, the compromise, was a mistake, however. Not only did it years later prove a health hazard, but its vaginal presence terrified me. I didn't trust it for a silly reason: it looked to me like a trilobite, and I did not knowingly want a trilobite or any other arthropod inside me. Nothing from the Paleozoic era with the advantage of all that history. I could not rest and felt compelled to check by the hour for the Dalkon's tail, fearing the trilobite was biting through the cervix, would chew up my fallopian tubes like sausage. And I loathed how closely checking copied masturbation. I had it removed within ninety days. I did not tell Wesley right away that it was gone. And after I did, we did not resume the use of condoms. We were engaged.

As a sophomore, I had a new major; this time education (with intention of specializing in audiology and speech pathology) instead of English and drama. I applied to and was selected for Teacher Corps, agreeing, after certification, to work in inner-city schools. In neighborhoods like my own. I went to Bellevue Elementary School in Syracuse and convinced the principal that my technique of teaching drama to fourth and fifth graders who had difficulty reading and behavioral problems associated with academic failure would transform their self-perception and improve their fluency and confidence in reading.

That day I was given a classroom where I worked for an hour every afternoon with fifteen tough girls and boys who were my size and who asked me whether I was a girl or a lady. We wrote a play together, *The Dangerous Woman,* with Rose, the toughest girl, as assistant director and stage manager. I had buttons made with these titles on them, and Rose was transformed by my vote of confidence in giving her power. The project was so successful that the principal made arrangements for the play to be performed at a nearby junior high school that had a larger stage and auditorium, where we gave three performances for all the Bellevue students and two more on two evenings for parents and the community. I was asked to consider Bellevue when I completed my studies. It was meaningful and fulfilling work. Most of the students did improve.

The class was therapeutic for both teacher and students. I thought

I'd found my place, my welcoming place. I still have a photograph of them, all their autographs on one copy of the play, their love, and they have mine. It was work I'd loved since I first attempted it during my first summer vacation at Ben Franklin school. Work I probably would have pursued further had I completed my degree at Syracuse.

When that same year I also auditioned for a play to be produced by the department of speech and drama, one of the assistant directors was quite frank in telling me even before I read from the script that I would not be cast, if cast at all, for a speaking role because I was black. The assistant director would give me, if merited, even the lead, but the decisions were not up to him. Mr. Gold was right. I got a part in *Midsummer Night's Dream* as a prop. I was onstage for the entire production, in front, reacting to everything, integrating at last one of the department's major productions, more stage time than any other actor, but I was a mute pixie of the woods, invisible to all but the audience. Vanessa Williams didn't have to endure such attitudes when she arrived years later on that campus.

For a speaking role, I had to audition for a production of *Midnight Special* by Clifford Mason, the world premiere of his play sponsored by the Afro-American studies department. I was cast in the lead female role: Francine, the prostitute who was pushed around and slapped by Grease, her pimp, but who in front of his dumpy wife flirted with him and let him grope her, behave too roughly; he had *carte blanche* with her. She had to kiss him to keep him from spitting on her.

Casting the pimp's wife was difficult as the directors had someone who did not audition in mind for the role, someone perfect because she was dark, what we used to call *Nubian* without realizing that it might be an honor; we meant to denigrate. But Nubians are people of the Nile River and the Nuba Mountains in Sudan; they are the oldest settlers, and in the South where they are called Nilotes, they endured (perhaps still endure) the indignities of the Arab slave trade. Shelby wasn't the more desirable blue-black dark, but was close enough, and, even better, was overweight, had short nappy hair, a kitchen on her neck no comb would enter: my dear friend. *Shelby would be perfect,* the directors said; *tell her we'd like her to be in the play. Tell her she might get interviewed on TV because Mason is coming for the premiere. She won't have to audition; tell her she's got the part.*

No one was interested in her ability as an actress, nor in my ability. We were cast according to the perception of our appearances, and the reputations necessarily attached to those appearances. I have regretted that I did not tell Shelby why she was courted for the production. She brought to the play exactly what the directors wanted; they had the authority to restrict what she could bring; it was their responsibility as directors to see to it that she brought nothing else, no language of her own, no bright personality. How submissively she played her part, so much wringing of her hands. Really, I was the submissive one, and Shelby was confident, a *Maud Martha* (the self-assured dark title character of Gwendolyn Brooks's only novel—didn't bleach her skin, didn't get a wig or hair weave, didn't have an inferiority complex, not ever).

To the pimp's wife, to Shelby who gave me Finnish glass (that we still have) as an engagement present, I said as Francine: "I can have him anytime I want him." And it was true. Two young men so desperately wanted to play Grease, and were equally talented for the role, that they shared the role, alternating each performance for the weekend run, two on Friday, two on Saturday, held over for one more on Sunday; perhaps they flipped a coin. For some performances, my costume included a short blond wig; for others just my own long dark hair. Perhaps to correspond to the preference of each Grease.

Mason did in fact attend the world premiere of his play, but was not interested in the pimp's wife; instead he liked Francine. He told me that I, at eighteen, was just what he had in mind when for Francine he wrote lines such as: *I can get more pleasure from a Coke bottle,* a line, one of the few without profanity, that Francine directs at Grease just before he knocks her to the floor. I went to dinner with Mason, sat right beside

him, thigh-to-thigh, and was seen in his televised interview, right beside
him, thigh-to-thigh, for which I was, of course, mute. He did not slap
me, however, nor did he invite me to his hotel room. The slapping was
just for the production, stage directions that were part of the script and
that we rehearsed until they were real.

While Grease slapped my character, Hollis, Hector, and Lytta
slapped me.

The theater was packed; there was quite an audience to hear me
say nothing that I really needed to say; nothing that I believed. My
opinions and voice were subordinate to the words that Mason, the directors, the male faculty producer, and two adolescent males fighting over
who gets to pimp wanted to hear me say. I obeyed the script and the
gestures, vulgar even when minimal. A cast of sixteen. Four women,
two significant female speaking roles but the speaking consistently de-
meaned women, two extras. Wesley was in the audience, witness to
one of the most denigrating experiences of my life. The applause, that
his applause supported, confirmed how good I was, how effectively I
suppressed my own voice. It surprised no one that I convincingly por-
trayed a whore.

Wesley, who was my fiancé and maintaining Ohio residency, knew
that I spent much time in Jeff's dormitory room. He didn't mind because
he also knew that Jeff wouldn't try anything carnal, although Jeff had
not, never did, officially come out. He didn't have to; everyone knew.
He seemed oblivious to the sissy sneers that I heard sometimes in town
with him. Jeff and I were like two girls hanging out, talking, laughing.
It was dangerous to be openly, unapologetically homosexual then, not
that conditions are significantly different now. I miss him. Instead of
trying to trace him through the alumni association or even a private
detective or just a phone book, I look for his panel in the Names Project
quilt. I've assumed much, perhaps unfairly. We kept in touch until 1983
when I received his last letter. He wasn't the type to just stop corres-

ponding; his etiquette was impeccable. He even blew bubbles delicately, the bubbles spilling from a tiny hoop and piling on the grass outside the dorm window in a mountain of clear eggs before popping.

In dormitory lounges, he would play the piano and I would sing show tunes, attracting quite a crowd. "Call Me Irresponsible," "On the Street Where You Live," "People," "It Ain't Necessarily So," "Everything's Coming Up Roses," "Alfie," "The Shadow of Your Smile." Once in a motel lounge. I felt so bright, vibrant; I never laughed so much as when I sang with Jeff. Tonic. He was to me a giant, standing in my memory about seven feet tall and skinny as a vector. Seated he was still taller than me standing. He looked good that night in a tie and black jacket, sporting an Afro as well tended as a celebrity's prize shrub, beside me in a cocktail dress returned in the morning. We sang loudly as we walked back to our dorms. *Geese and chicks and ducks better scurry, when I take you out in the surrey; We're off to see the Wizard, the wonderful Wizard of Oz. . . .* and we will ask him for the desires of our hearts. *Felix the cat, the wonderful, wonderful cat. Whenever he gets in a fix, he reaches into his bag of tricks. . . .* for the desires of our hearts. A night so perfect I must have dreamed it. Jeff didn't come to see *Midnight Special;* he had too much respect for me. I miss our music.

I have thought much about what seems to me the simplicity of delight in sameness. The calm. The companionship and affirmation. The equality involved. The greater pleasing that could grow out of the experience of having like physical equipment for all of one's life with one's mate. Delight in sameness seems to have a logic that is purer, as it is not tied into biological destiny and procreation, but rather into the delight of living with love. It places love above the welfare of the species. That is magnificent. I realize that domestic dispute exists within gay and lesbian households, and I realize that my first indiscretions were with Lytta, but the theory of sameness seems far less volatile than the theory of opposition, of adversaries attracting and overcoming the differences on which their very attraction depends.

The poetics of sameness seems beautiful, flawless, and the indulgence of angels. It seems sacred. All as one.

Besides Jeff, I did meet one nice man at college, Armenian and thirty, who stood only five foot seven and rode a motorcycle. He pulled up to me while I walked down the hill to my dormitory. He walked his bike so he could walk along with me while naming for me the constellations. He said that I was beautiful. Then he got back on his bike and rode away loudly, a knight in helmet and boots. He came around again, whenever I was walking alone at night down the hill, as if he spied on me to know just when I'd be alone in the dark. Finally, he said that he'd like to take me for a ride and I climbed on, having no choice but to hold on to his waist, timidly until his gloved hands pulled my arms around him in a big sure circle; he said that no one ever fell with him. He turned around to put the extra helmet on my head and minutes later we rode by a body of water that doubled the amount of available stars, before he disappeared.

Three weeks after I returned home from college for the summer, Wesley and I were married at the beginning of July, in my parents' dining room. We were unwilling to wait for a wedding at the end of August. My parents could sense the urgency. They regretted having allowed the engagement, although since I was eighteen, the age of majority, their permission was no longer required. Wesley had asked them out of respect. Now we were married. Wesley spent the July night in my room, ignoring my parents' objections. *But he's my husband,* I said, and closed the door.

This was all so rushed and exciting. The next day, we planned the wedding, reserved the storefront church, ordered flowers. I began shopping for the gown. For the sake of the wedding, we were to keep the marriage secret, and we did except for sleeping together in motels in the outskirts of town, registering, as we should have, as husband and wife. I would wear the wedding band at night, then give it back to Wesley in the morning. I was still too young, nineteen against his twenty-five years, three of them in the air force in London, well away from the napalm of his peers. He wouldn't let me reveal my real age to his family in Dunson when he took me to meet them. I had to be over twenty-one, significantly older than the two of his siblings who, like me, were teenagers.

Wesley did not want me to return to college unless I was legally bound to him, but once we were married, I didn't want to return, so I didn't. I just wanted him. I had been disappointed with college anyway; for the most part, it had been nothing that it should have been. A summer job to earn tuition became permanent, a second income so useful to newlyweds who had little besides each other. Wesley did not have a car and was dispatcher for a construction company. He married me to keep me. I married him to be kept. I wanted to belong to him. I wanted him to have dominion over me. We weren't really ready for that level of commitment.

No one in his immediate family had a formal wedding except Wesley. His father, then in good health, declined to travel to Ohio for our wedding; I don't think that my father-in-law realized it was to be such an event or that the marriage would be so enduring. Besides, his family did not have weddings; he had no context in which to understand one. Wesley's mother did come with her new husband, her cancer perhaps already beginning, but imperceptibly and entirely treatable then, though no action was taken. She was mesmerized by my wedding gown, *that dress* she said over and over. *That* size two *dress*. *That dress* nothing like the church clothes of her daughters' civil ceremonies. *That dress* with its beaded lace trim on bodice, skirt, and sleeves; the enormous satin bow at the waist in the back, and a headpiece that was a lace mantilla edged in tiny lace scallops that extended into a cathedral length train of lace and tulle. *That dress* and the eleven lavender dotted Swiss bridesmaid and flower girl dresses that I made, the sewing machine's small light defying darkness all night. Its hum of thriving hive. I sewed all July and through the 24th of August, the night before the ceremony, sleeping with Wesley that night in our new apartment. Sometimes I wonder what was the fate of all those dresses. As wedding gowns go, mine was modest, inexpensive, about five hundred dollars new.

After a prolonged dark spell, I put on brightness for my wedding and floated down the aisle, my hand resting on my father's bent arm for our last walk together; he was already ill. Before two hundred people, I kissed Wesley after he lifted the mist, the veil; his hands like crepuscular rays appearing from behind a cloud, promising an establishment of light.

Burian was persistent even into our marriage. She continued to need Wesley, perhaps believed herself in love with him, and ten days after our wedding, called him at lunchtime on his job—minutes before I called him—invited him to her house where she was waiting in just a robe and contraceptive foam. It was not their first sexual encounter (the others, however many there were, occurring before the marriage), but it was their last. I didn't know what made him go there, and he didn't know either, especially as he said that he did know the unstated purpose of the invitation. It was sex, but it wasn't intimacy. It was a mistake; I understood mistakes, having made so many. I knew that it was possible to do things that really you were opposed to doing. I knew that Burian didn't want to let him go just as I hadn't wanted to lose Hollis. But Burian knew me and was intimidated by both my intelligence and my looks. I knew that in a twisted way it probably enhanced her esteem to be able to seduce a man that was choosing me over her; I had become the kind of woman to whom Burian would always lose (I'm glad to say).

A coworker claimed not to know where Wesley was. I had called to invite my new husband to lunch as well. I was immediately suspicious, and that suspicion led me, during my search, to a love note from Burian that had accompanied the wedding present she gave only to Wesley; only his name was on the gift tag. I thought of Linda, Hollis's wife, my sister of circumstance; I thought of reaping what I'd sown. Wesley came home already prepared to tell me; I did not have to confront him although I was ready to confront him. Every day after, he brought me a rose at lunchtime, testing, as did Noah, to see if the ground was ready to again support life, and the seventh rose I kept. He said, as he held me in his arms, that he didn't kiss her nor caress her with his hands. I believed him. I knew that what he said could be true; it was possible not to touch and possible to feel only regret during sex.

When I got married, I was employed as a minimum wage–earning, $1.85 per hour, accounts payable clerk. I had vague ambitions and wanted undefined success but was unable to articulate anything. I had not forgotten old dreams of becoming: a violinist (*first* violinist, concert master) for a symphony orchestra, a geneticist, a singer (jazz), physicist, teacher, audiologist and speech pathologist, but I was so emotionally wrecked that I was unable to act upon dreams. Writing wasn't on my list (as it had been in elementary school), and I'm not sure why it wasn't. Perhaps because of the interface of darkness and poetry; I didn't really want to further embed myself in such miserable perception, but I could not create with words the hope I felt with Wesley. I don't know why my thinking remained so crippled. Perhaps I didn't yet have enough distance from all my disgraces. Perhaps I was denying being so trauma-tized by events that were more common than I had realized. I could not envision writing as a career since the writing was done by the person from whom I had separated myself, the one I watched in those films about Hollis and Lytta. She was the writer, not Wesley's wife. I had more growing to do before I could begin to embrace as complex an issue as my future that seemed to depend so heavily upon my past.

I called Wesley every day during my morning break and felt awkward about either accepting or declining invitations to lunch from male coworkers and other acquaintances we'd formed. He was as worried as he'd been while I was away from him at college, for I wasn't as emotionally stable as I needed to be in order to assert my own judgment. I still wasn't twenty-one. He told me that I was on my own; he couldn't be with me for lunch every day; he worked twenty miles from where I worked. But he said I could always call him if I was in trouble.

When trouble did come, I did not call as I should have. Instead, I went to the Pegasus Cafe with a pianist and looked into his eyes during lunch, let him brush my bangs out of my eyes with fingertips also capable of Chopin, submitted that evening to sorcery and a kiss I couldn't taste, refusal coating and incapacitating my tongue, tears clouding my vision. I let him drive me home to even the score. I was still naïve. It would not have happened had he not been a musician whose part-time career I coveted and needed to pilfer.

Wesley seemed to know immediately—from the way I walked by him, the quavering in my voice, awkwardness in my kiss, length of my shower. *You need to tell me,* he said sternly, picking me up, wrapping my towel around me. I told him that again I'd done something I didn't want to do. I said I doubted that he could forgive me although I had forgiven him, telling him then I could never do what he had done. I asked him to help me learn to refuse the encounters I didn't approve of, to overcome the easy surrendering that was poisoning me, and he told me as forcefully as he could that I was much more than what men had taken from me and taken from me. *No one else can touch you like this,* he said, touching me as only he can.

How incredibly gifted Wesley was in helping me to believe again in the potential for my life. He told me that night that he had seen in me, even that first time, some grand future in the way I spoke and held my head. He said he could imagine my doing great things, commanding attention and respect; there was more to me, complexity and sophistication to me, and he loved that more as much as he loved my body— what would I do without Wesley? He did not express the anger he felt; for my sake, he was kind, reassuring, bringing me soup on a tray, holding me tightly as if to say nothing could penetrate this defense. Then he let me go, and we slept that night with space between us.

Over the next few weeks, he nursed his wounds himself and looked at me differently, no longer directly in my eyes. We talked less during meals and when we did talk, his voice was quieter—I had hurt him so thoroughly. Every day, he still said he loved me, but felt, I could tell, rather foolish saying it. I loved him too. And that love really was everything; soon it became impossible for him to deny. From then on, our love prospered.

Within two years, I became the accounts payable data entry supervisor; a year later, a junior executive auditor, my salary quadrupled, and I could easily, as if writing reports, write poems and stories; and easily, as if conducting audits, leave the premises and go to the library where I learned of a poetry contest, the first I ever entered; the first I ever won. The judges of the Cleveland Public Library contest, who selected my poem "Coming of Age in Sandusky" as the winner of the $25 that helped change the direction of my life, happened to be editors from the Cleveland State University Poetry Center, who eventually published my first book. I was motivated by that prize—and the absence of compassion and ethics, more blatant at the executive level, in the company for which I worked—to return full time to college.

When I was supposedly conducting audits, I really researched college catalogues. There was something about Oberlin's having admitted blacks and women from, for women, the day the doors opened and, for blacks, not long afterward, that made me apply there with intentions of majoring in creative writing; dark outlook or not, I believed I could write; the library prize convinced me. A week after sending my application, I called the admissions office daily, and within two weeks, the director of admissions himself informed me of my acceptance, probably to prevent further badgering of his office. Immediately, as if writing a report, I typed a letter of resignation. Enrolling at Oberlin was not something I could have done if my husband had not helped me partially emerge from my dependence on desolation.

How my life was changing with Wesley beside me. He took over all the household duties so that I could devote myself to my studies full time, and we lived on only his blue-collar salary; fortunately, I commuted a hundred miles round trip three times a week, so had no room and board to pay, and for tuition had a combination of scholarships and loan. I don't believe that most men would have encouraged me the way that Wesley did, telling me that he knew all along, even if I didn't, that I was meant to have wings, and now that they were unfurling, I had an obligation to use them. He was proud of me for *deciding* on my own to go to Oberlin, and to prove his pride, he bought a car for me, a 1978 Toyota Corolla, and taught me how to drive it.

Once I enrolled at Oberlin College, I found that I could not speak in class just as I hadn't spoken in Ben Franklin school or in Thurgood Marshall High School. However, Professor Zagarell, in my first year there, could not tolerate silence. My other professors could. She would not excuse weakness, especially in young women. She would call on me at least twice each session, although I didn't volunteer. At first, I would be close to tears and would just shake my head. Once I left the room for a few minutes. She persisted in wanting me to not only have ideas, for I wrote acceptable papers, but also to verbalize them with conviction. She called on me early in the discussions; I would not be able to simply agree with what had been said by others. Finally, I thought to write down comments that I could then read aloud, a script (I never lost stage presence and the ability to take on roles, be someone other than myself), when she called on me. This worked. Her strategy was harsh, but by the end of the semester, I could speak extemporaneously; I even raised my hand in other classes.

But the poet Ai remained my mentor, and now there was more at stake in my writing; I had to produce it for my degree since I was majoring in poetry. My senior portfolio would be filled with tributes to Ai. I would be first in my class; an A in everything, several A pluses (worth 4.33 at Oberlin. I received them in literature, writing, and science courses. I graduated with a 4.11 average, lowered from 4.22 by one A- from Sandra Zagarell). My father knew that, for at the end of my junior year, I was already first; my father held the transcript and died a month later with partial restoration of a splendid vision. Deeper and deeper my writing took me into reprobation. Ai provided an outlet for my distress; through her poetry I learned to vent my accumulated frustration and anguish onto the page.

Seeing those poems now (I did not publish them and kept but a few) is horrifying to me, all the violence against women, all the monstrosity with which I endowed men, the depravity, the acceptance and glorifying of brutality, the self-loathing. Odious and licentious. So much pain.

MEETING HIM AFTER DARK

Cars approach without headlights.
Everything is ready to kill
as I duck down an alley whose stink
keeps me alert and hopeful. I suck it in
and it rushes, dislodges the cotton
in my jaw. The ache returns, this time
without you. Many footsteps; I don't recognize yours
till your cleats jab my hands. All night I love you
or you'll bleed me. After you, men use whips

that never touched horses and screw me one by one.
Today a snake ripped off its skin. Honey,
would you do that for me? Tonight do it,
tonight without danger of sunrise, where
water sloshes sweetened with palm oil
and cloves, running from my skull that
you crack going after sweetmeat
that you can't seem to find elsewhere.
The cock knows I'll strangle him
if he tries to crow.

Oberlin

1980

⁓

*P*erhaps it isn't quite this simple, but I don't think that I would have attended a graduate writing program at all if my advisor, Stuart Friebert, who was also director of the writing program at Oberlin College, had not suggested that I attend one despite his unuttered concerns (uttered to me years later) about the escalating encroachment of darkness in my poems; he had been worried. Although I went to graduate school because I was told to go, still believing that I wasn't to defy authority, still unaware that I could be the authority for myself, my graduate work was a necessary part of my emergence.

When it was time for graduate school, I remembered that Ai, my mentor with whom I never corresponded though I wrote hundreds of poems honoring the brutality she esteemed, used an excerpt of a poem by Charles Simic as the introduction to her first collection. If my mentor took as her inspiration this Charles Simic, then I could do no differently. In fact, I was eager to venture for a first time to New Hampshire to work with him; I was reading his poems and admiring them apart from

Ai's endorsement that led me to them. And Charlie called Stuart to tell him how much he wanted to work with me, that I'd *be some kind of poet.*

At the time, our niece was living with us, and we told the world she was our daughter even though one day she would have to return to her roots. But Wesley let me, not that I needed his permission, go to New Hampshire while he took care of our niece alone. Again, he proved himself remarkable, an element of dream, for he did not object to my leaving the marriage for two years nor to my living in the graduate dormitory; again, he encouraged me to discover how far my wings could take me. Evidently, he had wings of his own, because 800 miles of separation brought us closer. During my second year of study, our niece joined me in an apartment in family housing, and more of her truth emerged, her shocking, lurid history in an abusive home. Although Wesley and I each spent a year trying separately, we could not help her. She was yet another version of Lytta, and our lives improved once she went home; the air cleared as after a storm. Her life has not been so fortunate.

In graduate school, I continued to serve Ai faithfully, a protégée as I was in high school. Her poetic craft was better than mine, but I too relied on imagery of abuse, violence, disillusion, and acrimony. Ai was dark epiphany and in praise of what in me her poetry affirmed, for ten years my writing exclusively erected bleak monuments, recognized authenticity nowhere but in the brutal.

It was not easy to write the last essay that I had to write as a graduate student in 1983; in fact, Charlie had to call me to remind me that he needed the essay in order for me to complete the course and the course had to be completed in order for me to earn the degree. He urged me to write it, convinced me that I had something to say about Sylvia Plath; he did not agree that I should write about a poet whose work was more engaging to me. *Stick with Plath,* he said, so I, grudgingly obedient, did.

It was in that paper, assigned to me out of Charles Simic's genius, that I named the limitations of Plath *and Ai* (I felt compelled to include her), limitations that previously I had considered as their greatness, their gutsy, brutal honesty, their independence from sugar, their shattering of false light. I called, more for my own sake than for any actual shortcoming in the work, their poetry ultimately unsatisfying because it was dishonest in denying the existence of joy. I concluded that a celebration of darkness was insufficient to sustain humanity; there was something lacking: magic, the numinous, love that transcended pain and disillusionment, humor and laughter, even if the laughter were unstable, destined to breakdown; in their poetry—that was published—was a continuity that is false.

Finally writing that literary analysis, I realized that I was actually commenting on my own poetry; I made the connection (that I believe Charlie hoped I would make). And having made it, I could begin to sever those ties. I had been quite prolific, but the voice was spurious, wasn't completely mine—was more like Ai's. I borrowed her interpretation of cruelty to explain my own experiences; from her interpretation, I drew my conclusions about life. Her aesthetic, her interpretation of cruelty became the backdrop to my syntax and revealed an abiding triumph of Lytta despite Wesley's illusion of victory. The blue ink had been the liquefaction of the unraveling fibers of her dress. But Wesley couldn't exist if Ai's aesthetic defined validity, yet he was real; I married him; I loved him. He made me laugh. Such enrichment.

Now I knew the problem, and the prognosis was good, but the course of treatment proved wearisome as I tried to break free of Ai's— and Lytta's—sensational gravity. I was a tide, leaving her point of view only to return. But I knew now of this pull, and I worked on resisting it, a process that took years to complete. I fancied myself tested by the Van Allen radiation belts; after all, there is no universal destination that will not subject me to a consequence of gravity. Bodies fall toward the center of the earth with a uniform acceleration $g = GM/R^2$ where G is the universal gravitational constant, M is the mass of the earth, and R is earth's radius.

My poetry had tried to emulate Ai's perspective and had tried to deny joy until I was twenty-seven. In graduate school, I learned that humor was crucial from one Charles Simic, a fine poet who had survived the ugliest war when he was a boy in Nazi-occupied Yugoslavia. Because of Wesley and because of Charlie, I was a survivor of an ugliness too.

I want to show you something, Wesley, I say. He drives me to Lills, but the house on Lills Drive is gone without a trace as if the ground, in its contempt for what went on there, swallowed it to overcome some shame. Evidently there could be no more mercy in the wood, no more ability to shelter. In exchange for the house, the ground had yielded the most uncomplicated of wildflowers and grass indulged with clover.

Shame perhaps is not entirely overcome, however; for so many flowers are a shade of blushing. They are beautiful yet also somewhat ashamed of what appear to be their immodest acts, luring, seducing insects to get into their pollen, bump and grind with the anthers to help the plants reproduce. In shame, they have no voices. In triumph, they bloom.

There is, as I keep looking, pastoral invitation, an opportunity to respect whatever is buried in such a soft green grave.

⟋ The Relative Infinity of Now

In no way could I express to Wesley what were to become essential ways of my perceiving the world and my role in it. No way could I share with him goals and plans that did not exist when I was nineteen. I didn't know what I valued in a mate. I didn't know how vital it was to discuss our possibly conflicting matrimonial and parental ideologies. I didn't even have any. I was a wife before I was my own person, but I was able to become that person within my marriage, *because* of my marriage. What I've done better and longer than anything else is be Wesley's wife.

His is an uncommon generosity; right after graduate school, I remained in New Hampshire as a lecturer, and Wesley joined me there, although New England was a wrinkle in the plan for me to come home to Ohio after completing my studies. Wesley quickly adjusted his life to these changes, telling me that we would find the place for both of us once the dust of my emergence settled. Then came a series of teaching positions: at Phillips Academy in Massachusetts, at the University of New Hampshire as a visiting professor, and at Brandeis where I taught until coming to Michigan. Wesley was with me, pursuing his career in business and accounting wherever I was, giving me all the room I would need to grow into the woman writing this book, the woman so amazed that she found him. So amazed that there was a man like him to be found. Although I married without making a mature decision, Wesley was the conduit; the only way for me to get here, where I am comfortable with life and successful, was through him. And the journey is not over.

Within my life's present unified theory of being, splendor divests itself of its own integrity, splitting to belong to everything that notices it, each part as effective as the whole splendid thing. It belongs to whatever wants it and is inexhaustible even as someone lies dying, even as someone else cries thinking there is none, their tears becoming prisms. Splendor is generous, but we must be able to receive this generosity. Some are not yet able. For a long time, I was not able, disturbed by the competition between tyranny and compassion. But the duality that troubled me is simply a fact of existence. I must accept complexity as the purpose and a benefit of the journey. Events are neither good nor evil; they are just events, consequences of existing.

Most of those sentient have an expectation that meaning be attached to each aspect of the journey. We have the help and advantage, sometimes misfortune, of interpretation to make the journey meaningful and more splendid than it really may be. Otherwise, there'd be no joy, and I prefer how joy makes me feel, what I accomplish in joy's name, what I am willing to endure for a kept promise of joy. Perhaps for animals it is similar, a male mandrill aware that his colors have become the most vibrant in his troop (if that is the word for a group of mandrills), the bonobos touching and touching, massaging splendor into each other. For some, God, as traditionally depicted, provides this reassurance of meaning and joy, and that is fine; that is necessary for them, but God for me has become less concrete, less concerned with my petty daily activities; God has become for me the state of splendor. Glorious evanescence that no amount of tragedy or trauma can depose. Extremely personal splendor.

Splendor happens when I can let it happen and see it in the veins of the rock and hard place between which I am sometimes trapped. How can there not be pain in a world spinning madly, in the lovely calculable chaos that requires us to deteriorate? In the middle of the hurting, I find gems. Maybe it's just a small light seen through a crack in the window; maybe it's just recalling a dream of unforgettable and impossible loveliness; a thought is something real, a real thought; it need not be three dimensional to exist in splendor, for splendor itself is not three dimensional. And this small light, this impossibility can sustain; they are that breath of air that allows two divers with one tank of oxygen to attempt to reach the surface. It is their belief that is splendid; their faith. Splendor is not continuous, but of a frequency that will not force it to be doubted. That is what I understand now; that difficulty does not destroy splendor. That the purpose of difficulty is not the destruction of splendor. That splendor is not defined by tyranny, for I knew joy before I knew anything else, and I knew that it was joy that I knew. For having struggled, I do not know splendor better now, but I know now more than splendor, and despite the increase in knowledge, splendor does not become lost in the crowd. It is always there; it is incumbent upon me to notice it, the annoyance of my husband's snoring becoming a conch shell's amplified sound, a chorus of conch shells, his body huddled in sleep suggesting a walrus, suggesting Wonderland. Or that snoring is a revving, Evinrude, the boat in which I can be transported if I let it transport me.

I am not saying accept torment and tyranny—no; stop such forces if at all possible, but if those forces persist, as I believe they will, splendor, however muted its form, can help console, can help one survive to possibly plot and execute escape. I am saying that joy is too necessary to abandon. I am saying that it is best not to let tyranny dominate a life, that I spent too many years under the influence of the tyranny of a girl who no doubt forgot all about me within a week of my departure from her home. I am saying that if she suffered in her life, that it was not from recollections of my influence; I was null and void in her life. I perpetuated a tyrannical presence and followed it although splendor had not left me; I closed my eyes to loveliness that light revealed as often as it could.

Everyone cannot be physically removed from the threats and dangers, but the mind can feast on splendor even as the bullet that cannot be dodged lands as it does through a dining room window into the head and back of a woman playing cards, a winning hand in her hand as the new year started, that hand putting in her mind thoughts of how wonderful she was, how she itched to be strutting, how fulfilling it was to be with her daughter, smiling as she hadn't smiled in a long time since she didn't know where her man was, but she knew where the two jacks in her hand were and what they meant to her at this moment, what they meant *now*.

She hears the shot, knows what's coming, but can't duck that fast; it sounds like something cracking to reveal a sweet nutmeat. For a split second, she can taste something that's not anywhere on the table.

Now is all we have. Any moment perceived is called *now* at the time of its perception and is subject to all the uncertainty that accompanies *now*. How exciting uncertainty is; what opportunity for adventure it offers. No chance for boredom. The way we experience time turns every moment experienced into *now;* the *now* factor: perception of any entered moment as the present. Remembering happens now. Prognosticating happens now. Therefore, there is no time other than this moment. Wesley and I are now. Anything we'll ever have, do, or know must come to us now.

Including reconciliation with death. We know it's coming; it's on its way now, is somewhere right now. We must not fear a presence as continual as God's. So constant that death becomes trustworthy. And when death actually arrives here, I'll know just how strong I really am. Just how successful Wesley and I have been in empowering me will be revealed then. I want it to be splendid. A clear-cut dichotomy of life and death. I want a clean break, neither surrender nor compromise.

I believe that there is no seduction involved in death, that it arrives plain, with no pseudonym, no proxy. Death comes and says, *I am Death;* hearing that, I'll know what to do, as if answering a post-hypnotic suggestion made at conception; implanted in the genes. Accepting death is as easy as slipping away into morphine, yet death may hurt, may be brutal and unapologetic. It doesn't need to deceive me, for it alone, so far, is infallible and inescapable. So, it wears no mask. Only the executioners, only the euthanizers, but not death itself; these are transporters, not the commodity itself. The approach to it may take years, yet the moment of actual entry into it, the moment that establishes the direct link to it, is easy. Just a blink, a gasp. Fast.

But I don't know the size of death, whether it widens each time it is joined or instead becomes more dense and compacted. I don't know whether each separate death arrives at the same dead destination or elsewhere, nowhere. I don't know whether or not awareness persists nor the form awareness could take since the usual sensual avenues of awareness will not exist.

I assume that death is a cessation of the present boundaries in which consciousness operates, a severing (preferably a neat one), a cutting of another cord. It is transformation and merger into physics, the transfer of the energy of life into another form; the start of decomposition, flesh and bone becoming other justifications of matter. In the last seconds of life may arrive an awareness of perpetuation of the cycle of existence. The last splendor. The design, the art of the cycle may be revealed in the jolt of the shutting down of synapses; it may involve much color or the activation of deeper application of senses before the ability to know them dissipates. Or just nothing.

Not that I look forward to death, but if it occurs in advanced age when I am mentally and physically impaired, why would I argue against it? In such context, Huntington's is desirable for the dementia it imposes. Huntington's becomes a light. Not knowing of my decline, I would not have to suffer the knowledge. I would not be able to comprehend what had happened, would neither recall nor understand that I was ever some-one who wrote a book. I don't want to live to be a hundred years old unless at one hundred I would be much as I am right now in my early forties with able body and especially, mind. The few gray strands do prompt me to start adjusting to decline. They do serve to remind me that there are limitations to the abilities of lungs, liver, heart, brain, eyes, tissue; none of these things, even with optimal maintenance within the present confines of knowledge, can function indefinitely. But how good while they last.

The word doesn't bother me at all: Huntington's. A merciful fatal disease, it will usually sleep at least until you are forty and then slowly steal your mind and movement. Since it waits until middle age, you have time to know you've lived, time beyond regret, sane and agile long enough to witness your children's arrivals (unless, as I did, you have them late) into adulthood, to become grandparents blissfully demented before these grown children show signs, if any, of the disease. If it happens, Wesley will find himself vastly intellectually superior to me, enjoying that briefly, then will come for both of us: agonizing and irretrievable loss. I'm just at the age that I must wonder, that I begin to look for signs, especially signs in my memories of my father; for if he didn't inherit it from his father, then I can't possibly have received this dominant gene. But I don't know whether or not he did; he died too soon from something else in his late fifties, a good sign at that age that maybe he eluded inheritance; he had as much a chance of inheriting as not inheriting it.

My fear is that maybe it just hadn't yet manifested, that he might have been a late bloomer. I never asked how it was that he missed all the wars of his lifetime, a strange absence of military duty. He had never outright danced the Huntington's dance by his death, but who can say that he would not have danced it the next year or the next? Who's to say he would not have started forgetting the lyrics he sang to me on the Saturdays he saved for me as we walked to fetch bread? He had a great mind and died with it intact, the way I want to die. I shudder at a tap on the shoulder, a deep voice saying: *May I have this dance?* You just can't refuse—the wine, the music; they're perfect. Martha Reeves and the Vandellas: *"Dancing in the street."*

How ironic it is that I may have finally emerged just to decline. Because my mind is everything to me; my identity is rooted in my brain, in language; I'm nothing but language, and if language fails me, then

I'm no one I would care to know. To think that I will be feeble-minded, that I will become someone of no fairly reasonable claim to intellectual dazzle, someone ignorant and at first merely slow, ridiculed though I still try to excel, and then idiotic, in an institution for imbeciles as was my paternal aunt who had finished college with honors in her middle-adulthood. Just in time.

Huntington's is what I may face, but each day my mind stays sound decreases the likelihood of that inheritance. But if my father had gene IT15, identified shortly after I started my job at the University of Michigan, I may be a candidate for supreme humbling; for an antigift. And maybe that will be just fine, for then I will have had everything.

This is very much a life of cycles, a life that depends upon deterioration of what exists in order to sustain that which will exist. There is a system of destruction that is apparent even in weather, circuit breakers that allow for resetting, restarting, the shift, however slight, in focus that interruption creates. There is a violence that gets the job done, an effective aggression. Perhaps for that reason, some embrace aggression, recognizing it as the challenging friend it is, grateful for its help, its motion, its activity that constantly defeats stasis.

In this system, so far nothing is eternal, and while time may seem to be so, for it may be construed to contain the universe; it may not be. Distance and meaning take place in a moment in time, these moments influenced and even determined by the observer who is not eternal; it is not logical that time be exempt from the universal demise that finishes everything else.

Time seems linear, ever moving in one direction, unable to turn around, yet I, and many others, think of life as a circle, birth and death as part of a timed cycle that takes place in curved space. However, the circle of life is not a repetitive circle in which rugged acess to resplendence is smooth with each repetition. Instead, each season is a new circle (from which disturbances and beauty can erupt and protrude, such as trees, mountains, Saturnian rings, and solar flares), these circles spreading out concentrically from that first compact, reproducing round-ness that was the very first hot minute of existence. In a sense, we ride, in these cycles, the shock waves of that explosion. Winter returns, but a different winter, and I, who experience each succeeding winter, am different. I hope, better. Circles traveling, moving, each one a little farther into space (that expands with time), not a vicious circle whose track is fixed, or I'd be as I was twenty, thirty years ago.

I think of the interesting pairs of photos in Louise Young's book *The Unfinished Universe*. Near the end, in plates seventeen and eighteen are the Andromeda galaxy and a human cell that bear a striking resem-blance. Or plates one and two, at the beginning, that offer a whirlpool in the Bay of fundy and a similar whirlpool galaxy in Canes Venatici. Time and all of its components and constituents are making similar journeys, and these journeys are all of process; nothing is in a fixed or permanent or final form. All ephemeral. All rounding, moving mathemat-ically, seeking ideals. Seeking splendor.

As I seek ideals myself, I still walk through catalogues of miracles unable to rank the superlatives. In spring, I see new wings catch light and scatter it as they dry in the sun, attached to named magnificence: Monarch, Viceroy, Fritillary, American Painted Lady. Butterflies. Some-times the lawn is as full of small white butterflies as it is of dandelions, a butterfly resting on each yellow head. At home, headlights go by in the night; I see their brightness, through the partially open blinds, like pools, wells. So round and amazing; I am able to find my notebook and pencil, record the encounter, the entry, the bright guest always welcome, the shadow of the bed and shadow of my husband increasing tremen-dously in the visiting eminence.

I realize that what was true of my foundation is true again, was always true, that my ways of nurture are bright ones, that I will show my sons bright pieces of the world that they may connect with any other pieces they find as they live—as they seek earnestly if it becomes impor-tant enough to them that they find splendor. I hope to force no other belief upon these two boys: one with whom I see eye-to-eye, soccer player who plays saxophone, visual artist who calls me—if his friends aren't present—his buddy, and the other, a scientist trying to make a rock and a time machine so that a hundred years can be a minute, who says during dinner: *Pretend this salt shaker is the earth—there is only up; if you look down and look all the way through the earth, you're looking up again, up into the sky. We don't have to go to space; we're in space—right, Mommy?*

I too look up only, aware that each bird has a sound, melodious or cacophonous, and I listen to it, aural brightness or aural sting like salt spray of the ocean, the one calming, the other invigorating when not disturbing. Notes can disperse in breezes and seem to come from blossoms as if flowers are soft tubas. Plants, the welcomed and the weeds, lean toward light. I am a namer, assigning words, and therefore also value, to what is beheld; my real work is taxonomy.

Yes; this is my work: acknowledging the complexity, disputing the challenges to light, feeding a root that will produce as long as it is fed. Some challenges have such force it is as if they mean to dominate, devastate; it is not easy to defy them, yet for the sake and prosperity of light, they must be defied.

Even water that sparkles, full of glints of sun, may harm us, for it may hold unseen, tasteless and odorless sometimes, toxic agents that are soluble in it, that bond with the flesh of fin fish and crustaceans we eat, with roe we hold as delicacy, opalescent or shimmering like smoky topaz; for bright indulgence in deliciousness we may contract the beginnings of our cancers. It is even in the air, some viruses, some pollutants that impair our health. But isn't the deliciousness worth the risk? I have heard the lovers of blowfish, of fugu, say so. And isn't it usually splendid to breathe? I do not want to be afraid to live just to try to avoid unavoidable peril and pain. This is my only life.

Some of the challenges to splendor are distant. I read of a fire in which a little girl burned because her mother left an unattended candle lit on the bed, liking the flickering shadows moving across the page when reading into the night, rejecting electricity. I read this and was in my room in the attic again, realizing a potential for disaster that had not occurred to me, that surely just as easily did not occur to this mother. The ladder to the girl's upper bunk was so hot, no one could hold on to it and climb, and then the complex mass of smoke made of rescue just a sweet fantastic idea, the striving that is never actually to be reached, for then humanity would be finished, and the greatest dream is that there is no sublime limit to what humanity can become.

Such challenge can force growth once we put away the agony over what went up in smoke, from now on irretrievable: the last T cell, dollars, last drop of resistance, uneventful family reunion. The burned phone in the girl's house melted into a misshapen ear, one with a keloid. Judy's ear was like that, when we were in the junior choir, when Deirdre, Judy, and I all liked Jeremy-myah (his real name) and he did not care what we liked. By this transformed phone, I am connected to this challenge; it is part of my memory, part of the inevitable association I will now make when I recall Judy. Loss compounding loss. That nameless little girl becomes important to me but to hug her, I must also hug flames.

This fire enters my circle, blends into Gladys's flames, and though I did not feel its heat, I cannot forget it; my own thinking and remembering are forever changed, perhaps enhanced, because of it. This has touched me; I can't go back to a state of not having been touched. Laminated cards from the last bid whist game melt into the table.

But I must witness without losing faith in luminescence. I must love celestial light though I know of the violence necessary both for its continuation and for human survival. I must use this glow to devise arguments against any prevailing attitudes promoting man's corruption, his glorification of torture, mutilation, chauvinism, superiority. It must be as Anne Frank recorded (in version C of her diary) on the fifteenth of July 1944: *. . . in spite of everything I still believe that people are really good at heart. I simply can't build up my hopes on a foundation consisting of confusion, misery,* and death. I see the world gradually being turned into a wilderness, I hear the ever approaching thunder, which will destroy us too, I can feel the sufferings of millions, and yet, if I look up into the heavens, I think that it will all come right, that this cruelty too will end. . . . We must believe that we can effect change instead of waiting, those who do, for God, for Jesus to intervene, for there's no telling just how many millennia it will be before that massive holy invasion happens, and there's no need to continue the profiting of tyranny just to give God more purpose; some of the blessing we can do for ourselves. We are capable.

I believe in redemption and radiance even though solar light, the light of the world, is aggressively manufactured and the darkness of space is passive, peaceful, quiet, and gentle, the fill that provides a sense of vastness, of endlessness that can be troubling. Therefore, light, not a tame darkness, is the aspiration of the compassionate. Light reveals. Helps us see better. Aberration such as Lytta is a great challenge, as are other specialists: perpetrators of genocide and eugenics, ethnic cleansing, xenophobia, architects and patronizers of death camps, *Topt* maker of ovens, mass murderers, those whose joy has no bounds only at brutal exhibitions, gangsters; despite all this evidence, a small part of which I know firsthand, I must still be persuaded by light, still shored up by softness that isn't light, but is what light reveals. Though light can be dangerous, though electricity cannot be cuddled—its love, its voltage can kill, on the golf course, in the chair wired to conduct it—it may restart, used with discretion, a heart. Matters of degrees. Matters of perseverance. Brutality may be a natural capacity; it is helpful to survival to have physical as well as mental and emotional strength, but brutality must not control us. Yes; likewise for Lytta, for if she now feels no remorse, she cannot enjoy the redemption and affirmation of life and self-blessing. Remorse, so that forgiveness (what I offer you, Lytta) can be meaningful.

We populate much of darkness with demons that both fascinate and terrify us. God and angels both fascinate and terrify as well, but these we usually situate in light that we use as our metaphor for triumph and glory, since light seems unable to conceal anything; its visibility precludes conspiracy and treachery. No matter their differences, we cast both devils and gods as humanoids, permitting some of them to more directly capitalize on their animal connections as minotaurs, centaurs, gorgons, mermaids, werewolves, the new breed cyborg. Animals live as we do, in both darkness and light. Indeed do animals kill rivals in mating competitions for the sake of, the motion of species survival, the strongest male winning the most desirable female. The female often deciding just what is meant by "strongest male," seeing more strength when there is also physical symmetry. Some, like some of us, kill just for fun, I've heard; a certain primate, a certain polar bear, a certain elephant, for instance. I rather fancy the cunning movement of nature, the cuttlefish, for example, pushing a rival's sperm receptacle out of a female then inserting his own after destroying the rival in a battle for her. It is almost genius. And is not necessarily a challenge to the success of light. Perhaps it is evidence of light. After all, light is linked to darkness, and some forms of electromagnetic radiation, of which visible light is a part, are dark to us, entirely outside the visible spectrum, yet they are merely other wavelengths of light. Ultraviolet, infrared.

But we are not cuttlefish; we are willful beings, and I like this willfulness after not exercising any will for many years. We have more control over our behavior than most other animals apparently have over their behavior. We can use strength with more discretion, even to battle instincts. We can *decide* to change, *decide* not to maim nor malign, *decide* to forgive; therefore, instinct seems a function of our intellect rather than intellect being a function of our instinct.

But to succeed, we must rescind somewhat the scourge of emphasis we place upon rights. Rights sometimes help us not make compassionate decisions. For rights are what I do not encounter on my walks nor in my reading; no evidence of any rights except for those we have, often misguidedly, constructed. We don't *have* rights innately; we *give* ourselves rights, and rights are all contrived. Most likely there can be no entitlement in a world in which there is no permanence and no total separation of one thing from another. Even incarceration depends upon a system that connects the inmate to the outside world. At the point of connection there is relinquishing of individual rights by both parties or else there is conflict, perhaps violation. I try to see the interactions where things meet, the new entity that may be made through their interaction and that is possible to make only if each separate contributor is not overly protective of its right to maintain its individual integrity, forcing the other contributor to conform to it.

The connections make possible perceptions the individual otherwise might not have. There are cycles of being, cycles of awareness, movement from one state of being to another, transcendence of form, but no right to any of this. Arbitrariness is at work. Ordered randomness that cannot be defined as justice or injustice. Justice doesn't exist outside our making it. Rather are there hopes and dreams, desires, wishes, causes some of which people are willing to sacrifice their lives for, but not at the expense of continuing life indefinitely, for that is not allowed, not yet if ever possible. A right's being in place does not mean that the right necessarily should be acted upon; sometimes the humane choice is for the individual to forgo the right.

As long as there are any rules at all, there is no freedom from limitation; nor should there be. This in only logical. Limits impose urgency, and urgency forces action. Limits can raise the value of splendor.

I do not have rights; I have dreams. Sometimes I have needs (some of which are just more urgent dreams). I have dislike of suffering, dislike of pain, dislike of disease for everyone, but these are not yet escapable. I do not have the right to dress provocatively, but I may want to; it is not a right. I do not even have the right to criticize Lytta, Hector, or Hollis, but for the longest time I had deep-seeded desire for vengefulness, and during that time, I made no progress away from the things holding me back. There are not rights; there is dream, there is desire, and there is influence. Unless I am mentally or physically isolated, I am constantly influencing and being influenced. In influence, there are intersections and passings that are open to interpretation—herein lie our chances. I do not know things that do not come to me through some sensual avenue. Patty Duke as Helen Keller touched and was touched by water, then to her the world was revealed, in all its splendor.

I am choosing what light reveals; it is superseding challenges, for there is a beauty that lingers almost defiantly after tragedy; birds, soft fragrance, for instance, bounteous light in the cemetery after the ceremony. Many say that reality is harsh as if softness is fake and never formidable, always at risk, but that simply is not true; at the foundation of my life is softness, a cushioned root of splendid geometry fully able to support the entirety of my life, both its excesses and its inadequacies. A root that generates light so that the root may be seen, its warmth may be felt. It is beautiful, and is not passive.

~

As long as someone wants revelation, there will continue to be an outpouring of art that defines, revives, encourages, and elevates people. I want us to be more even if, at the end of existence, it is all for naught. When we are striving for a more, an ineffable existence beyond mortality, an unfettered potential for consciousness to exceed all known bounds, then do we produce our most striking and moving art: the poetry, for instance, that supplants the poet's intentions with an enduring resonance that glimmers, illuminating abundant water, and revealing meaning beyond the limits of the poet's mind. The products of struggle and striving are made of the grace sought.

Art names us as we struggle to name it so that we can produce it. It proves the reality of the more it makes. It both spawns and is spawned by the epiphany that appears quickly, a photon as the poet is struck by something, a meaning the poet understood for the split second of that seeing in the milk, for instance, a significance beyond milk, a significance that is not milk yet could not have existed without the significance passing through milk. The epiphany as quickly gone. My challenge is to discover what has struck me about milk, for what has struck me is the poem, the art, but as I write, I have nothing but an image of the milk, not an image of the revelation, the immensity. The revelation was just a flash. It does not remain. But it is the revelation that I need. I write the poem trying to recapture the revelation, but end up with an ode to milk. Sometimes a denunciation. The revelation should contain the poem; instead, the poem contains (and so reduces) the revelation.

This is ever my dilemma, the attempt to connect again with something that briefly unlocked everything and as swiftly sealed it up again. Meaning is so fleeting, and I receive the meaning for only a small part of something, and only the meaning in a particular moment, then that meaning is no longer valid. Still I search and think I have something until I examine that thing outside its moment. I seek anyway. Stumbling in the name of shimmer, splendor. Occasionally I come close. Only then it there some resonance in the three categories of poems (that are better when categories overlap) that this life has led me to produce: poetry of blessing in which I endorse delight and celebrate wonder, for what seemingly contradicts wonder, doesn't; poetry of necessity in which I acknowledge my obligation to humanity, in which I witness (I believe I am responsible for information; that awareness of something impels a response) ; and poetry of struggle in which I seek to discover meaning— perhaps by creating it.

I remember having my hand in a dolphin pool so that I could shake a fin when the dolphin swam by; the animal surfaced for me so that I touched more than a fin and imagined for a minute that my hand slid into a new existence formed by the contact, a place where hand and dolphin converged, gray turning silver and the water turning silver, then my hand becoming the chalice, also silver, from which this silver spilled, creating a trail that would lead me to all that could be silver and glowing, and then the dolphin passed. I could see, through the dwindling motion of the water, the bottom of the pool, of the same material as the penguins and polar bears' artificial ice bergs.

Then I realized I had touched dolphin skin that had a softness unanticipated. I saw cuts I hadn't expected; it had fought something and prevailed. A rigidity of fin where I had imagined frill. I wanted to embrace it, hoping it would then incorporate something of me in its song, but there were so many hands in the water, so much shrieking and laughter that I deferred to the pleasure of others, tucked away my dream, resurrected in its place an old one in which my father tore down our garage with his bare hands, built a tank for two dolphins that emerged from his body, his two lungs that turned silver in the light, leaping and diving, an arc of water following. It is a dream I had once; it is most precious.

This actual dolphin encounter was just a visit to Sea World of Ohio, factory day courtesy one of Wesley's former employers, but while my hand was in the water, while the dolphin took from my palm small fish and swam round again just to be barely touched, there was cease-fire, a questioning of the priority that would say that this moment did not matter, this moment which is the only moment of that day that I remember, the only moment to survive although its incredibly short-lived revelation did not—but for a second I was caught in the vibration of the water and emitted thoughts that were pure tones of fixed pitch. I've not been a tuning fork again.

This life is full of bright essences history would omit. This life has transformed, tasted, luxuriated, panicked, grieved, apologized, loved, hurt, helped, erred. This book is affirming; I can say my life; I can own it. I can use language to have everything that I need and to recover anything important that I lost. Language resurrected a beautiful life. I have never been so revealed yet that revelation is what most pleases me, for it exposes a commitment to make living mean more than it probably really does. Above all, this life has been privilege, despite all the mistakes I make. Despite the undiminished presence of tyranny.

During my silent years, during my dominated years, I did not exist. I could not think these burgeoning thoughts now without liberation of the word. I could not attempt to embrace a universe, could not try to move light-years without language and thought that is a form of electromagnetic radiation and moves also at C, the speed of light. So delectable are the words by which I know there are innumerable galaxies, the wondering I admire that has led to every discovery, every invention. They are not my inventions but I may speak of them, I may taste them when I say the words, my tongue deep in them. I celebrate fullness. I agree that it be called God's *Word,* that in the beginning *was the word;* that God said *let there be light,* and only after saying those words could God see *that it was good.*

Joy and evil may employ similar tools, but what is accomplished with them and the methods of utilization differ greatly. Does this imply that the ends justify the means? No. But within the confines of existence, there is a finite number of parts available to make whatever is to be made; we are limited, perhaps to existing matter, regardless of the form it takes. But, we have not yet, and probably never will, come close to exhausting the possibilities for this matter. There is relative infinity.

Before I wrote *Rainbow Remnants in Rock Bottom Ghetto Sky,* my fourth volume of poetry, I had denied the range of human emotion and endeavor. I had reduced both what humanity was and could become. What I was, had been, would be. I must not dwell and wallow in strife. As rigorously as I had worked on constructing bleak monuments, I now emphasize the architecture of joy, the domes and towers rising above the ashes. Built from dust, crumbs, scraps of blue cloth.

Sex first was pernicious, but sex also was a gateway to numinous rapture with a man; when we make love, we form a chrysalis where we transform our feelings, our commitment, our love, our energy, reaching the more that we can't hold on to, but we reach it again and again; we always return to the numinous and want to return; it is worth the work to enter that place of such concentration and transcendence that we forget where we are, time, our separate identities, using the vocabulary used only in that place, great sounds of existence and creation coming from our throats and tongues but originating in a place so deeply embedded it is beyond us, pushing up from a vastness into us then through us, orbs coming out of a cocoon of scream, condensations of experience and being, and lodging above us, radiating, radiating, suspended like any other stars maintaining their own lives in the universe through the thermonuclear conversion (cocooning) of hydrogen into helium, not having to eat or breathe, self-fueled for eons.

And when the hydrogen at the core of this passion is exhausted, and as the new pure helium core contracts, we make love a last time, spinning a final cocoon of gravitational collapse into black hole, entering absolute black perfection where light no longer escapes us and we become the more, pulling everything into an incredible attraction for each other, into our gravitational bliss, other black holes growing to the point where black hole intersects and sucks up black hole sucks up black hole until there is only one bliss, one ecstasy, the cocoon itself becoming the product produced by transformation and not merely the vehicle supporting changes.

Sometimes I look at Wesley, astonished by how pleased my eyes are, as if over night my hands in touching him have reshaped him more perfectly, more precisely to my ideal. I can look at him and find splendor in the way he holds a fork, chews, fastens his belt, slips a tie around his neck, stands before his share of the bathroom mirrors with a towel wrapped tightly around his waist, groin, thighs, raising his arms and hands in such graceful gestures to brush his hair that lies black in short sine waves; I can see him each day and find the new magnificence in the motions of his shining his shoes and motion of the turned steering wheel slipping through his fingers returning to its regular position. In the car, when I am passenger, I place my hand on his thigh to feel the ideal movement of the muscle as he shifts his foot from gas to brake pedal to gas again. It all seems calculated, so beautifully mathematical.

I make eye contact with his reflection and his reflection promises to do things to me that the eyes casting the reflection have not promised; there is different light on the reflection and it manages to hold me as tightly as the real arms that move me from the wattage to the dark covers of the bed, sometimes onto the counter, one arm moving parabolically to clear the counter of brushes, rollers, lotion, razor, dried flowers, the other arm lifting me, its strength keeping me from flying away, its coolness keeping me from incinerating.

⁓

10:30 A.M. I call Wesley. *Are you busy?* I ask.

Sort of, he says. He is preparing a budget report, doing spreadsheets.

There is a forecast of snow flurries, at times heavy squalls; first flakes are scheduled to appear at noon. The sky is light gray without interruption as if it has snowed into the sky, as if snow will be volleyed back and forth; a beautiful day.

In the refrigerator is the rest of last night's turkey meat loaf, plenty of fresh, uncooked broccoli, pears, strawberries from Florida, spinach. He loves this meat loaf. He commented last night, off-handedly, thinking his wife and sons did not hear him, that sometimes, he'd like a meat loaf *like that one* for lunch, all to himself, so I denied seconds and quietly put it away. He also said that I never prepare enough broccoli, that it's my little touches that make him crave it. I feed several of his appetites.

Sorry, I say; *I didn't mean to disturb you. I'll talk to you later.* I hang up the phone, turn up the volume on Samuel Barber's *Agnus Dei.*

10:33 A.M. Wesley returns my call. *What is it?* he asks. *I don't want you to think that I don't have time for you. Do you need me?*

—All these years. You're working too hard. Why don't you come home for lunch?

—I'd love to, but I have so much to do.

—Aren't eating and taking care of yourself part of what you have to do?

—I'll see what I can manage. Let me try to finish this report. I'll call you and let you know. I love you.

—I love you too.

11:25 A.M. Wesley calls back. *I'll be there at 11:45.*

—Great. Lunch will be ready.

Only twenty minutes. I wash up, redo my hair, freshen my cologne, lipstick, apply Revlon's color style light #2 to my face, change into my slimmest, shortest black skirt—Wesley's favorite—that I wear only for him, the sheerest black panty hose—Wesley's gift to me (that I've modified for his convenience)—black heels so that he will be only six inches taller than me, cream sweater that buttons, but not today, to six inches below the throat—it used to be his sweater—no bra, no panties. Wineglasses on the two cloth place mats I've put on the kitchen table. I fill them with Martinelli's. Cloth napkins in silver-plated napkin rings that seemed an enlargement of what we wear on our fingers; his napkin ring also holds a rose that had hidden almost a full day in the refrigerator. I set "I Like" by Kut Klose to play over and over. I tear then rinse romaine and leaf lettuce and spinach for his salad, slice baby carrots into lengths like slivers of miniature orange moon, slice two strawberries into thin partial roses. The broccoli is steamed with water and a half teaspoon of herb-enhanced oil, punctuation-size dots of imitation butter, pepper, a whisper of salt. The meat loaf warms as the garage opens. No time to write him a little note.

—I didn't expect this, he says as he comes in and kisses me. It's a long kiss for 11:45 A.M. I put away his coat. He could smell the meat loaf as he parked the car, more of the smell then escaping through the open garage door to the street.

—Did you finish your report? I ask, pulling out his chair as he washes his hands.

—*No. But I needed a break. Thanks for asking me to come home.*

—*Anytime,* I say, placing a plate of meat loaf and broccoli before him, leaning much closer than necessary; he can see into the unbuttoned sweater. He rubs my hips.

—*You smell even better than the food,* he says.

I sit to his right, singing quietly with Kut Klose. Our legs touch. Outside is brighter as the flakes begin to fall. He seems nervous and self-conscious about eating as I watch him, my deepening breathing increasingly audible. He lifts his glass. I can see myself on its convex surface. *Why that song?*

—*Because,* I respond, his timing of question perfect, (I'm singing the refrain with Kut Klose), *I like the way you sex me.* He tries to suppress a smile. He looks breathtaking to me, as he always does the minutes and days following a haircut. I like to watch his transformation in the bathroom mirror, thinking that I owe so much to his clippers. I can barely eat my own portion of lunch. I'm closer to him, barely on my chair at all. I keep overreaching for my fork, keep wanting to touch him.

—*What do you want?* he asks, looking directly at me, dabbing his lips with his napkin, smiling.

—*You have to ask a woman who's alone with you with nothing on under her skirt and sweater what she wants? You are getting old, aren't you?* I lean over him to clear the table. He pulls me onto his lap and kisses me. Kut Klose is still playing.

—*I have to go.*

—*Go where?*

—*I do have a job.*

—*I know; the work you must do as my husband.* I pull him to his feet. With the heels on, I am tall enough to slow dance with him the way I want, the way we always do. His hands are all over me. It is obvious why we can't ever dance in public. We kiss ardently through the bumping and grinding of our bodies. I repeat his name in labored puffs. After twenty-three years of marriage, I can't believe that my husband makes me feel like this. I can no longer stand up. There is no air left to breathe; there is only desire. Wesley maneuvers me to the couch. My heels fall to the floor as I straddle his legs, hold on to his shoulders and pull myself up, my breasts close to his mouth. The snow is so heavy now, it falls like a curtain; we don't close the blinds. The terrain of his shoulders, chest, and arms is stunning, a world hidden to all but me under the atmosphere of his blue dress shirt that I've unbuttoned and necktie that I've loosened. I undo his pants; the zipper does not slide easily past his erection that I stroke. I feel his finger deep inside me and have the first of several orgasms.

—*Don't you have to go to work?* I manage to ask.

—*Okay,* he says, *I'll get to work right now.* And he guides his penis inside me. Instantly, I explode within, more forcefully than a minute ago, moving rapidly, the couch moving too, Wesley's thrusting as powerful as my feelings.

It has stopped snowing. He holds me for a while. Soft kisses. I hear the mailbox close. *Mail's here,* I say.

—*I hate to leave you,* he says. *The way you are right now, exuding what you're exuding, I don't want anyone else to see you. Stay in this afternoon, until I get home.*

—*And then what?*

—*Whatever you want.*

—*You'll make love to me again?*

—*You make me want to make love to you again and again. You make me do things I wouldn't normally do, say things I wouldn't normally say.*

—*It's that way for me too, Wesley. The things I say to you—I can't believe it's me talking. I can't believe that I'm willing to tell the world what our love has achieved.*

—*What has it achieved?*

—*This,* I say. And we make love again. As if the world will end if we don't. As if ours is the only love left.